MW00637494

بسم الله الرحمن الرحيم

I LOVE ISLAM

ISLAMIC STUDIES TEXTBOOK SERIES - LEVEL FIVE

I Love Islam 5

بسم الله الرحمن الرحيم

In the Name of Allah, Most Compassionate, Most Merciful

I Love Islam © is a series of Islamic Studies textbooks that gradually introduces Muslim students to the essentials of their faith. It brings to light the historic and cultural aspects of Islam. The series covers levels one through five, which are suitable for young learners and includes a student textbooks and workbooks as well as a teacher and parent's guides.

The Islamic Services Foundation is undertaking this project in collaboration with Brighter Horizons Academy in Dallas, Texas. Extensive efforts have been made to review the enclosed material. However, constructive suggestions and comments that would enrich the content of this work are welcome.

All praise is due to Allah (God), for providing us with the resources that have enabled us to complete the first part of this series. This is an ongoing project, and it is our sincere wish and hope that it will impact our Muslim children today, and for many years to come.

ISBN 1-933301-24-2

PUBLISHER AND OWNER

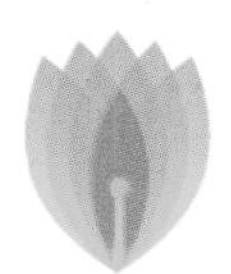

ISF PUBLICATIONS

Islamic Services Foundation
P.O. Box 451623
Garland, Texas 75045
U.S.A
Tel: +1 972-414-5090
Fax: +1 972-414-5640
www.myislamicbooks.com

PROGRAM DIRECTOR *

Nabil Sadoun, Ed.D.

WRITING TEAM

Ummukulthum Al-Maawiy
Lena Dirbashi
Nabil Sadoun, Ed.D.

REVIEWERS AND ADVISORS

Susan Douglass
Freda Shamma, Ph.D.

CONTRIBUTORS

Suad Abu Amarah
Sumayah Al-Khatib
Kacem Ayachi
Romana El-Rouby
Nicholas Howard
Sandra Schaffer
Omar Tarazi
Menat Zihni

CURRICULUM DESIGN

Nabil Sadoun, Ed.D.
Majida Salem

ENGLISH EDITOR
Sumaiya Susan Gavell

GRAPHIC DESIGN

Mohammed Eid Mubarak

ILLUSTRATIONS

Raed Abdulwahid
Special thanks to: Goodword Books

PHOTOGRAPHY

Al-Anwar Designs

* Names are in alphabetical order of the last names.

Tawheed: The Faith of All Prophets

MANY PROPHETS, ONE GOD

MUSLIMS UNDER SIEGE

WORSHIP WITH HEART

ISLAMIC CHARACTER

"I Love Islam" Friends and Family

Tawheed: The Faith of All Prophets

Tawheed: The Faith of All Tawheed

CHAPTER ONE

Word Watch

Tawheed Al-Khaliq	توحيد الخالق
Tawheed Al-Ibadah	توحيد العبادة
Tawheed Al-Asmaa' was-Sifaat	توحيد الأسماء والصفات
Shahadah (testimony of faith)	شَهادة
kufr	كُفر
shirk	شِرك

The Meaning of Tawheed

Tawheed is an Arabic word which means believing in and worshipping one God. Tawheed is the most important belief in Islam. The English word for tawheed is monotheism.

Surat Al-Ikhlas is one of the shortest suwar (plural of surah) in Al-Qur'an. But, it is one of the most important. This surah explains the idea of tawheed. Tawheed simply means the belief in one God, the true Creator of the universe, and worshipping Him alone.

Allah ﷻ is "One" without a partner and unique without a match. Allah ﷻ is the first and the last, and He knows everything. He is the only One worthy of worship, and no one is capable of being God except Him. Believing in tawheed (monotheism) is the most important part of being a Muslim. Do you know that a person cannot become a Muslim without saying the Shahadah?

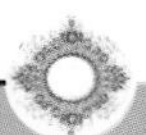

أشْـهَدُ أنْ لا إلهَ إلا الله وأشـهد أنَّ محمداً رسـولُ الله

I bear witness there is no god but Allah (God),
and that Muhammad is the Messenger of God.

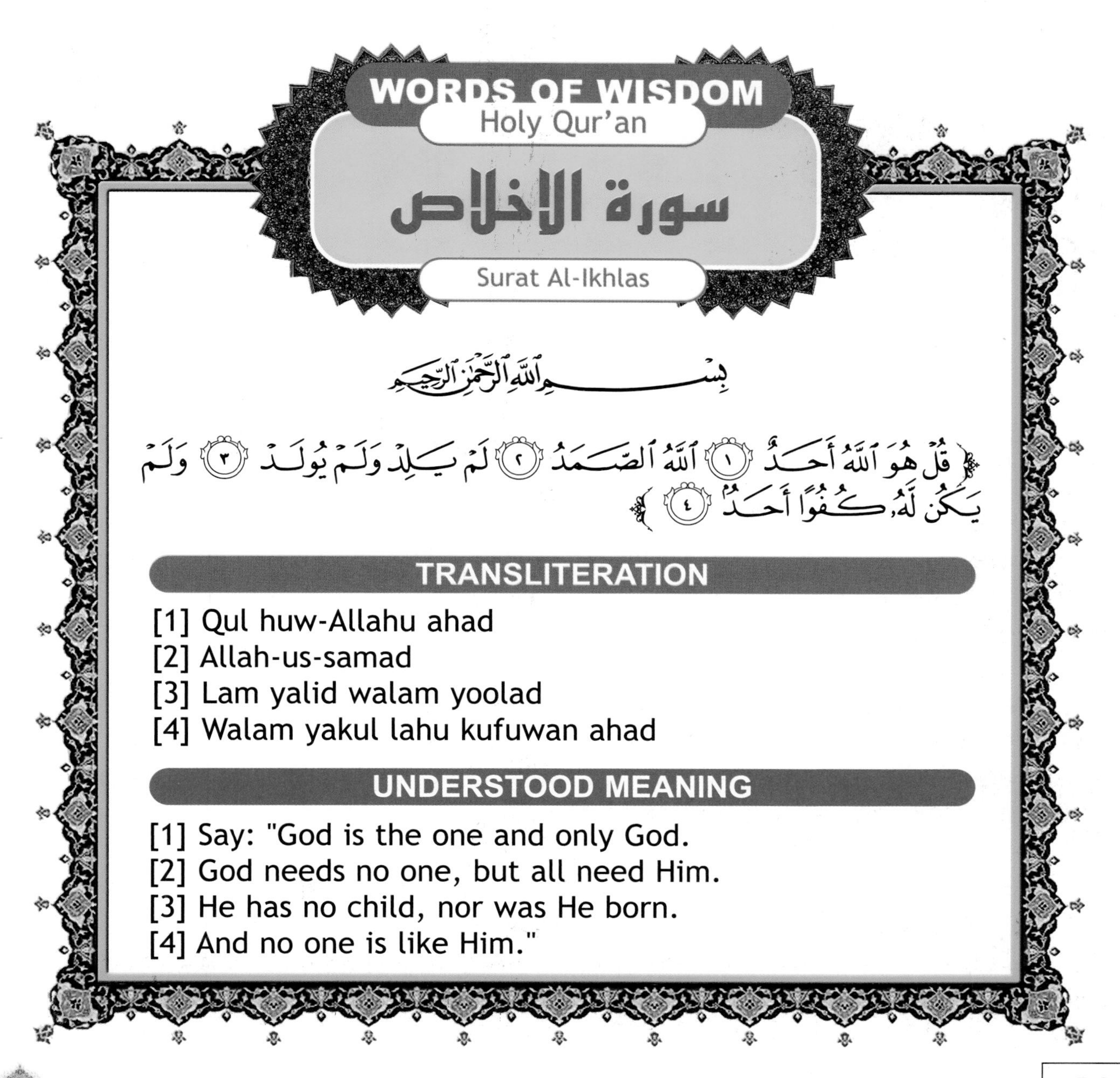

WORDS OF WISDOM

Holy Qur'an

سورة الإخلاص

Surat Al-Ikhlas

بِسْمِ اللَّهِ الرَّحْمَٰنِ الرَّحِيمِ

﴿ قُلْ هُوَ اللَّهُ أَحَدٌ ﴿١﴾ اللَّهُ الصَّمَدُ ﴿٢﴾ لَمْ يَلِدْ وَلَمْ يُولَدْ ﴿٣﴾ وَلَمْ يَكُن لَّهُۥ كُفُوًا أَحَدٌ ﴿٤﴾ ﴾

TRANSLITERATION

[1] Qul huw-Allahu ahad
[2] Allah-us-samad
[3] Lam yalid walam yoolad
[4] Walam yakul lahu kufuwan ahad

UNDERSTOOD MEANING

[1] Say: "God is the one and only God.
[2] God needs no one, but all need Him.
[3] He has no child, nor was He born.
[4] And no one is like Him."

Kufr and Shirk

Some people think that there is no god. They claim that the universe somehow just happened without a creator. This is called **kufr** كفر or disbelief. Others think that there are many gods who helped create this world. This is called **shirk** شرك (polytheism), and it is the opposite of tawheed (monotheism). Therefore, shirk is the act of believing in or worshipping false gods in addition to our true Creator, Allah سبحانه وتعالى .

All of these beliefs are rejected in Islam. In fact, to disbelieve in God or to believe in another creator or creators is the worst possible sin. Allah سبحانه وتعالى says:

﴿ إِنَّ ٱللَّهَ لَا يَغْفِرُ أَن يُشْرَكَ بِهِۦ وَيَغْفِرُ مَا دُونَ ذَٰلِكَ لِمَن يَشَآءُ ۚ وَمَن يُشْرِكْ بِٱللَّهِ فَقَدِ ٱفْتَرَىٰٓ إِثْمًا عَظِيمًا ﴾

"Allah does not forgive associating partners with Him; but He may forgive anything else, to whom He pleases; to set up partners with Allah is to commit a most heinous sin indeed." [An-Nisa':48]

The Three Parts of Tawheed

In order to understand the idea of tawheed, scholars in Islam have divided tawheed into three different parts.

Tawheed Al-Khaliq توحيد الخالق : Belief in One Creator

Tawheed Al-Khaliq, which scholars also call " توحيد الربوبية Tawheed-ur-Ruboobiyyah," is to believe that Allah سبحانه وتعالى (God) is the only creator of the world. Allah سبحانه وتعالى alone is the One Who created the

▲ *Stone Fish. Yes, this is a fish, NOT a stone. Can you see its mouth or eyes?*

universe. As you learned earlier, one of Allah's names is Al-Khaliq, or The Creator.

Tawheed Al-Khaliq also means that Allah ﷻ alone provides care to all of His creations. He alone controls the universe and allows things to happen. When something happens, it only happens with Allah's permission.

﴿ ٱللَّهُ خَٰلِقُ كُلِّ شَىْءٍ ﴾

"Allah is the Creator of all things." [Ar-Rad:16]

▲ *Do you know what this beautiful flower is?*

The Prophet Muhammad ﷺ explained the concept of Allah's control over the universe. He said: "If all of mankind gathered together in order to help you, they would only be able to help you as much as Allah had already permitted. Also, if all of mankind gathered together to harm you, they would only be able to harm you as much as Allah had already permitted."

2 Tawheed Al-Ibadah توحيد العبادة : Worshipping One God

Tawheed Al-Ibadah is one of the most important parts of Tawheed. Tawheed Al-Ibadah means that no one has the right to be worshipped but Allah. When we pray, give zakat (alms), and fast in Ramadan, it is all done in the name of Allah ﷻ.

All actions of ibadah should be done for Allah ﷻ alone. Worshipping others instead of Allah, or even worshipping others along with Allah, is the greatest sin anyone can commit. Many people worship people, saints, idols, animals, planets or other things. They think these things lead to God, or they are parts of God. This is not tawheed, and these

▲ *Salah is the act of worshipping the One True God.*

practices are rejected in Islam.

Ibadah should be done directly to Allah ﷻ, not through anyone or anything else. For example, many people think that they have to pray or communicate with Allah ﷻ through a religious person or a religious leader. When they ask Allah for forgiveness, they do it through a saint or a religious person. In Islam, you pray, make supplication (du'aa), and perform all acts of worship to Allah directly. Muslims repent and seek His forgiveness privately. Allah ﷻ can see and hear you whenever you say or even whisper your prayers, no matter where you are. He is very loving and very close to us.

Holy Qur'an

﴿قُلْ إِنَّمَآ أُمِرْتُ أَنْ أَعْبُدَ ٱللَّهَ وَلَآ أُشْرِكَ بِهِۦٓ ۚ إِلَيْهِ أَدْعُوا۟ وَإِلَيْهِ مَـَٔابِ﴾

Say, "I am commanded to worship Allah alone, and not to join partners with Him. Unto Him do I call, and unto Him is my return." [Ar-Rad:36]

Holy Qur'an

﴿ وَقَالَ رَبُّكُمُ ٱدْعُونِىٓ أَسْتَجِبْ لَكُمْ ﴾

And your Lord says, "Call on Me; I will answer your (Prayer)."
[Ghafir:60]

﴿ وَإِذَا سَأَلَكَ عِبَادِى عَنِّى فَإِنِّى قَرِيبٌ ۖ أُجِيبُ دَعْوَةَ ٱلدَّاعِ إِذَا دَعَانِ ۖ فَلْيَسْتَجِيبُوا۟ لِى وَلْيُؤْمِنُوا۟ بِى لَعَلَّهُمْ يَرْشُدُونَ ﴾

When My servants ask you about Me, I am indeed close (to them): I listen to the prayer of everyone when he calls on Me. Let them also listen to My call, and believe in Me so they may walk in the right way.
[Al-Baqarah:186]

Ahadeeth Shareefah

قال رسول الله ﷺ :

١- "إذا سألتَ فاسْألِ الله وإذا اسْتعنتَ فاسْتعِن بالله" رواه البخاري عن ابن عباس

٢- "من حلفَ بغيرِ اللهِ فقدْ أشْرك."

رواه الترمذي عن ابن عمر

The Prophet Muhammad ﷺ said:

1- If you ask (something) in prayer, ask only Allah, and if you seek help, seek it only from Allah. (Narrated by Bukhari)
2- Anyone who swears by anything other than God is committing an act of shirk, or disbelief. (Narrated by Tirmithi)

3 Tawheed Al-Asmaa' was-Sifaat توحيد الأسماء والصفات :

Belief in the high attributes of the One True God

Allah ﷻ is One, but He has ninety-nine names or attributes that we are made aware of. We understand who our Creator is through His many names. Each attribute has a meaning that is only for Allah ﷻ . Tawheed Al-Asmaa' was-Sifaat means that Allah's names and attributes can only describe Him and no one else.

For example, one of Allah's names is Al-Qawiyy, or the Powerful. A human being can also be described as powerful, or qawiyy. We can say that he or she is a powerful fighter, or a strong leader. However, they are not nearly as powerful as Allah ﷻ . The name of the attribute is perhaps the same, but the meaning and quality of it is extremely different.

Holy Qur'an

﴿ اللَّهُ لَا إِلَٰهَ إِلَّا هُوَ لَهُ الْأَسْمَاءُ الْحُسْنَىٰ ﴾

Allah! There is no god but He! To Him belong the Most Beautiful names. [Taha:8]

Benefits of Tawheed

1. It makes us depend on Allah ﷻ alone and not fear people. Tawheed teaches us that no one can hurt us without the permission of the Creator.

2. It makes people equal, since all are created by the same, One Creator.

3. It unites humanity since it teaches us to believe in the same God, the same message, and perform the same kinds of worship.

4. It frees man from worshipping other humans.

Hadeeth Shareef

عن ابن عباس قال: قال رسول الله ﷺ :
كنت خلف رسول الله صلى الله عليه وسلم يوما فقال يا غلام إني أعلمك كلمات احفظ
الله يحفظك احفظ الله تجده تجاهك إذا سألت فاسأل الله وإذا استعنت فاستعن بالله واعلم أن
الأمة لو اجتمعت على أن ينفعوك بشيء لم ينفعوك إلا بشيء قد كتبه الله لك ولو اجتمعوا
على أن يضروك بشيء لم يضروك إلا بشيء قد كتبه الله عليك رفعت الأقلام وجفت
الصحف. حديث حسن صحيح

Abdullah Ibn Abbas narrated: One day I was riding behind Rasulullah ﷺ.
and he said to me:

> Oh son, I am going to teach you a few words. Remember Allah so He will remember you. Remember Allah, so He will support you wherever you are. If you ask for anything, ask Allah [first], and if you seek help, ask the help of Allah [first]. And know that if all the people gather to do good for you, they will not be able to do that unless Allah wants it to happen; and if they gather to hurt you, they will not be able to do that unless Allah wants it to happen. The pens have been lifted and the ink on the pages has dried (This means, Allah has decided this, and no one can change it.) Reported in At-Tirmithi

Chapter Review

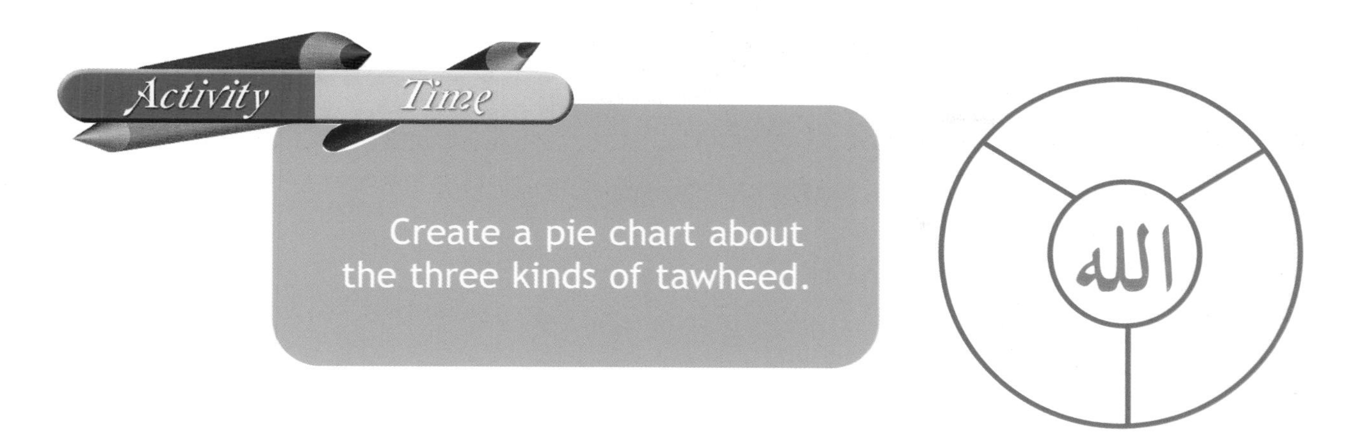

Explain the differences among the three kinds of tawheed.

1. What is the meaning of tawheed?
2. What is the first thing that a person says when he or she becomes a Muslim?
3. Explain kufr and shirk.
4. Name and briefly explain the three different parts of tawheed.
5. What are the benefits of believing in tawheed?

Ninety-Nine Names, One Creator (I)

CHAPTER
TWO

Pre-reading Questions

1. How many names does Allah ﷻ have?
2. What should we learn from Allah's names?
3. What rewards do we get if we learn these beautiful names?

Word Watch

[Al-Asmaa' Al-Husna الأسماء الحسنى]

The Ninety-Nine Names of Allah

Allah has 99 names. Each name describes one feature of Allah ﷻ . We cannot imagine what Allah is like. But He gave us these 99 clues so we can understand something about Him. These 99 names describe the One and Only God, the Creator of this wonderful universe. Allah's names are known as

الأَسْمَاءُ الحُسْنَى **Al-Asmaa' Al-Husna.** It is very important for Muslims to know these names and understand their meanings. Let's learn this important hadeeth:

Hadeeth Shareef

عن أبي هريرة رضي الله عنه قال: قال رسول الله ﷺ :

" إنَّ لِلَّه تِسْعَةً وَتِسْعينَ إسْماً، مِائَةً إلا واحداً ، مَنْ حَفِظَها دَخَلَ الجَنَّة "

رواه البخاري ومسلم

Abu Hurayrah narrated that Rasulullah ﷺ said:

> "Allah has ninety-nine names; one hundred, except one. Whoever learns them by heart [and lives by them] will enter Paradise."
>
> Reported in Al-Bukhari and Muslim

In the above hadeeth, Rasulullah (The Messenger of Allah) encourages Muslims to learn the great names of Allah ﷻ . This means learning them by heart, understanding their great meanings, and living by them.

Al-Aseeli, one of the great scholars of Islam, explains this hadeeth's meaning to us and makes this important point: "Learning the names of Allah means living by them, not just saying or memorizing them."

Calling on Allah by His Great Names

Learning and saying Allah's names is a form of thikr (remembering Allah). Thikr is very good for the heart. Allah says in the Qur'an:

Holy Qur'an

﴿ أَلَا بِذِكْرِ ٱللَّهِ تَطْمَئِنُّ ٱلْقُلُوبُ ﴾

"Indeed in remembering Allah, hearts find peace." [13:28]

It is also recommended that when we make du'aa' (supplication), we call Allah by His great names. For example, if you want Allah to forgive you and be merciful with you, call him by His names, Ar-Rahman, Ar-Raheem, Al-Ghaffar, Al-Ghafoor. If you want Allah to give you something in this life or in the next life, you call him by his names Al-Kareem, Al-Wahhab, Al-Mughni, and other similar names. It is very easy to call Allah, and to have him listen to you:

Holy Qur'an

﴿ قُلِ ٱدْعُوا۟ ٱللَّهَ أَوِ ٱدْعُوا۟ ٱلرَّحْمَـٰنَ ۖ أَيًّا مَّا تَدْعُوا۟ فَلَهُ ٱلْأَسْمَآءُ ٱلْحُسْنَىٰ ﴾

Say, "Call Him Allah, or call Him the Most Merciful; whatever name you use, to Him belong the most beautiful names" [17: 110]

His Names Are His Attributes

The names of Allah describe the attributes of Allah. You will know Allah better when you study His names and learn their deep meanings. These attributes include the Generous, the Forgiving, the Patient, and the Most Gentle. Some of the words used to describe the attributes of Allah are also used to describe good human characteristics. However, the qualities of Allah's attributes are far higher and better than those of humans. For example, you may say that Zaid is very generous, but, when you use the word generous to describe Zaid, it is very different from describing Allah as the Generous. Human generosity cannot be compared to that of Allah. Allah's generosity is at a level that no human can describe or match. Allah says about Himself:

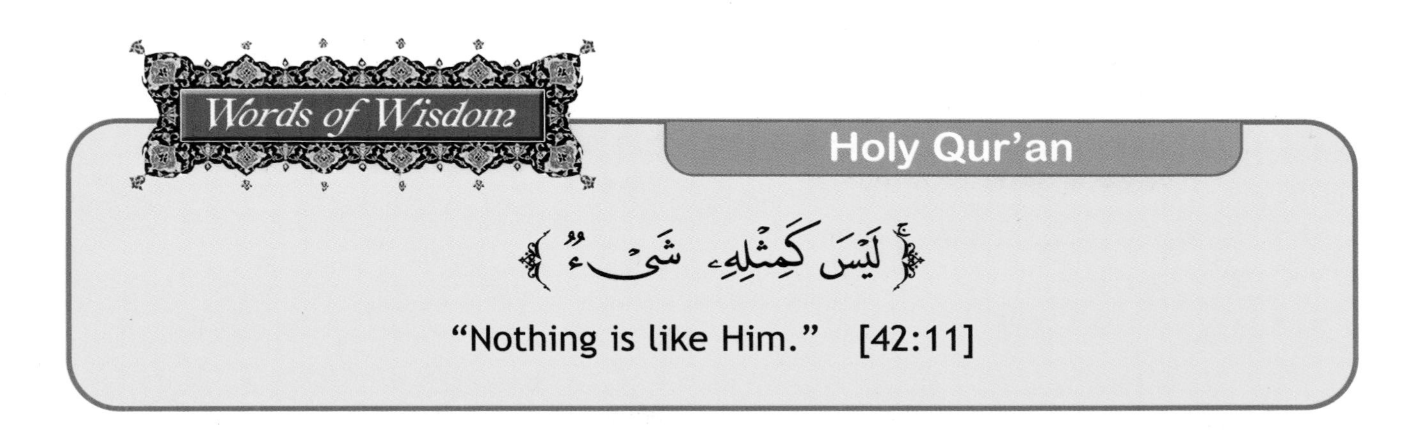

Words of Wisdom

Holy Qur'an

﴿ لَيْسَ كَمِثْلِهِۦ شَىْءٌ ﴾

"Nothing is like Him." [42:11]

The same rule applies to all the other names and attributes of Allah سُبْحَانَهُ وَتَعَالَىٰ . Let's learn the meanings of some of the beautiful names of Allah and see how we can live by them.

Learning Al-Asmaa' Al-Husna

As you learned earlier, Prophet Muhammad ﷺ encouraged us to learn about the names of Allah ﷻ. Learning Al-Asmaa' Al-Husna helps us to understand Allah better, and to love Him more.

1 Al-Kareem الكريـــــم, The Most Generous:

Allah is Al-Kareem because He is the Most Kind, Noble, and Generous. He continually gives the most precious gifts. He gives us loving parents, good health, delicious foods, refreshing drinks, beautiful clothes, and many other physical gifts. He also gives us the gift of Islam and all the great spiritual benefits that come with it. Allah gives His precious gifts even to those who may not deserve them, like evil people and criminals. He gives them many chances to choose to be good.

Holy Qur'an

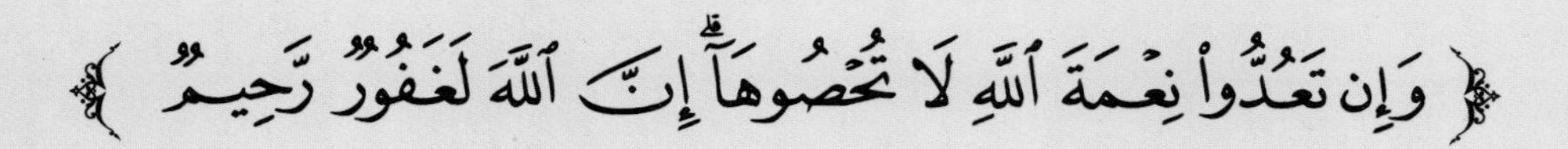

If you try to count up the favors of Allah, you will never be able to number them; for Allah is the Most Forgiving, Most Merciful. [Al-Nahl:18]

Related Names

- Al-Mughni | الـمغنـي | The Giver of Wealth
- Al-Barr | الـبـرّ | The Gracious Giver

Healthy Habit

1. Always be generous and giving, even to those who are not generous with you. This may make them change and become generous with you and others.

-or-

2. Make a donation from your allowance every month.

2 Ar-Raqeeb الرقيب , the Watchful:

Allah ﷻ is the Watchful because He can see and hear everything. He watches every activity in the whole universe at the same time. He is aware of all that we do, no matter where we are. Allah ﷻ watches over us at all times to protect us from others and from ourselves as well. For example, sometimes Shaytan wants to tempt us to do wrong, but we remember that Allah is watching, so we stop. Other times, Allah may stop us when we try to do bad things. Sometimes, bad people may try to hurt us but Allah ﷻ will not allow them to harm us.

Related Names

Al-Baseer	البصير	The All-Seeing
As-Samee'	السميع	The All-Hearing
Al-Aleem	العليم	The All-Knowing
Al-Khabeer	الخبير	The All-Aware
Ash-Shaheed	الشهيد	The Ever-Witnessing

Healthy Habits

1. Always remember that Allah ﷻ watches over you. So, try always to do the right thing and avoid doing wrong.

2. Try to watch over your younger brothers, sisters, and friends, and protect them when they are in danger. We learn this from Allah ﷻ, Who is always taking care of us.

3 Al-Waliyy الـولـي , The Protecting Guardian

Allah ﷻ is Al-Waliyy because He loves, assists, protects, guides, guards, blesses, and rewards all faithful servants. He is more loving and near to us than our parents or any of our dearest friends and relatives.

Holy Qur'an

﴿ ٱللَّهُ وَلِيُّ ٱلَّذِينَ ءَامَنُوا۟ يُخْرِجُهُم مِّنَ ٱلظُّلُمَٰتِ إِلَى ٱلنُّورِ ﴾

Allah is the Protector of the believers: He will lead them away from darkness into light. [2:257]

﴿ وَٱللَّهُ وَلِيُّ ٱلْمُتَّقِينَ ﴾

Allah is the Protector of the righteous people [45:19]

Related Names

- Al-Waali | الوالي | The Protective Ruler
- Al-Hafeeth | الحفيظ | The Protector

Healthy Habit

Always be a good friend and supporter of good people.

Storytime

Once, Prophet Muhammad ﷺ and Abu Bakr As-Siddeeq were hiding in Ghar Thawr near Makkah. There were some Quraysh gangs trying to capture and kill them. The kuffar came near the cave and Abu Bakr was very nervous. Rasulullah was very calm. Abu Bakr whispered to Rasulullah ﷺ , "If they look into this cave they will find us!" rasulullah comforted Abu Bakr and said,

﴿لا تحـزَن إنَّ الله مَعَـنـا﴾

"Do not be worried, Allah will protect us."

And this is exactly what happened; the kuffar didn't see them, and Allah ﷻ protected Rasulullah ﷺ and Abu Bakr.

4 As-Samee', السَّمِيع The All-Hearing:

Allah ﷻ hears, but not the way humans do. He hears the voices of humans, animals, and insects. He even hears your heartbeat and your silent prayers. Even if billions of people talk at the same time, and billions of animals call at the same time, Allah will hear every single one of them clearly.

Holy Qur'an

﴿ يَٰٓأَيُّهَا ٱلَّذِينَ ءَامَنُوا۟ لَا تُقَدِّمُوا۟ بَيْنَ يَدَىِ ٱللَّهِ وَرَسُولِهِۦ ۖ وَٱتَّقُوا۟ ٱللَّهَ ۚ إِنَّ ٱللَّهَ سَمِيعٌ عَلِيمٌ ﴾

O You who believe! Do not put yourselves forward before Allah and His Messenger. But fear Allah, for Allah is He Who hears and knows all things. [49:1]

Healthy Habit

Always try to listen to others carefully. Good listening skills help you learn more and grow smarter. People will like you more if you listen more than you talk.

5 Al-Hakeem الحكيم, the Wise:

Allah ﷻ is the Wisest. He has knowledge of all seen and unseen activities in the universe. He is the only One Who always makes the correct decision. And His decisions are always right.

﴿ تَنزِيلُ ٱلْكِتَٰبِ مِنَ ٱللَّهِ ٱلْعَزِيزِ ٱلْحَكِيمِ ﴾

The Revelation of the Book is from Allah, the Exalted in Power, One Full of Wisdom. [46:2]

Allah ﷻ gives knowledge and wisdom to some people. Those who are blessed with wisdom are granted great blessings. Listen to what Allah says:

﴿ يُؤْتِي ٱلْحِكْمَةَ مَن يَشَآءُ ۚ وَمَن يُؤْتَ ٱلْحِكْمَةَ فَقَدْ أُوتِيَ خَيْرًا كَثِيرًا ۗ وَمَا يَذَّكَّرُ إِلَّآ أُو۟لُوا۟ ٱلْأَلْبَٰبِ ﴾

"He grants wisdom to whomever He wants; and whoever is granted wisdom has indeed won overflowing goodness; but none will remember the guidance except those who have [wise] minds." [2:269]

Related Names

Al-Aleem	العليم	The All-Knowing
Al-Khabeer	الخبير	The All-Aware
An-Noor	النور	The Light

Healthy Habit

Try to learn what Allah wants you to do since He knows what is best for you. This way you may become wise, insha'Allah.

6,7 Al-Awwal & Al-Aakhir الأول والآخر , the First & the Last

Allah ﷻ is the first in everything. Al-Awwal also means the One whose existence is without a beginning. Everyone and everything in this world has a beginning and has an end, except Allah. When everything ceases to exist, Allah ﷻ remains. His creations may come to an end, but He stays forever. He is final and perfect in every way.

Holy Qur'an

﴿ هُوَ ٱلْأَوَّلُ وَٱلْـَٔاخِرُ وَٱلظَّـٰهِرُ وَٱلْبَاطِنُ ۖ وَهُوَ بِكُلِّ شَىْءٍ عَلِيمٌ ﴾

He is the First and the Last, the Evident and the Unseen: and He has full knowledge of all things. [57:3]

Related Names

Al-Aliyy	العلي	The Highest
Al-Mubdi'	المبديء	The Beginner of Creation
Al-Mu'eed	المعيد	The Renewer
Al-Muta'al	المتعالي	The Most High
Al-Baqi	الباقي	The Ever-Lasting

Healthy Habit

Always be the first to do good things.

8 Al-Hadi الـهادي , The Giver of Guidance

Allah ﷻ shows His servants the right way. He kindly guides them to their safe destinies. He sends prophets and messengers to guide mankind to the straight path with faith and knowledge. This guidance helps people to live happily in this life and win Paradise in the next life.

Holy Qur'an

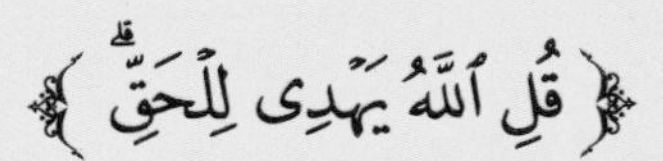

Say, "Allah guides to the truth." [10:35]

﴿وَٱللَّهُ يَقُولُ ٱلْحَقَّ وَهُوَ يَهْدِى ٱلسَّبِيلَ﴾

Allah tells (you) the truth, and He shows the (right) way. [33:4]

Related Names

- Ar-Rasheed الرشيد The Guide to the Right Path
- An-Noor النور The Light
- Al-Fattah الفتاح The Inspirer
- Al-Haqq الحق The Truth

Healthy Habit

Always guide others to do good deeds.

9 Al-Adl العـــدل , The Just

Al-Adl means the One Who always acts in a just and fair manner. Allah ﷻ delivers absolute justice. His justice is based upon complete knowledge of past, present, and future. Allah ﷻ never oppresses anyone in this life or in the Hereafter.

Holy Qur'an

﴿ إِنَّ ٱللَّهَ لَا يَظْلِمُ ٱلنَّاسَ شَيْـًٔا وَلَٰكِنَّ ٱلنَّاسَ أَنفُسَهُمْ يَظْلِمُونَ ﴾

Truly, Allah does not deal with mankind unjustly; rather, mankind transgresses against their own souls. [10:44]

Related Names

- Al-Hakam الحكم The Judge
- Al-Muqsit المقسط The Fair

10 Al-Haleem الحـلـيـم , The Tolerant

Al-Haleem is the One Who is infinitely tolerant and patient with His servants. He tolerates our mistakes and delays our punishments, and He gives us many chances. Though we may deserve punishment, He often forgives us out of great love.

Holy Qur'an

﴿ إِنَّ ٱللَّهَ غَفُورٌ حَلِيمٌ ﴾

Allah is truly Most Forgiving, Most Tolerant. [3:155]

Hadeeth Shareef

عن ابن عباس رضي الله عنه أن رسولَ الله ﷺ قال للأحنف بن قيس: "إن فيكَ خِصْلَتَيْنِ يحِبُّهما الله : الحِلْمُ والأناة"

رواه مسلم والترمذي

Ibn Abbas رضي الله عنه narrated that Rasulullah ﷺ called upon Al-Ahnaf Ibn Qays and told him:

"Allah loves two personal qualities in you: tolerance and patience. "

Reported in Muslim and At-Tirmithi

Related Names

- As-Saboor الصبور The Ever-Patient
- Al-Lateef اللطيف The Gentle
- Al-Afoww العفو The Pardoner

Healthy Habits

1. Always be fair with everyone, whether you are in a good or a bad mood.

2. Always be tolerant of others, especially when they make innocent mistakes.

الله

Chapter Review

Listen to a nasheed about Al-Asmaa'-ul-Husna, and try to memorize it.

If someone came to you and said "Muslims really believe in many gods because they believe in the 99 names" how would you answer him or her?

1. How many names of Allah سبحانه وتعالى did the Prophet tell us about?
2. What are Al-Asmaa' Al Husna?
3. What reward will Allah give you if you learn His names properly?
4. Which of Allah's names means the Protecting Friend?
5. What do we mean when we say that Allah سبحانه وتعالى is the Wise?

Ninety-Nine Names, One Creator (II)

The Beautiful Names of Allah

CHAPTER THREE

Names for Allah Alone

In the last chapter you learned many of Allah's great names. You know that there are many other names you must learn. However, there are some names that are for Allah ﷻ alone. People must not give these names to anyone other than Allah. These names include Allah, Ar-Rahman, Al-Khaliq, Al-Quddoos, Al-Jabbar, Al-Mutakabbir, Al-Qahhar, Ar-Raziq, and Ar-Razzaq.

1 Allah الله

Allah ﷻ is the proper name of God and means the One we worship. We must not worship anyone or anything other than Allah ﷻ . A related name with a similar, although not identical, meaning is Al-Wahid الواحد (the Unified).

Did You Know?

In other semitic languages, the name for God (Allah) is only slightly different. In Hebrew, the language of Prophet Musa, or Moses, and the Jews, Allah is called Eloh, or Elohim. In Aramaic, the language of Prophet Isa, or Jesus, Allah is called Alaha.

2 Ar-Rahman الرحمن , The Most Beneficent

Ar-Rahman is the One Who has unlimited mercy for everyone in this world, and especially for the believers in the Hereafter.

Holy Qur'an

﴿ هُوَ ٱللَّهُ ٱلَّذِى لَآ إِلَٰهَ إِلَّا هُوَ عَٰلِمُ ٱلْغَيْبِ وَٱلشَّهَٰدَةِ هُوَ ٱلرَّحْمَٰنُ ٱلرَّحِيمُ ﴾

He is Allah, no god but Him; Who knows (all things) both secret and open; He is The Most Gracious, The Most Merciful. [59:22]

Related Names

- Ar-Ra'oof الرؤوف The Kind
- Ar-Raheem الرحيم The Most Merciful
- Al-Ghaffar الغفار The Ever-Forgiving
- Al-Ghafoor الغفور The Forgiving

3 Al-Quddoos القدوس , The Holy One

"Al-Quddoos" is the One Who is pure from any weakness or imperfection. All people, animals, and things have shortcomings and weaknesses, but Allah is perfect. No one is holy but Allah.

Related Names

- Al-Jaleel الجليل The Glorious
- Al-Majeed المجيد The Majestic

Al-Jabbar الجبار , The Irresistible

"Al-Jabbar" is the One Who can force all others to submit to His power. Even kings, presidents, super heroes, and powerful people cannot resist His power. They all fail to even challenge Him. Al-Jabbar سبحانه وتعالى destroyed Pharaoh, Qaroon, the people of Aad, the people of Thamood, Abu Jahl, Abu Lahab, and many other tyrants when they dared to challenge Him. However, Allah uses His power only to support good and destroy evil.

STORY TIME

Pharaoh (Phir'oun) was a very evil ruler in Egypt. He oppressed his people, especially the Children of Israel, who were living in Egypt at that time. Allah chose Prophet Musa (Moses) to go to Phir'oun and invite him to the true faith. Pharaoh refused to obey Allah and claimed that he was God. Then Allah ordered Musa to flee with the Children of Israel from Egypt to Palestine. Prophet Musa obeyed. The flight began during the night. Pharaoh and his soldiers learned about the escape and chased Musa and the Children of Israel. The Children of Israel became very frightened as they came to the Red Sea. They knew that Pharaoh would have no mercy on them. They didn't have ships to help them escape across the sea. The Children of Israel came to their Prophet, Musa. They cried to him, "We will be captured soon!"

▲ *Satellite picture of Egypt, Sinai, and part of Palestine.*

Prophet Musa said with confidence,

﴿كلاّ إنّ معي ربّي سَيَـهْدِين﴾

"No, My Lord is with me, and He will guide me through!"

Allah immediately ordered Musa to strike the sea with his rod. Musa and his people were stunned to see the sea parting. A dry path opened for them to pass over to the other side. Allah protected all of them and destroyed Pharaoh and his army.

Related Names

- Al-Muqtadir | المقتدر | The Prevailing
- Al-Qahhar | القهار | The Conqueror
- Al-Qawiyy | القوي | The Powerful
- Al-Muntaqim | المنتقم | The Avenger

5 Al-Mutakabbir المتكبر, The Majestic

Al-Mutakabbir is the One Who is much greater than all His creation. He is the One whose acts and power are greater and higher than those of anyone or anything else.

Holy Qur'an

﴿ هُوَ ٱللَّهُ ٱلَّذِى لَآ إِلَٰهَ إِلَّا هُوَ ٱلْمَلِكُ ٱلْقُدُّوسُ ٱلسَّلَٰمُ ٱلْمُؤْمِنُ ٱلْمُهَيْمِنُ ٱلْعَزِيزُ ٱلْجَبَّارُ ٱلْمُتَكَبِّرُ سُبْحَٰنَ ٱللَّهِ عَمَّا يُشْرِكُونَ ﴾

He is Allah, other than whom there is no god, the King, the Holy One, the Source of Peace, the Guardian of Faith, the Preserver of Safety, the Exalted in Might, the Irresistible, the Majestic: Glory to Allah! (High is He) above the partners they attribute to Him. [59:23]

Related Names

- Al-Kabeer | الكبير | The Greatest
- Al-Atheem | العظيم | The Grand
- Al-Azeez | العزيز | The Mighty
- Al-Malik | الملك | The King
- Al-Muta'al | المتعال | The Most High

6. Al-Khaliq الخالق , The Creator

Al-Khaliq is the One Who brings everything from non-existence into being. He is the only true Creator of people, animals, plants, planets, all things, and the whole universe. No person can create living or nonliving things from nothing; Al-Khaliq, **subhanahu wa-ta'ala,** did and continues to do it.

Holy Qur'an

﴿ هُوَ ٱللَّهُ ٱلۡخَٰلِقُ ٱلۡبَارِئُ ٱلۡمُصَوِّرُۖ لَهُ ٱلۡأَسۡمَآءُ ٱلۡحُسۡنَىٰۚ يُسَبِّحُ لَهُۥ مَا فِي ٱلسَّمَٰوَٰتِ وَٱلۡأَرۡضِۖ وَهُوَ ٱلۡعَزِيزُ ٱلۡحَكِيمُ ﴾

He is Allah, the Creator, the Inventor, the Maker of forms. To Him belong the Most Beautiful Names: whatever is in the Heavens, praises Him; and He is the Mighty, the Wise. [59:24]

Related Names

Al-Badee'	البديع	The Awesome Inventor
Al-Bari'	البارئ	The Inventor
Al-Mubdi'	المبدع	The Originator
Al-Muhyi	المحيي	The Giver of Life
Al-Musawwir	المصور	The Image Maker

Look at Allah's creation. No one can do the same! None can even come close to it!

Allah's Creation

A food market in Uzbekistan.

7 Ar-Razzaq الرزاق , The Ever-Provider.

Ar-Razzaq is the One Who always provides His creation with all its needs. He gives people their food, water, and everything else. People, even our parents, cannot give us something if Allah objects. And no one can stop us from getting anything if Allah wants us to have it. Allah put enough food in this world to feed everyone. But many people don't have enough to eat because other people have a lot but don't share.

Holy Qur'an

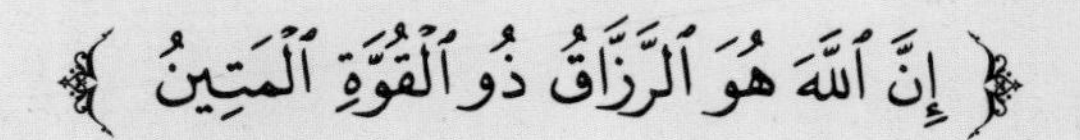

Allah is truly the One Who gives (all) sustenance, - [He is] the Lord of Power, the Steadfast.

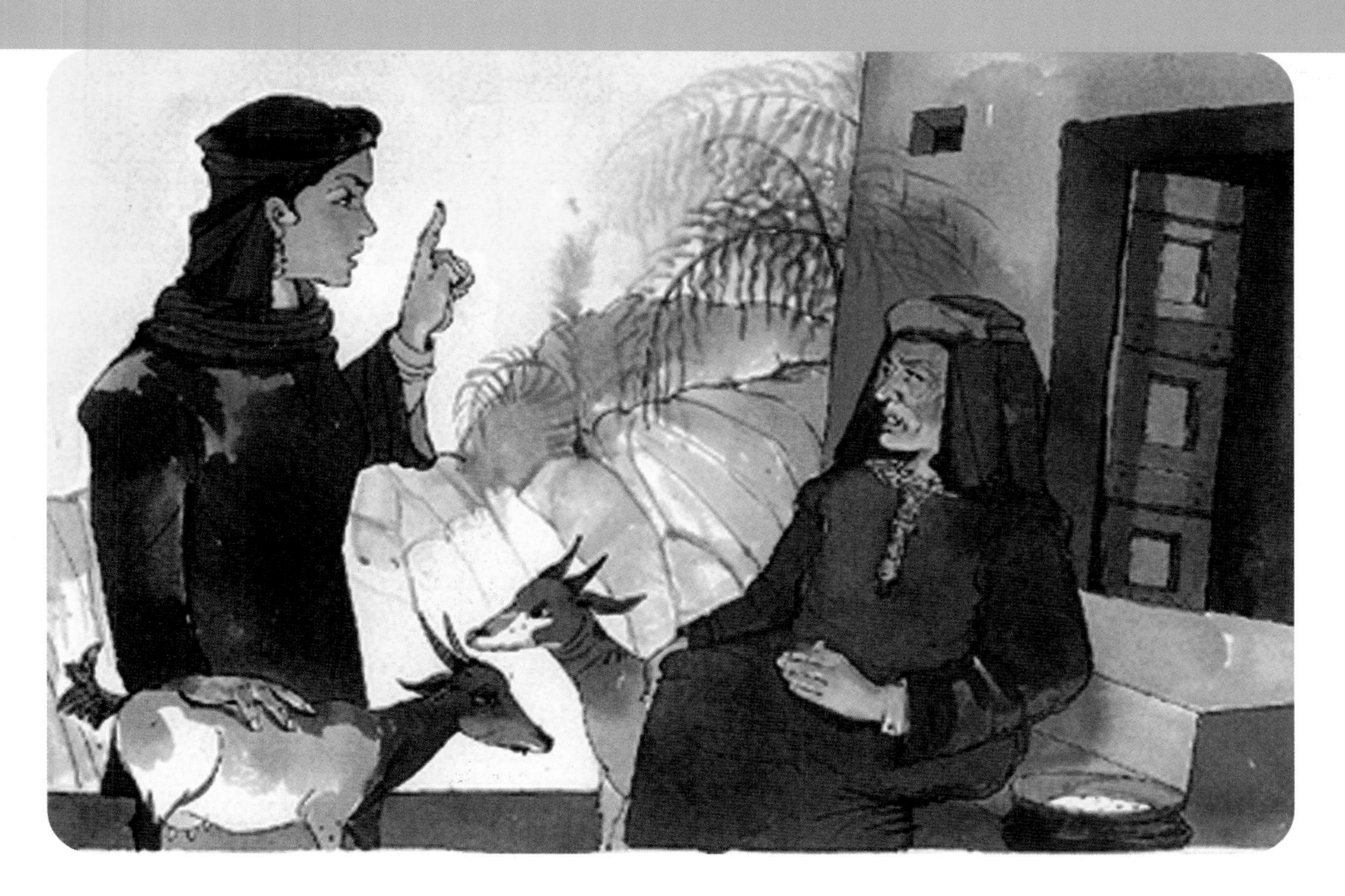

Story Time

Once a Muslim woman's dear husband passed away. He passed away and left her alone. A few days later, one of her friends asked her how she would take care of her family. How could she provide for herself and her children now that her husband had died? The woman answered, "My husband was not Ar-Razzaq, Allah is."

Related Names

Al-Wahhab	الوهاب	The Giver of Gifts
Al-Muqeet	المقيت	The Giver of Food

Importance of Knowing Allah's Names

1. Knowing Allah's names is the best knowledge that a person can have. Think about it: is there anything more important than knowledge of Allah? No other knowledge can compare to it.

2. One of the best ways to have knowledge of Allah is by understanding His most beautiful names. Knowing Allah makes a person love and appreciate Him more.

3. Remember in the tawheed lesson that one of the categories of tawheed is called Tawheed Al Asmaa' was Sifaat. Learning Allah's names increases our level of faith.

4. Allah سبحانه وتعالى created human beings and other creatures to know Him and worship Him. So, when a person learns about Allah, he or she is fulfilling his duty and obligation toward Allah.

5. Knowledge of Allah's names is the basis of all other knowledge. Allah is Al-Aleem, Al-Hakeem, which means the All Knowing and All Wise. Any past knowledge or future knowledge waiting to be discovered is already known to Allah.

6. Each of the 99 names of Allah سبحانه وتعالى represents a quality that Allah possesses. Some of these names represent qualities reserved for Allah alone (Al-Khaliq, Al-Tawwab, Ar-Rahman, Al-Quddoos and others). Other names represent qualities which are perfected in Allah سبحانه وتعالى ; these include As-Saboor, Ar-Raheem, Al-Kareem. People can acquire such qualities, but not as perfectly. Indeed, there is no comparison between people's patience, mercy, or generosity, with that of Allah سبحانه وتعالى . While no one can ever have as much patience, mercy, generosity, strength, or kindness as Allah, we should all strive to increase these qualities within ourselves.

Chapter Review

Make a poster of the 99 names of Allah. Write the names in Arabic and English.

1. How can the names of Allah ﷻ make you a better person?

2. Choose three names of Allah ﷻ and explain how you apply them in your life.

1. Why is it important to know Allah's names?
2. Write in Arabic and English seven names of Allah that are only used to describe Allah ﷻ .
3. Can you compare the qualities of Allah to those of a person? Why or why not?
4. List three points that show the importance of learning Al-Asmaa' Al-Husna.

Away from Tawheed

CHAPTER FOUR

Pre-reading Questions

1. What is the opposite of tawheed?
2. What does shirk mean?
3. How bad is it to believe in or worship anything other than God?

Word Watch

shirk (Polytheism)	شِرك
mushrik	مُشرك
Shirk Al Asghar	الشرك الأصغر
Ar-Riyaa'	الرّياء
Sihr	سِحر

Introduction

In the lesson about tawheed we learned how Islam stresses the importance of the One and Only God. In this lesson we are going to learn about shirk, which means believing in other gods along with Allah ﷻ and worshipping them. **Shirk** is a major sin in Islam, and in this lesson we will learn why.

Shirk Explained?

Shirk شرك is the opposite of tawheed. If tawheed is to worship the One and only God, then shirk is to worship something other than Allah ﷻ. Shirk is the worst sin in Islam. A person who falls into Shirk is called مشرك **Mushrik**. Allah says in the Qur'an:

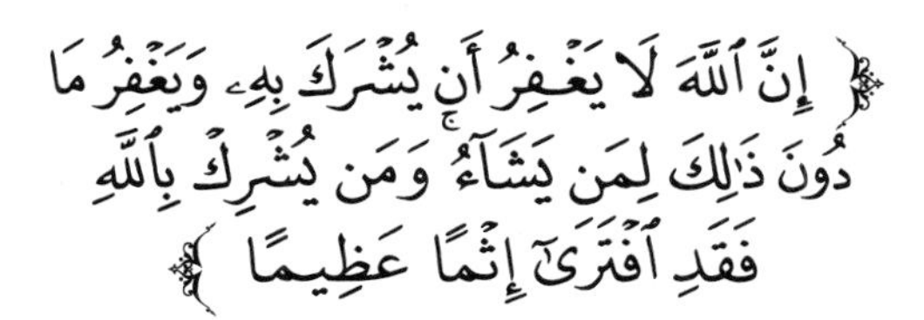

"Surely Allah does not forgive that anything should be associated with Him, and forgives what is besides that to whomsoever He pleases; and whoever worships anything with Allah, he indeed commits a great sin." [4:48]

Human beings were created to worship Allah, their only true Creator, Who is also the Creator of the whole universe. Allah ﷻ says in the Qur'an:

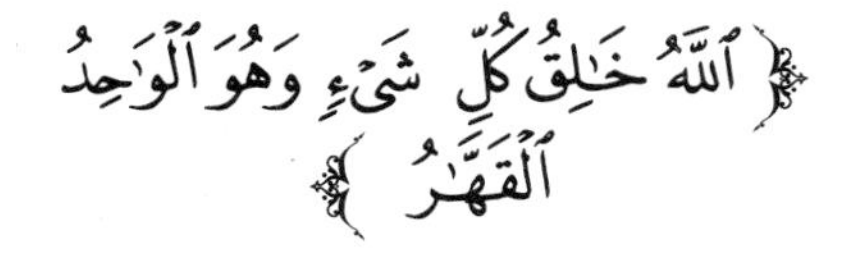

"Allah is the Creator of all things, and He is the One, the Supreme." [13:16]

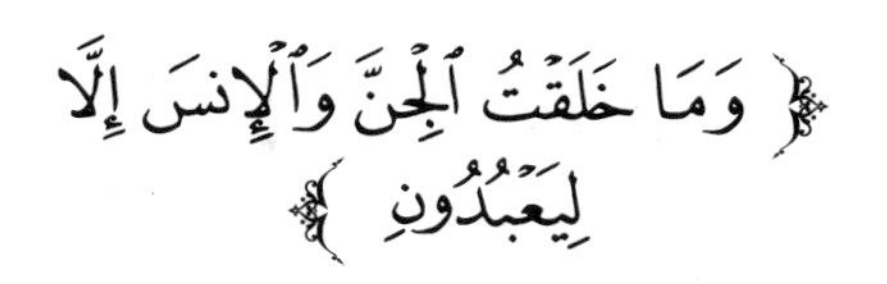

"I have not created jinn or mankind except for my worship." [51:56]

By committing, shirk a person is going against the statement of tawheed.

لا إله إلا الله

La ilaha illa Allah

People become Muslim when they believe in and declare the Shahadah, but they depart from Islam when they act against it. Believing in other gods beside Allah ﷻ is an act against Shahadah It causes a person to go away from tawheed and out of Islam.

Islam is a religion that teaches pure monotheism. Monotheism means the belief in only One God. Remember how the Arabs during Jahiliyyah used to practice polytheism, which is believing in and worshipping many gods. Both the Qur'an and Sunnah of the Prophet Muhammad ﷺ stress that there is only one God.

Some people during ancient times invented false religions. They called to worship many idols, instead of worshipping Allah, the One and only true Creator of man and the universe.

Types of Shirk

In the tawheed lesson we mentioned three different categories of tawheed. In the section that you are about to read, we will revisit the three categories of tawheed. This time we will look at how shirk can be committed by acting against the three different categories of tawheed.

1 Shirk in Ar-Ruboobiyyah شِرك الرُّبوبية

As Muslims, we believe that it is Allah alone Who creates, controls, and maintains the universe. The belief that other people or things have shared in the act of creating, controlling, and/ or maintaining the universe is a form of shirk. For example, ancient Greeks and Romans used to believe in many gods and goddesses. Their gods had names like Zeus, Athena, Eros, and Mercury. In Arabia and elsewhere, they used to worship idols and statues, hoping that they would help them get closer to God. In Hinduism, a religion followed in India and other parts of the world, people also believe in

Some idol worshippers made their false gods from gold, but this does not make their false beliefs true.

and worship many gods and goddesses. Each god or goddess has a role to play in creating or controlling parts of this world. Astaghfir Allah! This is a form of shirk and Islam rejects all shirk.

Many Christians believe that God has three parts:

1. **God the Father**
2. **God the Son, or Jesus Christ**
3. **God the Holy Spirit**

In Christianity, this is known as the Trinity. It says that the one God consists of three persons.

AstaghfiruAllah! This is also a major form of shirk. As Muslims, we know that Allah ﷻ is the only Creator of the Universe. God or Allah does not have a father or a son, and He cannot be divided into two or three parts.

Many of the people who worship idols, people, or other things believe in God as the Creator of the world. But they think that God somehow is also part of these things or people that they worship. Others do not believe in one God, but believe in many gods. These imagined gods and goddesses sometimes fight and disagree.

2 Shirk in Ibadah شِركٌ في العِبادة

There are a few categories of shirk in ibadah, or worship.

Types of Shirk in Ibadah

Anyone who directs any act of worship to something other than Allah falls into shirk. Worshipping humans, animals, idols, or anything else is strictly forbidden in Islam. Actions involving prayer, supplication, bowing, and prostration are clear examples of worship. Those who commit this type of shirk have moved away from Islam. However, there are other examples of worshipping other than Allah which can be also described as acts of shirk. Sadly, some Muslims worship saints or travel to graves to ask for help from dead people. They make tawaaf around these graves and they sacrifice in the name of the dead people. All of these are major forms of shirk and must be avoided. We must offer our worship only to Allah, not to anyone or anything else.

In the Qur'an, Allah says

﴿ قُلْ إِنَّ صَلَاتِي وَنُسُكِي وَمَحْيَايَ وَمَمَاتِي لِلَّهِ رَبِّ الْعَالَمِينَ ﴾

"Say, 'Truly, my prayer, my sacrifice, my life and my death are all for Allah, Lord of the worlds'." [6:162]

As you learned earlier, shirk will not be forgiven and whoever dies while committing it will not be able to enter Jannah. But remember, Allah is Al Ghafoor, which means the Most Forgiving. Allah ﷻ will accept the repentance of those who repent before they die, and they will inshaAllah be forgiven.

Ash-Shirk Al-Asghar

الشِّرْكُ الأَصْغَر

(The Minor Shirk)

There are other types of shirk in worship and they are described as **Ash-Shirk Al-Asghar**. Although these acts do not necessarily automatically take the person beyond the path of Islam, they are still very serious sins.

Mahmood Ibn Lubayd reported that Prophet Muhammad ﷺ said:

> "The thing that I fear for you the most is minor shirk." The companions asked "O Messenger of Allah, what is minor shirk?" He replied, "Showing off (Ar- Riyaa'), for Allah will say on the Day of

Judgment, when people are receiving their rewards, 'Go to those whom you were showing off to in the world, and see if you can get any reward from them.'"

Ar-Riyaa' is having insincere intentions and performing acts of worship in order to show off to other people. A person is committing riyaa' if he/she prays in front of people, just so the people can think that he or she is a very good Muslim. It is very important for a person to make sure that he/she has pure intentions to only please Allah, and nobody else.

Healthy Habit

Always purify your intention when you perform good deeds. Avoid riyaa', or it will wipe out your rewards.

Other forms of minor shirk involve:

▶ **Swearing by other than Allah.** Once, Abdullah Ibn Omar رضي الله عنه saw a man swearing by his father, and another swearing by Al-Ka'bah, so he told them not to do that. Then he said: "I heard Prophet Muhammad ﷺ once saying:

'Whoever swears by other than Allah has committed an act of shirk.'"

Here, Rasulullah means minor shirk.

▶ **Following one's desires while not obeying Allah and His Prophet.** Some people love money,

games, fame, and other worldly things more than they love Allah. They will do forbidden things to have more fun. They do such things, even if they have to disobey Allah and displease Him. Some people even skip prayers in order to keep playing video games or watching TV. To them, their desires are more important than Allah ﷻ. Allah says in the Qur'an,

﴿ أَفَرَءَيْتَ مَنِ ٱتَّخَذَ إِلَٰهَهُۥ هَوَىٰهُ وَأَضَلَّهُ ٱللَّهُ عَلَىٰ عِلْمٍ ﴾

"Have you then seen the one who follows his low desire as god, and Allah has made him go astray although he has knowledge?" [45:23]

Healthy Habit

Always obey Allah first, and avoid disobeying Him for a little fun in this life.

▶ **Wearing charms or using spells to weaken jinn or evil spirits.** Some people wear certain charms and use spells to protect themselves or children from jinn. They think that these things have the power to protect them from the harm of devils. These people are committing minor acts of shirk. Instead, they should pray, read Qur'an, or make du'aa to Allah ﷻ, asking Him for His protection. This is what Rasulullah used to do when he wanted Allah's protection against evil powers.

▶ **To believe in fortune telling and fortune tellers.** Prophet Muhammad ﷺ once said,

من أتى كاهناً فصدّقه بما يقول فقد كفر بما أنزل على محمد ﷺ.

رواه أبو داود

"Whoever visits a fortune teller and believes in what he says, he has disbelieved in what has been revealed to Muhammad." (Reported by Imam Abu Dawood.)

Reading horoscopes, for example, is a type of fortune telling. Muslims must avoid reading them and believing them.

****

It is important to understand that just because these forms of shirk are called minor shirk, it does not mean that they are not serious. The reason they are called minor shirk is because they are not as obvious when compared to major shirk. Sometimes it is hard for a person to know they are committing Ash-Shirk Al-Asghar. So, we should be very careful not to commit Ash-Shirk Al-Asghar.

3 Shirk in Al-Asmaa' was-Sifaat شِرك في الأسماء والصفات

You learned earlier that Allah has the greatest names and attributes. They are also called Al-Asmaa' Al-Husna. Therefore, you know that Allah is unique, and none is like Him. However, many people fall into shirk because they do not believe in the names and attributes of Allah ﷻ properly. They may give Allah some names or attributes that are unfitting to Allah ﷻ. Here are examples of shirk in Al-Asmaa' and As-Sifaat.

▶ An-Nafi: Denying the great attributes of Allah. Some people deny that Allah has the greatest qualities and attributes. They say the names of Allah ﷻ like Ar-Rahman, Al-Kareem, or Al-Qawiyy have no actual meaning. They claim that God is not merciful, generous or powerful, and that these are just empty names. This is the worst type of shirk in Al-Asmaa' and As-Sifaat. Allah has the best names and attributes, and He is so great because these attributes are real and actual.

▶ **At-Tashbeeh:** Giving Allah ungodly attributes. Some people give God human qualities, like getting sick, tired, jealous, or greedy. Astaghfirullah! For example, some religious books say that God created the world in six days, got tired, then rested on the seventh day. This is very wrong. God is like no other, and that means we cannot compare Him to humans, or to any of His creations.

▶ **At-Tahreef:** Changing the meaning of God's attributes. Some people understand the meaning of God's names or attributes in an incorrect manner. We should always understand the meaning of Allah's names and attributes the way God or the Prophet explain then. For example, some would say that God's name Al-Wadood does not mean the loving, because that makes God emotional, like people or animals. Therefore, when Allah describes Himself in the Qur'an as loving this thing or that, they say it means that Allah wants it. That is also wrong. Allah loves people and His good creation, but the quality of His love is greater and different than that of people or animals.

Effects of Shirk

1 Shirk puts humans in a very low status.

Allah created jinn, animals, humans, and many other things. But Allah says that man is created in the highest of forms. This means that human beings are put above all other creations. Humans are known as Khaleefat Allah fil Ardh (the vicegerents of Allah on Earth). When a person commits shirk, then he falls from a very high status to the lowest one.

Allah says:

﴿وَمَن يُشْرِكْ بِاللَّهِ فَكَأَنَّمَا خَرَّ مِنَ السَّمَاءِ فَتَخْطَفُهُ الطَّيْرُ أَوْ تَهْوِي بِهِ الرِّيحُ فِي مَكَانٍ سَحِيقٍ﴾

"Whoever claims partners unto Allah, it is as if he had fallen from the sky and the birds had snatched him or the wind had blown him to a very low place." [Surat-ul-Hajj 22:31]

2 Shirk is the cause of evil and superstition.

It is because of shirk that many people believe in the powers of jinn and spirits. Some people think fortune tellers can predict the future, or cause something to happen or not to happen. They do that because they don't have proper faith and tawheed in their hearts. All these are forms of evil practices that lead to shirk.

Abu Hurayrah رضي الله عنه narrated that rasulullah ﷺ said:

" اجْتَنِبوا الموبقات: الشِرْكُ بالله والسِّحْرْ"

رواه البخاري

"Avoid the destructive sins: shirk and witchcraft."

(Reported in Al-Bukhari)

3 Committing shirk is injustice.

Injustice means to deny someone's right or to treat someone unfairly. By worshipping and praising something instead of Allah, we are being ungrateful and unjust to Allah. Only Allah has the right to be worshipped.

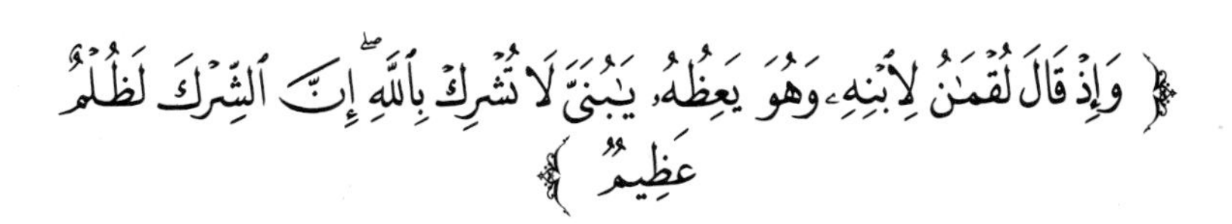

"Luqman said to his son while advising him, 'Oh my son! Do not call partners to Allah. Indeed shirk is a great injustice.'"
[Luqman 31: 13]

4 Shirk causes anxiety and fear.

A person who commits shirk lives in constant fear and anxiety. He fears powers like an idol, a fire, or a spirit. While trying to make one idol happy, he is afraid another one will be angry with him. Remember that we should only fear Allah.

Idols that used to be worshipped by disbelievers in Arabia and around the world

5 Shirk wipes out rewards in the Hereafter.

Heaven is forbidden to those who associate partners with Allah. No person who commits shirk will be allowed to enter Paradise. Also, Allah does not accept the good deeds of a mushrik. Therefore, those who commit shirk will have no rewards for whatever good deeds they do in this life. Allah ﷻ will reward them during this life only by giving them more wealth, health, and entertainment. But they will not win any rewards in the next life, and they will never win Jannah. This is because they disbelieve in Allah ﷻ or worship others with Him. Allah describes this in the Qur'an:

﴿ وَقَدِمْنَآ إِلَىٰ مَا عَمِلُوا۟ مِنْ عَمَلٍ فَجَعَلْنَٰهُ هَبَآءً مَّنثُورًا ﴾

"And We will come to what deeds they have done, so We shall make them as scattered floating dust." [25:23]

Create a table for the shirk against the three types of tawheed. List three examples of shirk under each type. Use the example below to create your table.

	Tawheed Ar-Ruboobiyyah	Tawheed Al-Ibadah	Tawheed Al-Asmaa'
1.			
2.			
3.			

STORY TIME

The People of Prophet Musa

The people of Prophet Musa had to leave their homes in Egypt to escape the evil Pharaoh. While searching for a new home, Musa's people wandered in the desert of Sinai for many years. One day, Musa عليه السّلام received Allah's order to climb a high mountain there. Prophet Musa عليه السّلام had to stay there for forty days and nights, praying to Allah and listening to what Allah would tell him and his people. But forty days and nights seemed a very long time. And while Musa عليه السّلام was away, his people became impatient. They decided to make a calf out of gold and worship it. When Musa عليه السّلام came down from the mountain, he saw the calf and became very angry. He smashed the calf into pieces and scolded his people so much that they felt ashamed of themselves. "You must never, ever worship anything else apart from Allah," Musa عليه السّلام instructed them.

Musa عليه السّلام had brought a book to his people which Allah had revealed to him on the mountain. This book is called At-Tawrah, or the Torah. In At-Tawrah, it is stated that men should never worship anything else except Allah. They must never kill a fellow man. They must not take things which do not belong to them. They must be good to their parents and to one another.

Prophet Musa's people understood then that they had been very ungrateful to Allah. It was Allah Who had created them and saved them from Pharaoh and his soldiers. They prayed to Allah and thanked Him for what He had done for them. They asked for His forgiveness and made a promise that they would do good deeds.

Allah سُبحانه وتعالي forgave those who were ashamed of the bad deeds they had done and wanted to return to Allah.

Chapter Review

1. Why is shirk the worst sin man can ever commit?

2. Why do you think Allah would not accept the good deeds of a person if he or she is a mushrik?

1. What is shirk?
2. Describe how one can commit shirk in tawheed-ur-Ruboobiyyah?
3. Describe how one can commit shirk in tawheed-ul-Ibadah?
4. Describe how one can commit shirk in tawheed-ul-Asmaa' Wassifaat?
5. Does Allah forgive shirk? Support your answer with an ayah from the Holy Qur'an.
6. Is Ash-Shirk-ul-Asghar not very important?
7. What are the five effects of committing shirk?
8. How did the people of Musa عليه السّلام commit shirk?

UNIT A CHAPTER 5 LESSON ONE

Surat Al-Mulk: The Kingdom (1)

Introduction

Surat Al-Mulk was revealed in Makkah. It has several other names. One of them is "Tabarak." The Messenger of Allah ﷺ called it "Al-Mani'ah," meaning that it helps prevent people from committing sins, or it protects them from being punished for them. He also said: "It is Al-Munjiyah (Savior) because it saves the person who knows it from the punishment of the grave".

(Reported in At-Tirmithi)

Rasulullah advised Muslims to read Surat Tabarak every day.

Some Signs of Allah's Power

WORDS OF WISDOM

Holy Qur'an

سورة الملك

Surat Al-Mulk 1-5

بِسْمِ ٱللَّهِ ٱلرَّحْمَٰنِ ٱلرَّحِيمِ

﴿ تَبَٰرَكَ ٱلَّذِى بِيَدِهِ ٱلْمُلْكُ وَهُوَ عَلَىٰ كُلِّ شَىْءٍ قَدِيرٌ ﴿١﴾ ٱلَّذِى خَلَقَ ٱلْمَوْتَ وَٱلْحَيَوٰةَ لِيَبْلُوَكُمْ
أَيُّكُمْ أَحْسَنُ عَمَلًا وَهُوَ ٱلْعَزِيزُ ٱلْغَفُورُ ﴿٢﴾ ٱلَّذِى خَلَقَ سَبْعَ سَمَٰوَٰتٍ طِبَاقًا مَّا تَرَىٰ فِى
خَلْقِ ٱلرَّحْمَٰنِ مِن تَفَٰوُتٍ فَٱرْجِعِ ٱلْبَصَرَ هَلْ تَرَىٰ مِن فُطُورٍ ﴿٣﴾ ثُمَّ ٱرْجِعِ ٱلْبَصَرَ كَرَّتَيْنِ
يَنقَلِبْ إِلَيْكَ ٱلْبَصَرُ خَاسِئًا وَهُوَ حَسِيرٌ ﴿٤﴾ وَلَقَدْ زَيَّنَّا ٱلسَّمَآءَ ٱلدُّنْيَا بِمَصَٰبِيحَ وَجَعَلْنَٰهَا
رُجُومًا لِّلشَّيَٰطِينِ وَأَعْتَدْنَا لَهُمْ عَذَابَ ٱلسَّعِيرِ ﴿٥﴾ ﴾

TRANSLITERATION

Tabarak-allathee biyadih-il-mulku wahuwa 'ala kulli shay-'in qadeer (1) Allathee khalaq-al-mawta waalhayata liyabluwakum ayyukum ahsanu amalaw-wahuwal-azeez-ul- ghafoor (67-2) Allathee khalaqa sab'aa samawatin tibaqam-ma tara fee khalq-ir-rahmani min tafaawot, far-ji'il-basara hal tara min futoor (67-3) Thumm-arji'il-basara karratayni yanqalib ilayk-al-basaru khasi'-an wahuwa haseer (67-4) Walaqad zayyannas-sama'a-ddunya bimasabeeha waja'alnaha rujoomal-lishshayateeni wa'aatadna lahum athab-as- sa'eer (67-5)

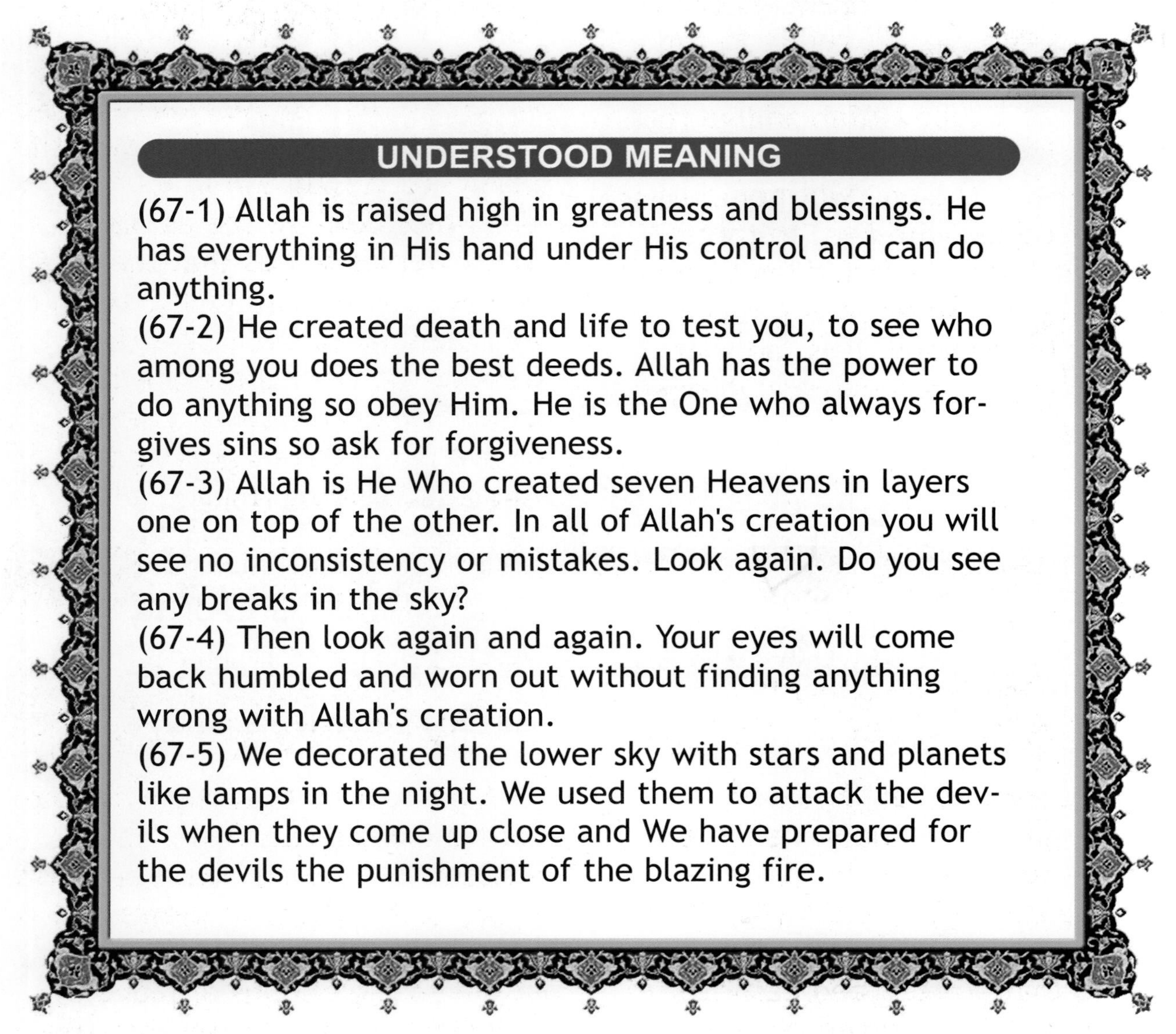

UNDERSTOOD MEANING

(67-1) Allah is raised high in greatness and blessings. He has everything in His hand under His control and can do anything.
(67-2) He created death and life to test you, to see who among you does the best deeds. Allah has the power to do anything so obey Him. He is the One who always forgives sins so ask for forgiveness.
(67-3) Allah is He Who created seven Heavens in layers one on top of the other. In all of Allah's creation you will see no inconsistency or mistakes. Look again. Do you see any breaks in the sky?
(67-4) Then look again and again. Your eyes will come back humbled and worn out without finding anything wrong with Allah's creation.
(67-5) We decorated the lower sky with stars and planets like lamps in the night. We used them to attack the devils when they come up close and We have prepared for the devils the punishment of the blazing fire.

Tabarak تبارك : He is great and full of blessings.

Al-Azeez العزيز: It is a name of Allah that means the One Who is so great and powerful. Nothing can stop Him from punishing those who are sinful.

Shaytan شيطان: Satan or the Devil, and he is a jinn. The word literally means someone who is getting farther away. Allah gave him this name because he is getting farther away from what is right, and from Allah's love and mercy. His original name is Iblees. Shayateen is the plural of Shaytan. It refers to the soldiers of Iblees, who try to get people to disobey Allah and go to Hell. Iblees is the leader of all of them. He is the one who tempted Adam and his wife Eve, to forget and eat from the forbidden tree in Paradise. Ash-Shaytan is the worst enemy of mankind. It is sad that many people obey him and disobey Allah ﷻ .

As-Samaa' السماء : It means "the sky." The plural is As-Samawati السماوات which means "the Heavens." In the past, people thought that over the Earth was a roof and in it were the white dots we see as stars. These verses tell us that the first Heaven contains all of the stars and planets we see in the sky. Beyond the stars there are six other Heavens. Each of these Heavens has angels praying to Allah and serving Him.

Main Lessons

1 Allah Is the Only Creator of the Universe.

These verses remind us of Allah's greatness and power. Then we are told that Allah ﷻ alone is the Creator of life and death. This is the concept of Tawheed Al-Khaliq that you learned earlier in this unit. Allah created life and death as a test for us. Will we spend our life doing good deeds? Are we going to develop good habits? If we do so, we live and die doing good deeds for the sake of Allah. But if we develop a habit to sin regularly, we may die when we are doing something bad. That would be very dangerous for us as we meet Allah on the Day of Judgment.

2 We Know Allah Through His Wonderful Creation.

Allah tells us that the evidence for his existence is found in His wonderful creation. His creation is huge, with billions of plants and animals on Earth. We can see His power in the billions of planets and stars. Scientists say that there are hundreds of billions of galaxies. Each galaxy has hundreds of billions of planets. They all revolve, without crashing into each other. Allah ﷻ made the universe perfect, and no one can find faults in His creation. The perfection in creation shows us Allah's power and wisdom. Everything He made is for us to learn about and use. This shows us Allah's love and mercy.

3 Allah's Creation Is Flawless

Allah ﷻ tells us to look again and again at His creation. This is because every time we look, we are impressed with His perfect creation and adore Him. Sometimes we find things we don't understand. The disbelievers might think it is a mistake. If we look again, we may eventually understand why Allah ﷻ did it that way.

4 We Must Offer Allah Our Best Worship and Work

We will discover that Allah's way is always the best.

Notice that Allah encourages us to do the "best" of deeds. He isn't asking us for the "most" deeds. This is because how many good deeds we do depends on how long we live. But how good our deeds are depends on how much effort we make to obey Allah's guidance.

Healthy Habits

1. Always learn about Allah's creation, and praise Him with your tongue and in your heart.

2. Always remember that Allah gave you your life as a gift and a test. He wants to see how good your deeds are. Therefore, worship Allah properly, and do the best of deeds.

The Punishment of the Disbelievers (Kuffar)

WORDS OF WISDOM

Holy Qur'an

سورة الملك

Surat Al-Mulk 6-11

﴿ وَلِلَّذِينَ كَفَرُوا بِرَبِّهِمْ عَذَابُ جَهَنَّمَ ۖ وَبِئْسَ الْمَصِيرُ ﴿٦﴾ إِذَا أُلْقُوا فِيهَا سَمِعُوا لَهَا شَهِيقًا وَهِيَ تَفُورُ ﴿٧﴾ تَكَادُ تَمَيَّزُ مِنَ الْغَيْظِ ۖ كُلَّمَا أُلْقِيَ فِيهَا فَوْجٌ سَأَلَهُمْ خَزَنَتُهَا أَلَمْ يَأْتِكُمْ نَذِيرٌ ﴿٨﴾ قَالُوا بَلَىٰ قَدْ جَاءَنَا نَذِيرٌ فَكَذَّبْنَا وَقُلْنَا مَا نَزَّلَ اللَّهُ مِن شَيْءٍ إِنْ أَنتُمْ إِلَّا فِي ضَلَالٍ كَبِيرٍ ﴿٩﴾ وَقَالُوا لَوْ كُنَّا نَسْمَعُ أَوْ نَعْقِلُ مَا كُنَّا فِي أَصْحَابِ السَّعِيرِ ﴿١٠﴾ فَاعْتَرَفُوا بِذَنبِهِمْ فَسُحْقًا لِّأَصْحَابِ السَّعِيرِ ﴿١١﴾ ﴾

TRANSLITERATION

Walillatheena kafaroo birabbihim 'athabu jahannama wabi's-al-maseer (67:6) Itha olqoo feeha sami'oo laha shaheeqaw-wahiya tafoor (67:7) Takadu tamayyazu min-al-ghayth, kullama olqiya feeha fawjun sa'alahum khazanatuha alam ya/tikum natheer (67:8) Qaloo bala qad ja'ana natheerun fakaththabna wa-qulna ma nazzal-Allahu min shay-in in antum illa fee dalalin kabeer (67:9) Wa-qaloo law kunna nasma'u aw na'qilu ma kunna fee as-hab-is-sa'eer (67:10) Fa'tarafoo bithanbihim fasuhqal-li'as-hab-is-sa'eer (67:11)

UNDERSTOOD MEANING

(67:6) And those who disbelieve in Allah will suffer the punishment of Hell which is a terrible place to be in.
(67:7) When they are thrown into it they will hear its scary breath as it blazes with fury
(67:8) It is about to burst itself to pieces out of anger. Every time a group is thrown in, the guards will ask them, "Didn't a messenger

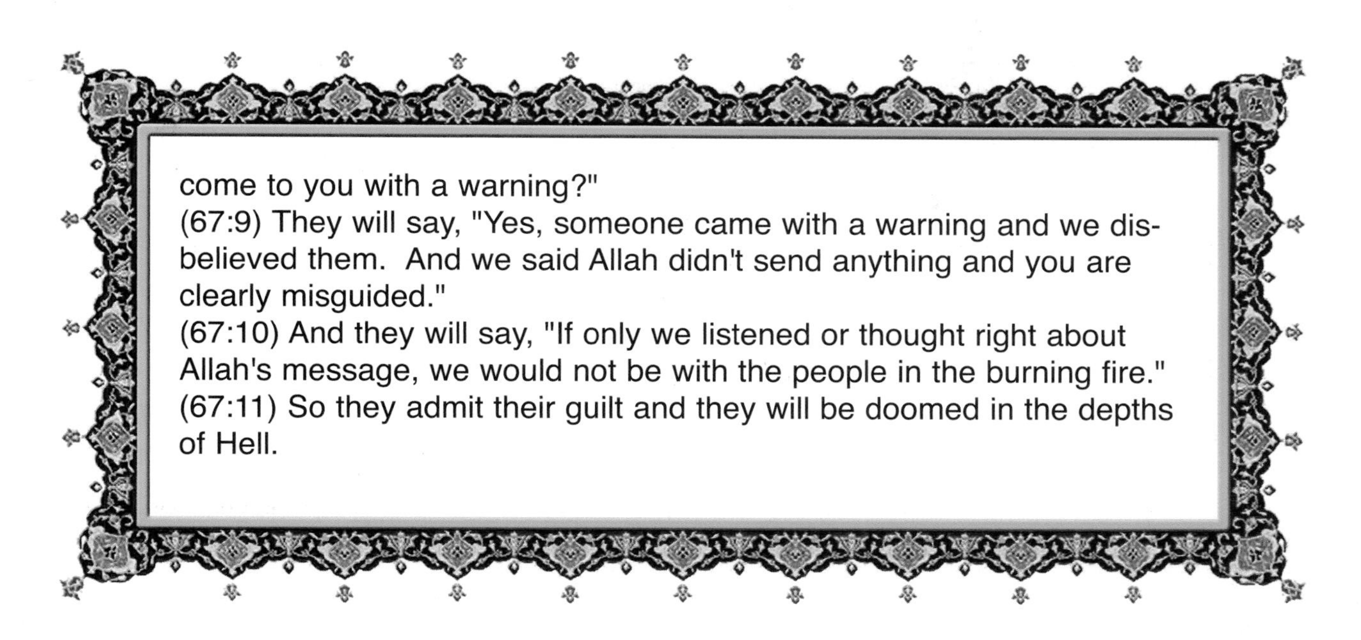

come to you with a warning?"
(67:9) They will say, "Yes, someone came with a warning and we disbelieved them. And we said Allah didn't send anything and you are clearly misguided."
(67:10) And they will say, "If only we listened or thought right about Allah's message, we would not be with the people in the burning fire."
(67:11) So they admit their guilt and they will be doomed in the depths of Hell.

Shaheeq شهيق **:** Noisy inhalation. Hell will make a terrible sound when it is sucking in all those who didn't worship Allah properly.

Ghayth غيظ **:** Severe anger.

Sa'eer سعير **:** This is one of the names of Jahannam (Hell).

Main Lessons

1 Hellfire is the destination of those who disbelieve and disobey Allah ﷻ.

In the previous ayaat, Allah told us that the Shayateen will be punished in Hell. Now, Allah tells us in these verses what happens to the people who listen to them. They will be punished in the horrible Fire of Hell, too. Everyone who goes into it knows he or she deserves it. That is because Allah ﷻ warned people against disobedience, but they did not listen.

2 Disobeying Allah leads to punishment in Jahannam

Allah ﷻ ordered us to listen to the Qur'an and Sunnah, and implement them in our lives. Allah ﷻ made His guidance available to all people. If people refuse to obey Allah, they will suffer the punishment in Jahannam. This is an important lesson for both Muslims and non-Muslims. We must learn and understand Allah's religion and put it into practice. On the Day of Judgment, we will not have any excuses.

3 Allah will not punish people if they did not receive Allah's Message.

These verses also show that Allah will not put people in Hell without sending them a messenger first. Allah ﷻ says:

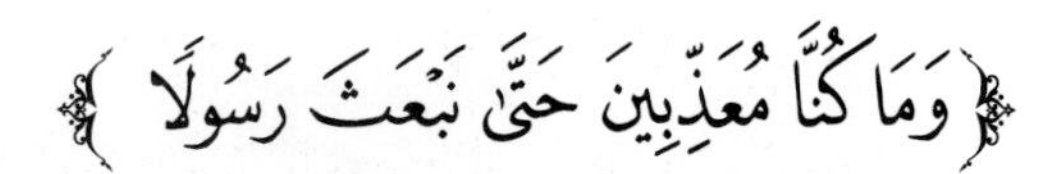

"And I will not punish anyone until I send them a Messenger." (17:15)

Today, people can learn easily about Islam. Books, schools, computers, and copies of the Qur'an are available almost everywhere. However, if some people still did not know about Islam, Allah ﷻ will be fair and merciful with them.

Healthy Habits

1. Always listen to good advice, especially when it comes from parents, teachers, and scholars. Give their advice your best attention, and implement it immediately.

2. Always fear Allah's punishment and do not let Shaytan fool you and convince you to disobey Allah.

Lesson Review

Do some research on stars and planets, which Allah created. Find out how many galaxies there are in the universe. Also, find out how many stars and planets there are in each galaxy.

Why do you think the Prophet advised us to recite Surat Tabaraka once every day?

1. What are the other names of Surat Al-Mulk? Explain these names.
2. Why did Allah ﷻ create life and death? How should this affect your behavior in this life?
3. What does the word "Shaytan" mean?

UNIT
A
CHAPTER
5
LESSON
TWO

Surat Al-Mulk: The Kingdom (2)

Allah watches us when we are alone or in public.

TRANSLITERATION

Inn-allatheena yakhshawna rabbahum bilghaybi-lahum maghfiratuw wa 'ajrun kabeer (67:12)
Wa 'asirroo qawlakum aw-ijharoo bihi innahu 'aleemun bithat-issudoor (67:13)
Ala ya'lamu man khalaqa wahuwa-llateef-ul-khabeer (67:14)
Huwa-llathee ja'ala lakum-ul-arda thaloolan famshoo fee manakibiha wakuloo mir-rizqihi wa-'ilayh-in-nushoor (67:15)

UNDERSTOOD MEANING

(67:12) Those who fear and obey Allah, even when no people are watching them, they will be forgiven and they will get a great reward.
(67:13) So keep secret what you say or say it out loud, Allah knows what is in your hearts.
(67:14) Doesn't He know well what He created? Remember, He knows the smallest details and He is aware of everything.
(67:15) He made the Earth easy for you to live on. So go explore it and eat of what Allah has blessed you with, to him you will return, after you die.

Yakhshoun يخشون : It comes from the term خشية khashyah, which means fear. And here it means fearing Allah's punishment. There is a big difference between fearing the punishment of Allah and the punishment of others. When you fear people or things, you run away from them. But when you fear Allah, you run to Him asking Him to forgive you and accept your repentance.

Al-Ghayb الغيب : The unseen. Here it means that believers obey Allah ﷻ in private, even when no one is watching.

Ajr أجر : Reward, and here it means a reward from Allah. Ajr, or Allah's rewards, are to be exchanged for Jannah in the next life. The more rewards you have in your account, the higher and better you will be in Jannah. If someone wants to be in Al-Firdaws Al-A'la, which is the best place in Jannah, then they must earn great rewards in this life. Al-Firdaws Al-A'la is where prophets, sahabah, and great people dwell in Jannah.

Al-Lateef اللطيف : Someone who is aware of little and minute things. It also means the Gentle. Allah ﷻ is Al-Lateef because He takes care of even very small things in our life to make us comfortable and happy.

Al-Khabeer الخبير : People sometimes think they know everything and they know it well. Later they discover that they know very little, and their knowledge is not perfect. To be Al-Khabeer is to know things very well. Allah is Al-Khabeer because He knows everything very well. This word can also be used to refer to scientists or experts who often know better how things really work.

Reason for Revelation

Ibn Abbas رضي الله عنه (a companion) said: "Some of the kuffar of Quraysh used to say bad things about the Messenger of Allah ﷺ. Then Jibreel told him what they said. So, they would say to each other 'speak softly so that Muhammad's God doesn't hear you.'" So Allah ﷻ revealed: "So keep secret what you say, or say it out loud, Allah knows what is in your hearts."

Gifts of God are sold in a food market in Uzbekistan.

Main Lessons

1 Muslims watch for Allah in private and in public.

Allah سبحانه وتعالى promises a great reward for the believers who obey Allah even when no one else is watching. What makes the believers different from others is that they fear Allah in private and in public.

You can fear Allah and love Him at the same time. Children always fear their parents, but they still love them so much. We fear our parents when we make mistakes. Similarly, we love Allah سبحانه وتعالى, yet we fear His punishment for our mistakes and disobedience. However, we love and fear Allah much more than our parents or anyone else. Being fearful of displeasing Allah makes us better. It straightens up our behavior.

2 Allah gave us a great planet.

Allah سبحانه وتعالى tells the believers to go out and get the good of this world through serious work. When we do this, we will better understand how merciful and generous Allah is. He gave us a great planet that is full of gifts, blessings and beauty. However, we have to learn about our world and work hard to make a living. For example, for certain foods we must first cultivate the land and harvest the crops.

3 Allah takes care of you, but you should do your part first.

Some people think that if they really depend upon Allah, this means they shouldn't do any work. Omar Ibn Al-Khattab answered them saying, "The person who depends upon Allah is the one who plants his seeds in the ground and then puts his trust in Allah." So we have to do our part and depend upon Allah at the same time. We should be like a bird which gets that wakes up early in the morning to work hard all day. The bird works very hard and then puts its full trust in Allah.

The Messenger of Allah said, "If you put your trust in Allah like you are supposed to, Allah will feed you like He provides for the birds. They set out in the morning hungry and come back full."
(Reported in Ahmed)

Faith in Actions

1. When you think of doing something wrong because nobody is watching, remember that Allah is watching.

2. Always remember that you are returning to Allah after death, and He is going to question you about your deeds.

WORDS OF WISDOM

Holy Qur'an

سورة الملك

Surat Al-Mulk 16-21

بِسۡمِ ٱللَّهِ ٱلرَّحۡمَٰنِ ٱلرَّحِيمِ

﴿ ءَأَمِنتُم مَّن فِي ٱلسَّمَآءِ أَن يَخۡسِفَ بِكُمُ ٱلۡأَرۡضَ فَإِذَا هِيَ تَمُورُ ﴿١٦﴾ أَمۡ أَمِنتُم مَّن فِي ٱلسَّمَآءِ أَن يُرۡسِلَ عَلَيۡكُمۡ حَاصِبٗاۖ فَسَتَعۡلَمُونَ كَيۡفَ نَذِيرِ ﴿١٧﴾ وَلَقَدۡ كَذَّبَ ٱلَّذِينَ مِن قَبۡلِهِمۡ فَكَيۡفَ كَانَ نَكِيرِ ﴿١٨﴾ أَوَلَمۡ يَرَوۡاْ إِلَى ٱلطَّيۡرِ فَوۡقَهُمۡ صَٰٓفَّٰتٖ وَيَقۡبِضۡنَۚ مَا يُمۡسِكُهُنَّ إِلَّا ٱلرَّحۡمَٰنُۚ إِنَّهُۥ بِكُلِّ شَيۡءِۭ بَصِيرٌ ﴿١٩﴾ أَمَّنۡ هَٰذَا ٱلَّذِي هُوَ جُندٞ لَّكُمۡ يَنصُرُكُم مِّن دُونِ ٱلرَّحۡمَٰنِۚ إِنِ ٱلۡكَٰفِرُونَ إِلَّا فِي غُرُورٍ ﴿٢٠﴾ أَمَّنۡ هَٰذَا ٱلَّذِي يَرۡزُقُكُمۡ إِنۡ أَمۡسَكَ رِزۡقَهُۥۚ بَل لَّجُّواْ فِي عُتُوّٖ وَنُفُورٍ ﴿٢١﴾ ﴾

TRANSLITERATION

Aa 'amintum man fissama-ie ay-yakhsifa bikum-ul-arda fa-itha hiya tamoor (67:16)
Am amintum-man fissama-ie an yursila 'alaykum hasiban fasata'lamoona kayfa natheer (67:17)
Walaqad kaththab-allatheena min-qablihim fakayfa kana nakeer (67:18)
Awalam yaraw ilattayri fawqahum saffatiw wayaqbidna ma yumsikuhunna illa-rrahmanu innahu bikulli shay-'in baseer (67:19) Amman hatha-llathee huwa jundul-lakum yansurukum min dooni-rrahman inil-kafiroona illa fee ghuroor (67:20)
Amman hatha-llathee yarzuqukum in amsaka rizqah, bal lajjoo fee 'utuwwiw wanufoor (67:21)

UNDERSTOOD MEANING

(67:16) How can you feel safe if you disobey Allah and reject His messengers? Allah, Who is in Heaven, may cause you to sink into the Earth, with an Earthquake, then it will be shaking.
(67:17) Or do you feel safe if you know that Allah, who is in Heaven, may send a strong wind with rocks to blow you away? Then, you will truly understand this warning.
(67:18) People before you rejected the message. Look how I destroyed them. (like Pharaoh and his people for example)
(67:19) Don't they see the birds over them how they fly with their wings spread out and close in? Nothing holds them up except the Most merciful. Allah sees everything and even takes care of every bird in flight.
(67:20) Where is this army that will help defend you from Allah, the Most Merciful? The only defense you have is Allah's mercy, so turn to Allah and ask forgiveness. Those disbelievers who reject Allah's message are only fooling themselves.
(67:21) And who will give you food and blessings, other than Allah, if He stops His blessings? And they continue in stubbornly running from the truth.

Main Lessons

1 Beware of the punishment of God.

It is true that Allah ﷻ made the Earth easy to live on. However, it is also true that Allah uses this Earth to punish people who disbelieve and disobey. The Earth is a blessing, but if we are too disobedient, Allah can punish us with it by sinking us into the Earth, or flooding us with water. Allah destroyed ancient nations with earthquakes, floods, diseases, destructive winds and other types of punishments. In these verses, Allah ﷻ continues to give severe warnings to the kuffar. He reminds them how the people before them were destroyed. Allah wants them to be aware that they may be next.

2 Disobeying Allah leads to punishment in Jahannam.

Allah ﷻ is also merciful. He gives people chances to ask for forgiveness and to be forgiven. The wise person is the one who avoids sin as much as he or she can. And if we sin, we should repent immediately. This way we please Allah and protect ourselves from His punishment in this life and in the next one.

Hadeeth Shareef

عن أنس رضي الله عنه قال: قال رسول الله ﷺ :

"كُلّ ابن آدم خَطَّاء وَخَيرُ الخَطّائين التَّوابون"

رواه الترمذي وأحمد

Anas رضي الله عنه narrated that Rasulullah ﷺ said:

"All the sons of Adam make mistakes, and the best of sinners are those who repent continuously."

(Reported in At-Tirmithi and Ahmad)

3 Allah gave the disbelievers many examples to make them believe in Him as the One True God.

Among these examples Allah ﷻ lists the following:

* He is the One Who keeps Earth stable under their feet.

* He is the One Who protects them from destructive storms, like those that came to nations before them.

* He is the One Who enables birds to fly up high and not fall.

* He is the One Who feeds them and gives them wealth every day.

Lesson Review

Pick a kind of bird and do a research project about all the different skills and special abilities Allah gave it to survive. Present your findings to the class.

What are the differences between the behavior of a person who is always mindful of Allah سبحانه وتعالى and another who is not?

1. Who are those to whom Allah سبحانه وتعالى is promising forgiveness and great reward?
2. How should a Muslim depend upon Allah سبحانه وتعالى ?
3. What are the examples that Allah gave to the disbelievers to make them believe in Him?
4. What should a Muslim do when he or she disobeys Allah سبحانه وتعالى ? Quote a hadeeth to support your answer.

UNIT A CHAPTER 5 LESSON THREE

Surat Al-Mulk: The Kingdom (3)

The Disbelievers Will Fail on the Day of Judgment

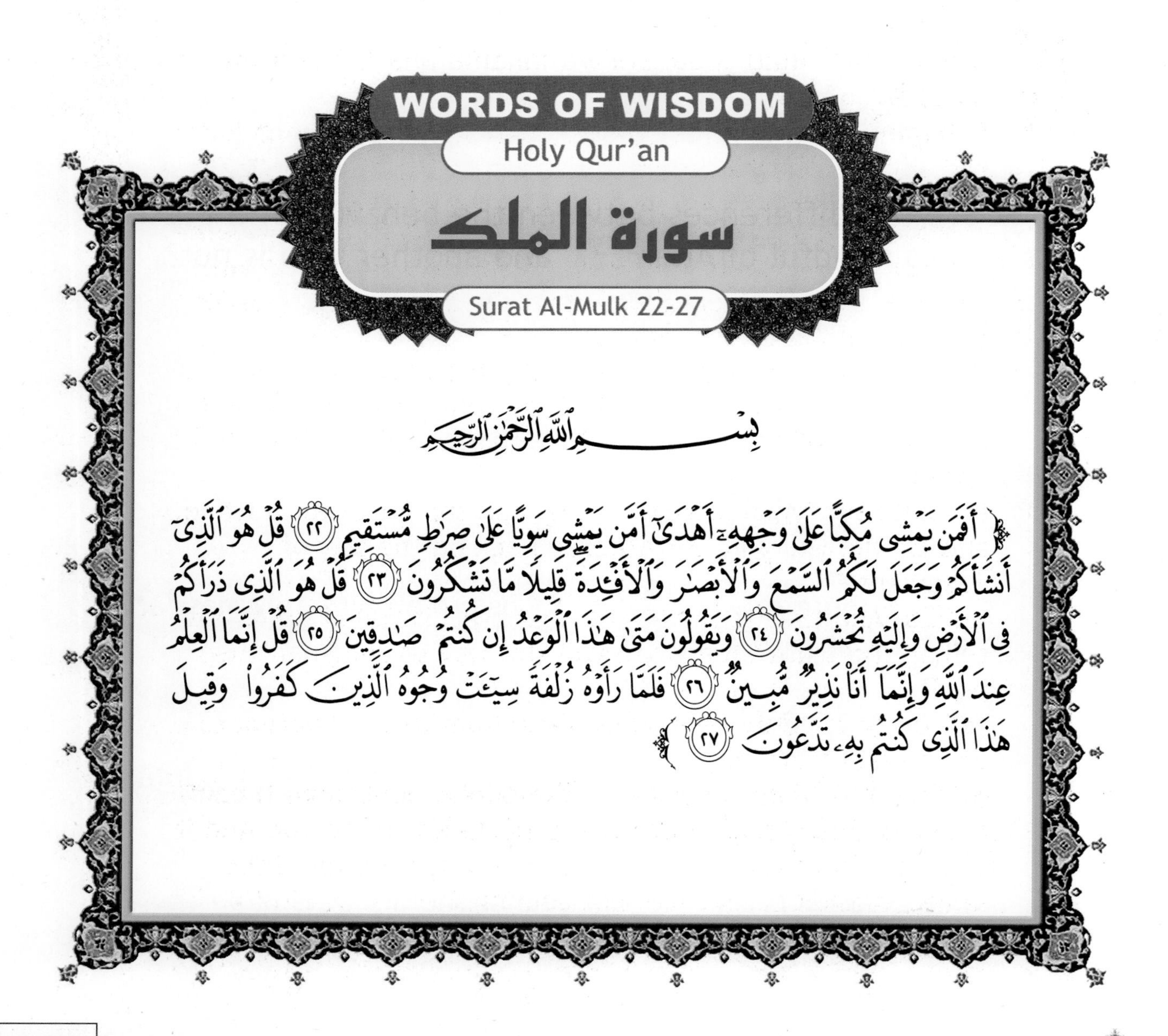

TRANSLITERATION

Afamay-yamshee mukibban 'ala wajhihi ahda ammay yamshee sawiyyan 'ala siratim mustaqeem (67:22)
Qul huwa-llathee ansha-akum waja'ala lakumu alssam'a wal-absara wal-af-idata qaleelam ma tashkuroon (67:23)
Qul huwallathee thara-akum fi-ardi wa-ilayhi tuhsharoon (67:24)
Wayaqooloona mata hathalwa'du in kuntum sadiqeen (67:25)
Qul innamal-ilmu 'indallahi wa-innama ana natheerum mubeen (67:26)
Falamma raawhu zulfatan see-at wujoohu-llatheena kafaroo waqeela hathallathee kuntum bihi tadda'oon (67:27)

UNDERSTOOD MEANING

(67:22) Is the disbeliever, who is made to walk in life with his face down, better guided than the believer who walks normally along the straight path?
(67:23) Say to the disbelievers: "Allah created you and gave you ears, eyes, and hearts, so you can hear, see and think about Allah's message. But you are still not thankful nor obedient."
(67:24) Say: "Allah spread you out on the Earth for a while, and to Him you will be gathered back on the Day of Judgment."
(67:25) And they (the disbelievers) ask, "If you Muslims are telling the truth then when will this Day of Judgment happen?"
(67:26) Say: "Only Allah knows and I am just delivering to you a clear warning."
(67:27) And when they see it (the punishment in hell) coming near them, their faces will turn dark from terror. And it will be said to them: "This is the punishment you disbelieved in and thought was not coming."

As-Sirat-ul-Mustaqeem الصراط المستقيم : This term is repeated in the Qur'an 30 times. Surat Al-Fatihah includes the famous ayah "إهدنا الصراط المستقيم" which means: "guide us to the straight path." This term literally means the straight path. Here it means the religion of Islam. To follow the straight path, one must practice Islam and obey Allah and His Prophet in all aspects of life.

Main Lessons

1 Following As-Sirat Al-Mustaqeem, the straight path, leads you to Jannah.

In this world the disbelievers seem to be walking with their faces down. They do not look ahead of them, and they have no real direction in life. They follow their desires and they keep falling into sin. The believers walk with clear guidance from Allah. They see the world as a test, so they do the right things to please Allah. They follow the straight path, which is Islam. They obey the rules of Allah and His messenger Muhammad ﷺ. Therefore, they succeed in this world and the next. Allah will grant them a happy and blessed life here, and in Jannah after death.

2 Following wrong paths leads to Jahannam.

Those who choose wrong paths away from the straight path will be punished in Hellfire. Allah ﷻ gave them faces with eyes to see and ears to hear, but they did not use them wisely. Instead, they used them just to enjoy their lives, even if they were led to disobey Allah ﷻ and harm themselves. Allah says about them, "They have hearts with which they don't understand, eyes with which they don't see, and ears with which they don't hear. They are like animals, even more misguided." [6:170] Therefore, Allah punishes them on the Day of Judgment by making them walk with their faces down like animals.

The Messenger of Allah ﷻ was asked, "How are the kuffar gathered together, walking on their faces on the Day of Judgment?" The Messenger of Allah said: "Isn't the One who made them walk on their feet in this world capable of making them walk on their faces on the Day of Judgment?"

(Reported by Bukhari)

Hadeeth Shareef

عن أنس بن مالك رضي الله عنه قال : قال رسول الله ﷺ :
" حُفَّت الجنَّة بالمكارِه و حُفَّت النّار بالشّهَوات "
رواه البخاري ومسلم

Anas Ibn Malik narrated that Rasulullah ﷺ said:

"Paradise is surrounded by [good but] disliked deeds, while Hellfire is reached by [prohibited] desires."

(Reported in Al-Bukhari and Muslim)

Explanation

This Hadeeth means that Paradise can be reached through doing the good deeds which we may dislike to do out of laziness. Imam An-Nawawi* said that these good deeds that we may dislike performing include "Carrying out required worship consistently, tolerance, forgiveness, charity, being good to those who are bad to you, and avoiding haram desires and practices."

People may also fall into Hellfire by engaging in prohibited desires and entertainments which we might enjoy. Imam An-Nawawi gave the following examples of the prohibited desires, "Drinking intoxicants, looking upon haram sights, backbiting others and enjoying haram pastimes."

** Imam Yahya An-Nawawi, who lived in the 13th century, is a great medieval Muslim scholar. He wrote many great books including Riyad-us-Saliheen and Sharh Saheeh Muslim, from which we took the above quotes. He also wrote many other books.*

Believers see life as a test.

Disbelievers see life as a game.

Allah Controls Our Lives

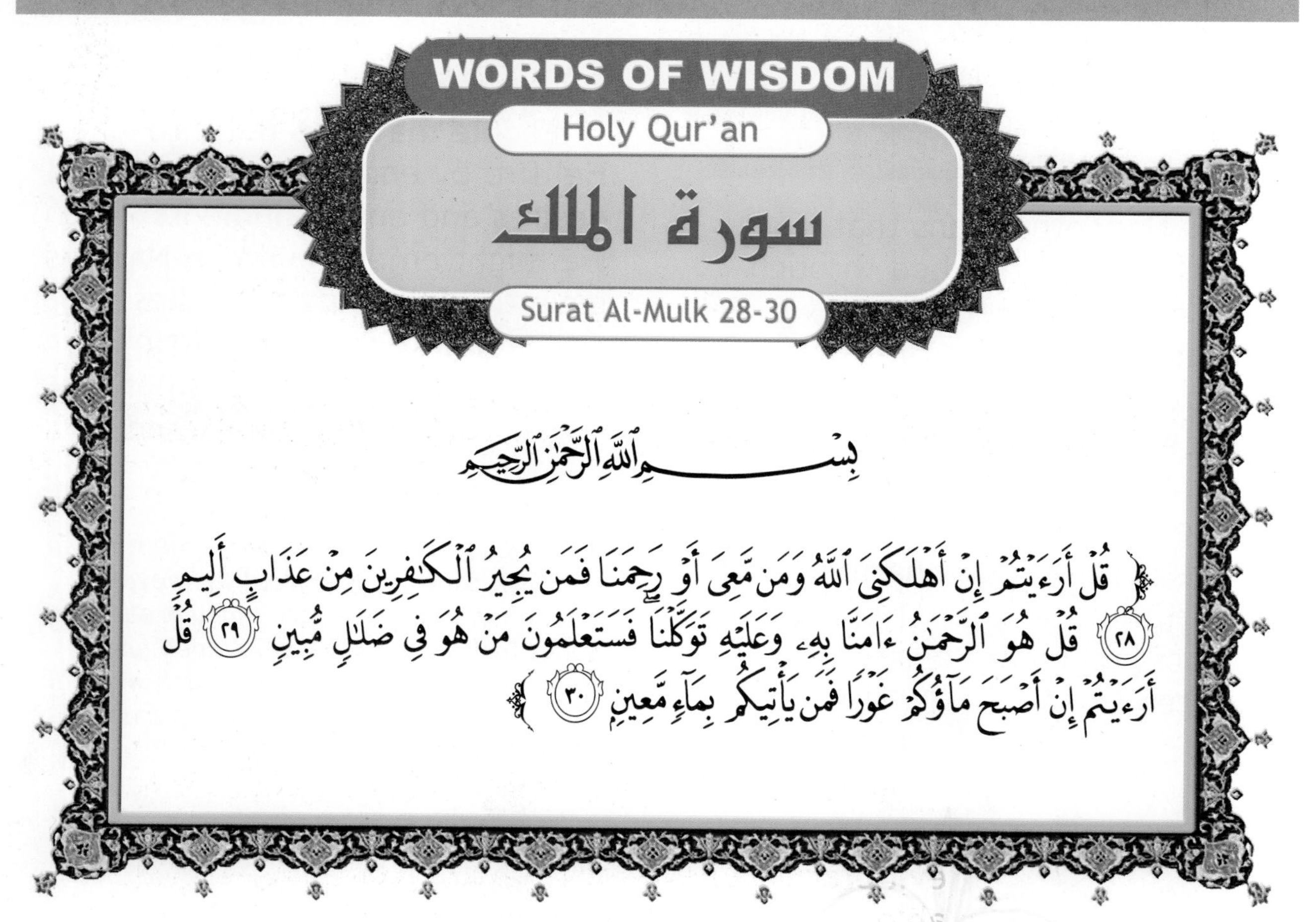

TRANSLITERATION

Qul araaytum in ahlakani-Allahu waman ma'iya aw rahimana, famay yujeer-ul-kafireena min 'athabin aleem (67:28)
Qul huwa-rrahmanu amanna bihi wa'alayhi tawakkalna fasata'lamoona man huwa fee dalalim mubeen (67:29)
Qul araaytum in asbaha ma-okum ghawran famay yateekum bima-in ma'een (67:30)

UNDERSTOOD MEANING

(67:28) Say:"Have you considered if Allah should destroy me and those with me--rather He will have mercy on us; yet who will protect the unbelievers from a painful punishment?"
(67:29) Say: "He is Allah the Most Merciful. We believe in Him and we rely upon Him. You disbelievers will soon know which one of us is clearly misguided."
(67:30) Say: "What if your water sunk deep into the Earth and you couldn't reach it? Who would send you flowing water to drink?"
(The answer they have to say is that only Allah can do this, so tell them, "Then why don't you leave your false gods and turn only to Allah for support and guidance.")

Healthy Habit

Always do the right thing and good deeds even if they look difficult. And always avoid haram things or evil practices, even if they look tempting or enjoyable.

Tawakkul توكل : To rely on or put your trust into someone else to help you. As Muslims, we must put our full trust in Allah ﷿ . We realize that there is no real power except the power of Allah. We also do the best we can to utilize the tools and means Allah has given us to serve Him and be successful, in this life and the next.

Reason for Revelation

It has been reported that the kuffar of Makkah used to pray to their idols that the Muslims would just die and go away. So Allah revealed the verse, "Say: "whether I and those who are with me die..."[67:28]

Main Lessons

1 The believers always trust Allah

The believers always trust Allah, rely on Him, and practice real tawakkul. They do not fear any other than their Creator. They do not fear their enemies, even if they are so powerful. True Muslims would never change their religion or disobey Allah ﷿ to please the disbelievers.

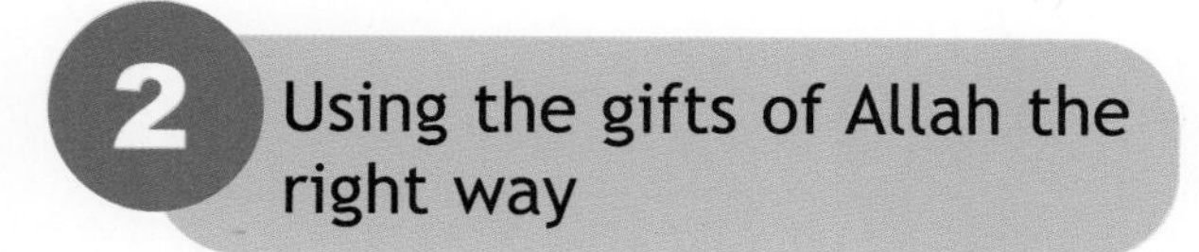

2 Using the gifts of Allah the right way

These verses remind us that we owe Allah ﷿ thanks for all His blessings. He reminds us with one of His gifts, water. What would happen to us if water were sucked deep into the Earth and we could not reach it?

Think about Allah's many gifts, like our hearts, minds, eyes, ears, food, health, and many more.

We must be grateful to Allah ﷿ for the food and water that keep us alive and healthy. We must use our healthy bodies to worship Allah and serve Him forever. We must be thankful for our ears by listening only to what Allah wants ﷿ to listen to. We must be thankful for our eyes by only looking at what we are allowed to look at. We must be thankful for our hearts by working to memorize and learn things that will help us in this world and the next.

Allah ﷻ gave us eyes, ears and brains to learn with. Do some research about the benefits of these gifts of Allah, and write a paragraph about each one of them. Water is a must for our life. Imagine if people woke up one day and found no water on Earth. How would their lives be that day? Have a discussion with your class-mates about this subject.

1. Why do you think the Quraysh were hoping to see the Muslims destroyed?

2. Are there misguided people today that have the same feeling towards Islam and Musims as those who are described in Surat Al-Mulk? How should we treat them?

1. What is As-Sirat Al-Mustaqeem?
2. Name the gifts that Allah ﷻ gave us to help us do right and avoid wrong in this life.
3. Explain tawakkul.
4. Why do people sometimes fail to do good deeds and insist on doing wrong things?

1 ادم
2 إدريس
3 نوح
4 هود
5 صالح
6 ابراهيم
7 لوط
8 إسماعيل
9 اسحاق
10 يعقوب
11 يوسف
12 ايوب
13 ذوالكفل
14 شعيب
15 موسى
16 هارون
17 داوود
18 سليمان
19 الياس
20 اليسع
21 يونس
22 زكريا
23 يحيى
24 عيسى
25 محمد

MANY PROPHETS, ONE GOD

Prophets of Islam

CHAPTER
ONE

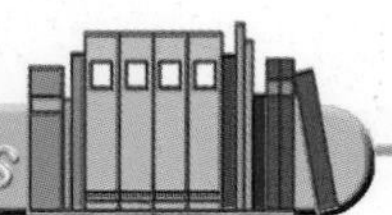

Pre-reading Questions

1. What is the main message of all prophets?
2. Were the prophets ordinary men?
3. What are the characteristics of prophets?
4. What were some of the miracles our prophets brought with them?
5. Are the prophets mentioned in the Qur'an similar to those mentioned in the Bible?
6. Who was the last and final prophet?
7. How should we respect our prophets?

Introduction

As you learned earlier, the concept of tawheed (monotheism) is the most important concept in Islam. The key to Heaven is to understand and believe that there is no god but Allah سبحانه وتعالى, the One True Creator. Allah wanted the message of Islam and the belief in one God, tawheed, to spread among mankind. He did this by appointing prophets and messengers.

Allah Sent Prophets to All Nations

Islam teaches that Allah sent prophets and messengers to all nations. Since the beginning of time, Allah سبحانه وتعالى has communicated His guidance through these chosen people. They were human beings who walked and lived among their people. They taught nations about

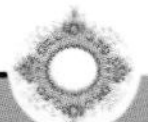

faith in One Almighty God and how to be good. From the first prophet, Adam, to the last prophet, Muhammad ﷺ, Allah's message eventually reached all corners of the world. Allah says in the Qur'an:

﴿ وَلِكُلِّ أُمَّةٍ رَّسُولٌ ﴾

"And for every nation there is a messenger." [10:47]

﴿ إِنَّآ أَرْسَلْنَٰكَ بِٱلْحَقِّ بَشِيرًا وَنَذِيرًا ۚ وَإِن مِّنْ أُمَّةٍ إِلَّا خَلَا فِيهَا نَذِيرٌ ﴾

"Indeed We have sent with you the truth conveying to people Our good tidings and warnings. And there is no nation, which has not been sent a warning (messenger of warning)." [35:24]

The Qur'an itself tells us that it has mentioned only some of the prophets:

﴿ وَرُسُلًا قَدْ قَصَصْنَٰهُمْ عَلَيْكَ مِن قَبْلُ وَرُسُلًا لَّمْ نَقْصُصْهُمْ عَلَيْكَ ﴾

"And We told you about some messengers, while We did not tell you about others." [4:164]

Since prophets appeared over thousands of years, and there were many in each nation, to make a full list of names is impossible. There are some ahadeeth of the Prophet which say that Allah sent thousands of prophets and messengers. Therefore, Muslims have to believe in and respect all the prophets that are mentioned in Al-Qur'an. And, they should also believe that Allah ﷻ sent many other prophets and messengers whose names are not known. The Holy Qur'an stated:

Holy Qur'an

﴿ ءَامَنَ ٱلرَّسُولُ بِمَآ أُنزِلَ إِلَيۡهِ مِن رَّبِّهِۦ وَٱلۡمُؤۡمِنُونَۚ كُلٌّ ءَامَنَ بِٱللَّهِ وَمَلَٰٓئِكَتِهِۦ
وَكُتُبِهِۦ وَرُسُلِهِۦ لَا نُفَرِّقُ بَيۡنَ أَحَدٖ مِّن رُّسُلِهِۦ ﴾

"The Messenger (Muhammad) believes in what has been revealed to him from his Lord, as do the men of faith. Each one (of them) believes in Allah, His angels, His books, and His messengers. We make no distinction (they say) between one and another of His messengers." [2: 285]

Hadeeth Shareef

عن أبي وهب الجشمي قال: قال رسول الله ﷺ قال:
"تَسَمَّوا بأسْماءِ الأنبياء ، وأحَبُّ الأسْماءِ إلى الله: عبد الله وعبد الرحمن."
رواه أبو داود والنسائي وأحمد

Abu Wahm Al-Jashmi narrated that Rasulullah ﷺ said:
"Choose the names of prophets for yourselves. And the names that Allah loves the most are Abdullah and Abdur-Rahman."
(Reported in Abu Dawood, Nasa'i and Ahmad.)

All Prophets Were Human Beings

Prophets and messengers were human beings who were very noble and pious role models. They were neither divine, angels or jinn. Every prophet was born to a mother and a father, except Prophet Isa عليه السلام, who had no father, and Adam عليه السلام who had neither. Some prophets had brothers like Prophet Musa عليه السلام. Prophet Musa's brother was also a prophet, and his name was Haroon عليه السلام. Ismaeel and Ishaq were also brothers and prophets. Other prophets got married and had children, like Prophets Adam, Nuh, Ibraheem, Musa, Muhammad ﷺ and others. Although prophets and messengers were ordinary men, Allah سبحانه وتعالى gave them special qualities. They all had high morals, manners, and attitudes. They were faithful, honest, patient, tolerant, and honorable. Additionally, some of them had long lives. Prophet Nuh عليه السلام lived for 950 years, and Prophet Ibraheem lived more than 200 years! Other prophets died much younger than that, such as Prophet Muhammad ﷺ. He became a prophet at the age of 40 and died at the age of 63. Prophet Isa عليه السلام is the only prophet who has yet to die. Instead, Allah سبحانه وتعالى raised him to Heaven. He will come back to Earth before the Day of Judgment, and he will confirm Islam as the true and final religion of Allah. He will also win over all evil people and powers.

All Prophets Were Men

Being a prophet or a messenger was not an easy task. It was a very serious responsibility, which required a great deal of perseverance and strength. Some prophets were killed, like Prophets Zakariyya (Zachariah) and Yahya (John) عليه السلام. Others were put in prison for years, like Prophet Yousuf (Joseph). Almost all prophets were persecuted and harassed, including Nuh (Noah), Ibraheem عليه السلام (Abraham), Younus (Jonah), Musa (Moses), Isa (Jesus), Muhammad ﷺ, and others. Therefore, Allah سبحانه وتعالى in His glorious wisdom, carefully selected those individuals who would be most suited to serve as prophets. Allah سبحانه وتعالى also stated that He chose only men to be prophets and messengers.

Holy Qur'an

﴿ وَمَآ أَرْسَلْنَا مِن قَبْلِكَ إِلَّا رِجَالًا نُّوحِىٓ إِلَيْهِم مِّنْ أَهْلِ ٱلْقُرَىٰٓ ﴾

And We have not sent before you but men from (among) the people of the towns, to whom We sent revelations. [12:109]

However, Allah ﷻ chose certain faithful women to play great and historical roles. Asiah, the wife of phar'oun, Maryam, Khadeejah, and many others were exceptional role models. They were not prophets, but they were women of great faith.

The Message of Prophethood

▲ *The Cave of Hira, where Prophet Muhammad received the first verses of Al-Qur'an.*

▲ *Mount Sinai, where Prophet Musa received the Torah.*

How did prophets find out that they had been selected as prophets or messengers? There were two ways in which Allah ﷻ reached out to his prophets. The first way was by sending an angel to them. For example, Prophet Muhammad ﷺ received the message of prophethood from the Angel Jibreel while he was in Cave Hiraa'.

At other times, Allah ﷻ spoke directly to His chosen prophets. For example, Prophet Musa عليه السلام went to a desert or a mountain where Allah ﷻ spoke to him directly.

All the prophets received the same basic message: That Allah ﷻ is the only true Creator and Sustainer of the universe, and that He is the only One worthy of complete obedience and worship. Adam, Nuh, Ibraheem, Musa, Isa, Muhammad, and all the prophets brought their people this same message. None of them claimed to be divine or God-like in any way, and they all taught a pure belief in the One True God.

Characteristics of Prophets

What Are the Characteristics of Prophets?

1. The prophets of Allah ﷻ were the best in their communities. They were the most moral and the most intelligent among their people because the life of a prophet served as a model for his followers. His personality had to be pleasant in order to attract people towards his message, rather than drive them away.

"And most surely you are of a great moral character." [68:4]

2. They usually came from well-known and highly respected families. Most prophets came from great lineage. Prophets Musa, Haroon, Yousuf, and Yaqoub were the offspring of Prophet Ibraheem, the Father of Prophets, through his son Is'haq. Prophet Muhammad was the descendent of Prophet Isma'eel. Isma'eel was also the son of Prophet Ibraheem.

3. Prophets had to possess strong personalities. They had to be strong and resilient in the face of challenges and difficulties. Many Prophets had to face fierce and evil enemies.

4. Prophets had to be patient and tolerant. Each prophet had to bring the message of tawheed to his people and teach this message for many, many years. Many prophets, including Prophet Muhammad ﷺ, were persecuted

and ridiculed for teaching Allah's message. Others, like Nuh, taught for hundreds of years, but only gained a few followers. In the case of Prophet Younus, the persecution and harassment got so bad that he fled, abandoning the people whom he was supposed to teach.

Prophet Younus: A Lesson in Patience

Prophet Younus, or Jonah عليه السلام، could not convert his people to the way of Allah. Eventually he got very frustrated and gave up. Prophet Younus left his people and sailed away on a ship. Allah was very disappointed in Younus. Although he had tried to teach Allah's message, he had abandoned his job without Allah's permission, and that is a serious mistake for a messenger. In order to teach him a lesson in patience and perseverance, Allah made the ship run into stormy weather. The people of the ship had to throw one passenger into the ocean to save the ship. They selected Younus and threw him into the sea. A whale came by and swallowed him .

The story of Prophet Younus and the boat on an ancient classic piece of art.

Miraculously, Prophet Younus was kept alive in the belly of the whale. Prophet Younus realized that his impatience had caused him to disobey Allah. He repented and asked for forgiveness. Allah forgave him and made the whale throw him ashore. Prophet Younus عليه السلام fell sick for a while later returned to his people and continued teaching tawheed. They eventually followed him and became Muslims.

Prophets and Miracles

Allah ﷻ provided some of His prophets with miracles. These miracles usually had one of two purposes:

- To help people during times of danger or trouble (Prophet Ibraheem, Nuh, Younus)

- As proof of Allah's greatness, and to prove that the prophet is a true prophet (Prophet Musa, Isa, etc.)

Prophet Ibraheem عليه السلام was saved from the huge fire that was lit to burn him. Prophet Nuh عليه السلام was miraculously saved with his family and followers from the flood.

The nature of the miracles depended upon the time and society in which the prophet taught. Allah knew that people would be most impressed by miracles that accomplished valued tasks in society. So He chose miracles that would be relevant to the society of His messengers. For example, Musa's contemporaries were excellent at magic. So his major miracle was to defeat the best magicians of the day in Egypt. Isa's contemporaries were recognized as skillful physicians. Therefore, his miracles were to raise the dead and cure incurable diseases. The Arabs, the contemporaries of the Prophet Muhammad ﷺ, were known for their eloquence and magnificent poetry. So Prophet Muhammad's ﷺ major miracle was Al-Qur'an. The people of Arabia were impressed by the eloquence of Al-Qur'an, and Arab poets and orators could not make even a few verses like it. Later, all Arabia became a Muslim nation.

Prophets in the Bible

There are 25 prophets mentioned by name in the Qur'an, although Allah tells us clearly that there were many more in different times and places. Christians and Jews also believe in most of the same prophets and their miracles. Provided here are the 25 mentioned in the Qur'an and their English names from the Bible, where applicable:

	Qur'anic Name	Biblical Name
1	Adam	Adam
2	Idrees	Enoch
3	Nuh	Noah
4	Hud	-----
5	Salih	-----
6	Ibraheem	Abraham
7	Isma'eel	Ishmael
8	Is'haq	Isaac
9	Loot	Lot
10	Ya'qoob	Jacob
11	Yousuf	Joseph
12	Shu'ayb	-----
13	Ayyoob	Job
14	Musa	Moses
15	Haroon	Aaron
16	Thul-kifl	Ezekiel
17	Dawood	David
18	Sulayman	Solomon
19	Ilyas	Elias
20	Al-Yasa'	Elisha
21	Younus	Jonah
22	Zakariyya	Zecharias
23	Yahya	John
24	'Isa	Jesus
25	Muhammad	-----

As you can see, most of the prophets in the Qur'an are recognized by the Bible. Some of the prophets have the same name in both the Qur'an and the Bible, like Prophet Adam عليه السلام. However, most prophets have names which sound different. For example, Prophet Sulayman عليه السلام is known as Prophet Solomon in the English translation of the Bible. Prophet Younus عليه السلام is known as Prophet Jonah. Also, Prophet Ayyoub is known as Job.

There are some prophets mentioned in the Qur'an that are not mentioned in the existing form of the Bible. for example, Prophets Muhammad ﷺ, Shu'ayb عليه السلام, Salih and Hud عليه السلام .

Respecting our Prophets

1. Believing in all of the true prophets and admiring them is a Muslim's way of showing appreciation. Muslims appreciate the many sacrifices that these prophets made. We must be grateful that they worked so hard to bring Allah's message to mankind.

2. The best way to respect prophets and messengers is to follow their guidance and manners. If you want to give great respect to Prophet Muhammad, for example, you must obey him and try to follow his manners and Sunnah.

3. When Muslims mention the name of Prophet Muhammad ﷺ or any other prophet, they make a prayer for them out of respect. This is a prayer asking God to grant the prophet His peace and blessings. In Arabic we say:

صلى الله عليه وسلم or عليه السلام

"Salla Allahu 'alayhi wa sallam or Alayhi-ssalam"

The Tomb of Prophet Yahya (John) عليه السلام *in the Omayyad Mosque in Damascas, Syria.*

4. Muslims do not draw pictures of the prophets. In addition, Muslims do not portray the characters of the prophets in movies or plays. Muslims believe that portraying a prophet of Allah ﷻ in a movie is disrespectful. No matter how good an artist or an actor is, it would be impossible to accurately portray the prophet's greatness. Also, Muslims do not want to

create images of prophets as other groups have done, because that could lead to idolizing those images. People in the past used to create statues of their great leaders and then ended up worshipping them.

That is why we do not see any actor playing Prophet Muhammad ﷺ in the famous movie "The Message." And even in the animated movie "Muhammad: The Last Messenger," no image of the Prophet is ever depicted.

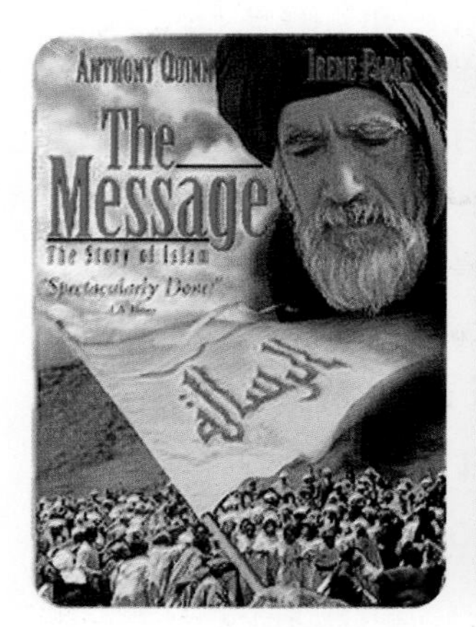

Healthy Habits

1. Always show love and respect for all the prophets of Allah ﷻ .

2. Always follow the Sunnah and manners of Prophet Muhammad ﷺ .

3. Say "Salla Allahu ‘alayhi wa Sallam" or "Alayi Salam" whenever you hear or say the name of Prophet Muhammad or other prophets.

Chapter Review

Why do you think Allah chose humans, not angels, for example, to be prophets and messengers?

1. What does Islam teach about prophets? Quote two verses from the Qur'an.
2. How many prophets are mentioned in the Holy Qur'an?
3. Explain how prophets were ordinary men. Why did Allah choose these individuals?
4. What were two ways in which these ordinary men learned that they were prophets?
5. Why did Allah provide some of His prophets with miracles?
6. What are some of the characteristics of a prophet?
7. Which prophets are not mentioned by name in today's Bible?
8. What are the English Biblical names for Prophets Younus, Dawood, Yahya, Thul-Kifl, Ayyoub, and Ya'qoub?
9. What is the significance of Prophet Muhammad ?
10. List three ways Muslims can show respect to the prophets.

Prophets and Messengers

CHAPTER TWO

Introduction

Prophets and messengers were great people selected by Allah to show other the straight path. They came from different places and spoke different languages, but they all conveyed the same message of Islam. They all focused on the most important concept of Islam, tawheed. Some of them were **anbiyaa'**, or prophets, and others were **rasul**, or messengers.

Word Watch

Prophet: Nabiy نبِي
Prophets: anbiyaa' أنبياء
Messenger: rasul رسول
messengers: rusul رُسُـل

Many Messengers, One Message

After the creation of Adam, just one original message has been repeatedly delivered to mankind throughout the history of humanity. All prophets taught their peoples about the oneness of Allah ﷻ, or tawheed, and the proper way to worship Him. They also taught people how to be righteous and lead positive and happy lives. Allah's message has been the same message from the first prophet, Adam, to the last prophet, Muhammad ﷺ. Allah gave them all His guidance and charged them with the task of conveying that guidance to His people. Each Prophet's ﷺ mission was to encourage people to believe in the One True God, obey Him, do good, and avoid evil.

In Surat Al-'A'raf, Allah tells us that although He sent different prophets to different peoples in different times, they all had the same message: "Allah ﷻ is One, and He is the only One to worship."

Holy Qur'an

﴿لَقَدْ أَرْسَلْنَا نُوحًا إِلَىٰ قَوْمِهِ فَقَالَ يَا قَوْمِ اعْبُدُوا اللَّهَ مَا لَكُم مِّنْ إِلَٰهٍ غَيْرُهُ إِنِّي أَخَافُ عَلَيْكُمْ عَذَابَ يَوْمٍ عَظِيمٍ﴾

We sent Nuh to his people. He said: "O my people! Worship Allah! You have no other god but Him. Truly I fear for you the punishment of painful day." [7:59]

﴿وَإِلَىٰ عَادٍ أَخَاهُمْ هُودًا ۗ قَالَ يَا قَوْمِ اعْبُدُوا اللَّهَ مَا لَكُم مِّنْ إِلَٰهٍ غَيْرُهُ ۚ أَفَلَا تَتَّقُونَ﴾

To the people of Aad, (We sent) Hud, one of their (own) brethren. He said: "O my people! Worship Allah! You have no other god but Him, will you not, then, seek protection." [7:65]

﴿وَإِلَىٰ ثَمُودَ أَخَاهُمْ صَالِحًا ۗ قَالَ يَا قَوْمِ اعْبُدُوا اللَّهَ مَا لَكُم مِّنْ إِلَٰهٍ غَيْرُهُ ۖ﴾

To the people of Thamood (We sent) Salih, one of their own brethren. He said: "O my people! Worship Allah; you have no other god but Him." [7:73]

﴿وَإِلَىٰ مَدْيَنَ أَخَاهُمْ شُعَيْبًا ۗ قَالَ يَا قَوْمِ اعْبُدُوا اللَّهَ مَا لَكُم مِّنْ إِلَٰهٍ غَيْرُهُ ۖ﴾

To the people of Madyan, We sent Shu'ayb, one of their own brethren, he said: "O my people! Worship Allah; you have no other god but Him." [7:85]

﴿وَمَا أَرْسَلْنَا مِن قَبْلِكَ مِن رَّسُولٍ إِلَّا نُوحِي إِلَيْهِ أَنَّهُ لَا إِلَٰهَ إِلَّا أَنَا فَاعْبُدُونِ﴾

Not a messenger did We send before thee without this inspiration sent by Us to him: that there is no god but I; therefore worship and serve Me. [21: 28]

Allah, the One True Creator

Prophets	The Message
Adam	God is One
Nuh	God is One
Abraham	God is One
Moses	God is One
Jesus	God is One
Muhammad	God is One

The Difference Between Prophets and Messengers

The terms "prophets" and "messengers" are sometimes used as if they always mean the same thing. This is not always the case. All prophets shared one common message, Islam. And all prophets were required to implement Islam in their own lives and guide their families too. However, some of the prophets were also messengers. Those messengers were ordered by Allah to deliver Allah's message to many other people.

A rasul means a person who is assigned to deliver Allah's message to the people of his tribe or in his area. The rasul, then, is a prophet whom Allah ﷻ ordered to guide a large number of people to worship Allah ﷻ and practice Islam. This was a very important role given to messengers in addition to the responsibilities of prophethood.

Of the many prophets Allah ﷻ sent, only 25 are mentioned by name in the Qur'an. All of them were messengers except Prophet Adam. He lived alone on Earth with his small family. Therefore, he was not ordered to convey Allah's message outside of his family. All the other prophets mentioned in the Qur'an from Nuh to Muhammad were rusul, or messengers. It should be noted here that Prophet Nuh was the first of Allah's messengers.

Contrasting Prophets and Messengers

Description	Prophets	messengers
Great people	*	*
Human beings	*	*
Men	*	*
Given divine messages	*	*
Must deliver the message to many other people		*
Perhaps given books		*

CORRECTION

Many people think that messengers are only those who received books from Allah. That is not true. There are messengers who did not receive books. Allah said in the Qur'an that Prophets Isma'eel, Lut, Yousuf, Ilyas, Younus, Salih, Hud and others are rusul, or messengers, although they did not receive books. Look at the following ayaat:

﴿ وَٱذۡكُرۡ فِي ٱلۡكِتَٰبِ إِسۡمَٰعِيلَۚ إِنَّهُۥ كَانَ صَادِقَ ٱلۡوَعۡدِ وَكَانَ رَسُولٗا نَّبِيّٗا ﴾

And mention Isma'eel in the Book; surely he was truthful in (his) promise, and he was a messenger, a prophet. [19:54]

﴿ وَإِنَّ إِلۡيَاسَ لَمِنَ ٱلۡمُرۡسَلِينَ ﴾

And Ilyas was most surely one of the messengers. [37:123]

﴿ وَإِنَّ لُوطٗا لَّمِنَ ٱلۡمُرۡسَلِينَ ﴾

And Lut was most surely one of the messengers. [37:133]

﴿ وَإِنَّ يُونُسَ لَمِنَ ٱلۡمُرۡسَلِينَ ﴾

And Younus was most surely one of the messengers. [37:139]

The Role of a Messenger

The main role of the messenger is to convey the message of Allah to his people. Allah ﷻ says:

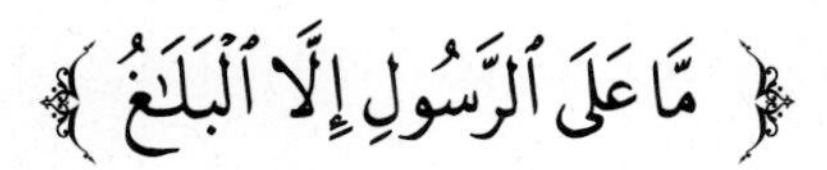

"The Messenger's duty is but to convey (the Message)..." [3:81]

Allah ﷻ also says:
"O Apostle! Proclaim the (Message) which has been sent to you from your Lord. If you do not, you will not have fulfilled (your obligation) and taught His message." [5:67]

As you learned earlier, messengers were given the responsibility of teaching their people Islam. Each messenger was only responsible for conveying Allah's message to his people. They were not responsible for bringing the message to people outside of their areas, unless Allah ordered them to do so. The situation of Prophet Muhammad ﷺ was different. He was sent as a messenger and guide for his people and for all of humankind. Allah says:

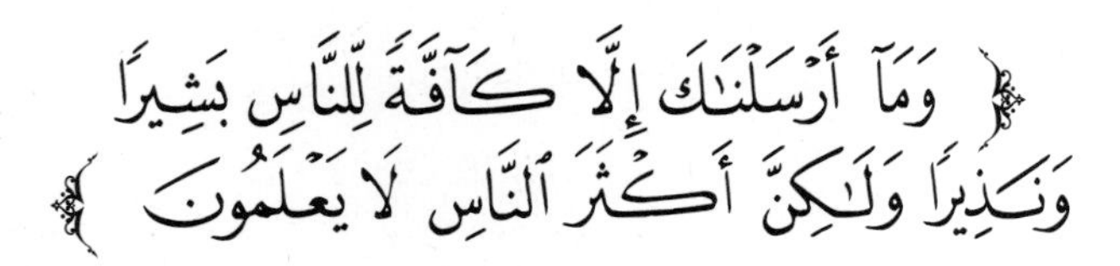

"We have not sent you but as a universal (Messenger) to mankind, giving them glad tidings, and warning them (against sin), but most people do not understand." [34:28]

During his 23 years as a messenger, he taught the people of Arabia the message of Islam, and all of Arabia became a Muslim nation. Before he died, he sent his ambassadors with messages to the kings of Persia, the Roman Empire, Egypt, and other nations outside of Arabia inviting them to Islam. Some of these nations, as well as others not mentioned, accepted Islam after the passing away of Prophet Muhammad ﷺ .

Messengers are sent to:
1. Teach Allah's message of faith
2. Teach people how to worship their Creator
3. Show people how to live moral and happy lives.

The Prophet's Mosque in Madinah

Prophet Muhammad ﷺ :The Final Prophet and Messenger

All prophets were chosen by Allah ﷻ , and their messages were equally true. However, their missions varied. The messengers before Prophet Muhammad ﷺ were only given teachings for their nations. During those times, except for trade or war, nations didn't interact with each other. Furthermore, the teachings of each prophet lasted for a limited time, after which Allah ﷻ would send another prophet to revise some of the teachings for the new circumstances.

But eventually the time came to unite all nations with a single religion. Allah wanted humankind to live in peace as one nation. For this purpose Allah sent Prophet Muhammad ﷺ to all mankind. Allah entrusted him to deliver His teachings to the whole world and for eternity. This teaching is Islam in its complete form.

Prophet Muhammad's ﷺ mission was to confirm the basic teachings of Islam that other prophets had taught. He also came with additional teaching and guidance for the good of mankind. Islam as we know, it now is a comprehensive and perfect way of life. If people follow this guidance they will live happily in this life, and win the wonderful Paradise in the after-life.

Prophet Muhammad ﷺ is the final Prophet and Messenger. He brought us the final message from God, the Qur'an. No true prophet or messenger will come after Prophet Muhammad ﷺ , and no divine message will come after Al-Qur'an. Allah سبحانه وتعالى says in Al-Qur'an:

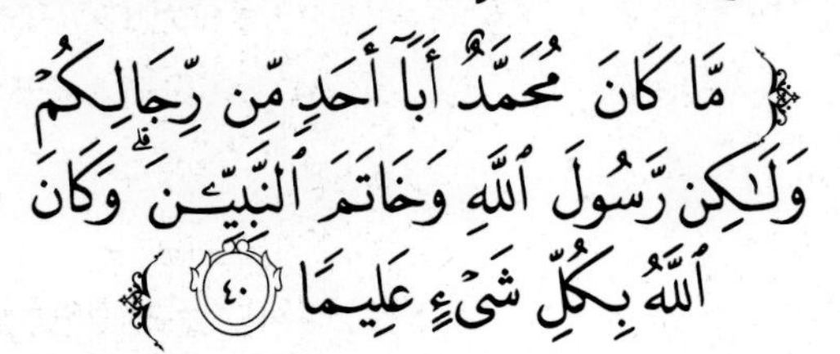

"Muhammad is not the father of any of your men, but he is the Messenger of Allah and the Last of the Prophets; and Allah is knowledgeable of all things." [33:40]

Al-Qur'an's message confirms but replaces all former holy books and scriptures that people changed or were lost over time.

▲ *Inside the Prophet's Mosque in Madinah*

Anyone who claims to be a prophet after Prophet Muhammad ﷺ is a false prophet. And any claimed divine message after the Qur'an is not from Allah سبحانه وتعالى .

It is unfortunate that there are a few groups that claim to be Muslims, but they believe in a prophet after Prophet Muhammad. These groups cannot be Muslim. The Qur'an confirms that Prophet Muhammad ﷺ is the last and the seal of all prophets and messengers. Al-Qur'an, too, is the final message from Allah سبحانه وتعالى .

The Messengers and Their Books

While all prophets and messengers taught the same message of tawheed, only five were given revelations in the form of a book. These books contained the message of tawheed along with other teachings such as morality, worship, the Day of Judgment, and the belief in Heaven and Hell. The messengers whom we are told received books are Prophet Ibraheem, Prophet Dawood, Prophet Musa, Prophet Isa, and Prophet Muhammad peace be upon all of them. These messengers received special books that had specific names:

Prophet	His Book	
Prophet Ibraheem	Al-Suhuf (Scrolls)	صحف إبراهيم
Prophet Musa	At-Tawrah (Torah)	التوراة
Prophet Dawood	Zaboor (Psalms)	الزبور
Prophet Isa	Al-Injeel (Bible)	الإنجيل
Prophet Muhammad	Al-Qur'an	القرآن

As you learned earlier, Prophet Nuh was the first messenger. However, the first messenger who received a written message was Prophet Ibraheem. He was given the first scripture known as the Suhuf, or the scrolls. The Suhuf contained the true message of tawheed along with other teachings of Allah ﷻ. However, many years after he died, people began to corrupt and change the true teachings described in the Suhuf. This caused the people to eventually forget the true message of Allah ﷻ. The need for another written message or a book became urgent. Prophet Musa was chosen to be the next messenger. Allah ﷻ gave him At-Tawrah (the Torah) as a guide for his people. Some time after his death, Prophet Dawood and Prophet Isa were appointed as messengers. They too offered to their peoples books of Allah ﷻ. As before, their people after them corrupted the original teachings.

The last and seal of all prophets was Muhammad ﷺ. Allah ﷻ provided Prophet Muhammad ﷺ with Al-Qur'an. Al-Qur'an has never changed since its revelation more than 1,400 years ago, and it will remain unchanged until the Day of Judgment. It is exactly the same as it was when first revealed by Allah ﷻ. Allah promised in the Qur'an that He will protect His last book against any change or loss.

Allah says:

﴿إِنَّا نَحْنُ نَزَّلْنَا الذِّكْرَ وَإِنَّا لَهُ لَحَافِظُونَ﴾

"We revealed this book and We will surely protect it." [Surat Al-Hijr 15:9]

Subhan'Allah! This is why there is no need for another prophet or messenger after Prophet Muhammad ﷺ.

Chapter Review

Draw a map which shows where at least twenty prophets and messengers delivered their messages.

1. Compare and contrast the characteristics of Allah's prophets and messengers.
2. What are the similarities and differences between prophets and other great Muslim personalities?
3. List all the suwar in the Qur'an that are named after prophets or messengers.

1. What is the message that all prophets taught to their families and peoples?
2. What are the similarities between prophets and messengers?
3. What is the difference between a prophet and a messenger?
4. How many prophets and messengers are mentioned in the Qur'an altogether? How many were prophets, and how many were messengers?
5. Did all messengers receive books from Allah سبحانه وتعالى ? Explain.
6. Draw a table showing the names of the messengers who received books, and the names of these books.

The First Messenger: The Story of Prophet Nuh عليه السلام

CHAPTER
THREE

Pre-reading Questions

1. Who was the first prophet of Allah?
2. Who was the first messenger of Allah?
3. How did Prophet Nuh call his people to Islam?
4. Did the people of Nuh obey Allah?
5. What did Allah do to the disbelievers?
4. What did Allah do to the believers?

Prophet Nuh: The first Messenger of Allah

Prophet نوح Nuh, or Noah عليه السلام, was the second of the 25 prophets mentioned by name in the Qur'an. Prophet Adam was the first prophet ever. After Prophet Adam passed away, human society became corrupt and evil. Most of the people did not worship Allah ﷻ and there was much evil and ignorance among people on Earth. Prophet Nuh and his people lived in present day Iraq. The people at the time of Prophet Nuh had been worshipping idols for many years. So Allah ﷻ appointed Nuh عليه السلام to be a prophet among his tribe to guide them back to the straight path.

Prophet Nuh was the first rasul, or messenger, that Allah ﷻ sent to help people return to the straight path. Prophet Nuh was a patient and wise man.

Did you Know?

Prophet Nuh عليه السلام was the first rasul (messenger).

Prophet Nuh Calls His People to Islam

Prophet Nuh invited his people to believe in the One True God, Allah, and to worship Him alone. He told them:

"My people, I am coming to you with a clear warning. Worship Allah, fear His punishment by staying away from sin, and obey me. Allah will forgive some of your sins, and will grant you life until the appointed time of death. When death comes from Allah, it cannot be postponed. If you only knew." [71:3-4]

The People Refuse to Believe Prophet Nuh

People refused to listen to Prophet Nuh. When he said that they should worship only Allah ﷻ and do good, they paid no attention. Prophet Nuh was very sad, and he told Allah ﷻ :

"Oh my Lord I have called my people by night and day. And all my calling did was to get them to run away faster from the truth. And whenever I called them so that they would believe and You would forgive them, they put their

fingers in their ears and their clothes over their heads. And they insisted on disbelief and became very arrogant in rejecting (Islam)."
[Surat Nuh 71:5-7]

Prophet Nuh then tried different ways to persuade his people, but all that did not work. He said:

"Then I called them openly. Then after that I would call sometimes openly and sometimes individually." [Surat Nuh 71:8-9]

Arrogant and Rude People

Prophet Nuh عليه السلام even told his people that if they listened to his message of tawheed, much good would happen to them.
Allah سبحانه وتعالى would provide them with rain for the crops to grow, more wealth, and children.

He said, "Ask your Lord for forgiveness because Allah is ever-forgiving. If you do, Allah will send lots of rain to you regularly. And will give you more money, He children, orchards, and flowing rivers."

The people of Prophet Nuh still ignored his message. But Prophet Nuh did not give up. He was very patient, and he pointed out the blessings of Allah ﷻ that had been bestowed upon them.

Prophet Nuh tried to reason with his people. How could they not see the everyday miracles of Allah ﷻ ? How could they not see how He created mankind in stages in the womb? How could they not see the sky and the stars, or the light of the sun, and the beauty of the moon?

▲ *A waterfall in Iraq*

Hadeeth Shareef

عن عبد الله بن مسعود رضي الله قال: قال رسول الله ﷺ :

" لا يَدْخُل الجنَّة مَن كان في قَلْبه مِثْقالَ ذَرَّة مِن كِبر"

قال رجل: "إنَّ الرَّجل يُحبّ أنْ يكونَ ثَوْبه حَسناً ونعله حَسنة"

قال رسول الله ﷺ :

" إنّ الله جَميلٌ يُحبّ الجمال ، الكِبْرُ بَطَرُ الحقّ وغَمْطُ الناس "

رواه مسلم والترمذي وأحمد

Abdullah Ibn Mas'ood reported that Prophet Muhammad ﷺ said: "Anyone who has in his heart so much as the weight of a seed of arrogance will not enter Paradise." A man then asked the Prophet, "If I want to look good by wearing a good outfit or shoes, is this arrogance?" The Prophet answered: "[No] Allah is beautiful and likes beauty. Arrogance is rejecting the truth and downgrading others."

(Reported by Al-Bukhari and Muslim)

Prophet Nuh's People Reject Tawheed and Worship Many Idols

Nuh's people still refused to listen. They denied Allah's favors and insisted on being rude and ungrateful to him. They continued to worship their idols. These idols had special names: Wad, Suwaa', Yaghooth, Ya'ooq, and Nasr.

Prophet Nuh complained to Allah ﷻ and said:

"My Lord, they have disobeyed me and followed those who lost their souls because of their wealth and children. They committed great sins, and the leaders said, "Do not leave your gods; especially do not leave Wad, or Suwaa', or Yaghouth, or Ya'ooq, or Nasr'."

▲ *Idols from ancient Iraq*

Prophet Nuh's Great Perseverance

With a lot of patience and determination, Prophet Nuh continued his mission of teaching and guiding his people. A small group of people accepted his message, but many others did not. Instead, they decided to torture him. They did not know that because of their disbelief and evil deeds, they would drown in the flood and go to Hellfire. Prophet Nuh lived and preached for 950 years!

When Prophet Nuh realized that his people would suffer the punishment of Allah, he was both sad and angry that his people would not listen to his message.

Healthy Habit

Learn to be patient and persevere, especially when doing good work for the sake of Allah.

Did you know?

Prophet Nuh called his people to Islam and tawheed for over 900 years. He lived the longest of all of the known prophets.

Allah Orders Nuh to Build the Ark

Allah informed Prophet Nuh عليه السلام that he should not feel sad. Allah revealed to him that he should build an ark:

Allah سبحانه وتعالى says in Al-Qur'an:

"None of your people will believe except those who have believed already! So grieve no longer over their (evil) deeds. But make an ark under Our eyes and Our inspiration, and do not talk to Me (further) about those who are in sin for they are about to be drowned (in the Flood)." [11:36-37]

In obedience to Allah's instructions, Nuh began to build an ark on land. The people who saw it when they passed by made fun of him and his ship. They said:

"Oh Nuh! You used to say that you were a prophet, but how come you've become a carpenter today? Perhaps you've come to hate prophethood and become interested in carpentry!"

Prophet Nuh answered:
"You ridicule us now but we shall laugh at you soon."

Nuh and the Believers Move into the Ark

When the ship was completed, Almighty Allah ﷻ then sent his revelation:
"When Our command came and the fountains of the Earth gushed forth! We said to Nuh:

'Board therein of each kind [of animals], a male and female and your family - except those against whom the word has already gone forth - and the Believers.' [Surat Hud 11:40]

Then it started to rain heavily, and the waters on Earth began to rise. Allah ﷻ told Nuh عليه السلام to board the ship, together with his family and all who believed. Nuh was also ordered to take one male and female from each kind of animal on Earth. Prophet Nuh عليه السلام did as he was told, and then he said, "In the name of Allah, we shall now sail away, and when the time is right, we shall return again to the land."

Allah Destroys the Disbelievers with the Great Flood

The waters rose higher and higher until all the valleys were flooded. Nuh saw Yam, one of his sons, who had not yet boarded the ship, and he called out to him:

"O my son! Come aboard with us and be not with the unbelievers!" [11:42]

The son replied, "I will protect myself by climbing the mountain; it will save me from the water."
Nuh said, "This day nothing can save you from the command of Allah!" [11:43]

Prophet Nuh عليه السلام cried out to his son Yam. His son refused to listen. Prophet Nuh was very sad and pleaded to Allah سبحانه وتعالى :

"My Lord! My son is of my family! And Your promise is true and You are the Most Just of Judges!" [11:45]

Allah replied to Prophet Nuh:
"He is not of your family. For his conduct is evil. So do not talk to Me about what you have no knowledge of. I advise you not to be ignorant!" [11:46]

It continued to rain for a very long time. The water rose so high that it covered all the mountains. The winds were violent, and thunder shook the Earth.

Many people in Turkey and around the world believe that this picture shows the remains of Prophet Nuh's Ark. The area now is called Mount Judi. This site is about 18 miles from the famous Ararat Mountain in eastern Turkey.

Allah Saves the Believers

When Allah's punishment reached its height and everything was destroyed, it stopped raining. Allah سبحانه وتعالى commanded the Earth to swallow all the water. Finally, Prophet Nuh's عليه السلام ship landed safely at the side of a mountain, which is in modern-day eastern Turkey. The mountain is called mount Judi. Then the word came from Allah:

> "O Earth! Swallow up your water, and O sky! Stop your rain! And the water abated, and the matter was ended."
>
> The ark rested on the [Mount] Judi, and the word went forth, "Away with those who do wrong!" [11: 44]

> "O Nuh! Come down (from the ark) with peace from Us and blessing on you and on some of the peoples (who will spring) from those with you" [11:48]

All the people and animals that had been on the ship came out. Prophet Nuh عليه السلام and his followers thanked Allah with all their hearts because they had been saved by Him. This was a great miracle.

Healthy Habit

Obeying your parents is very important in Islam. No matter how much you know, they are still much wiser than you and know much more than what you know. Disobeying parents often leads to destruction, as you learned from the story of Nuh and his disobedient son, Yam.

Chapter Review

Why do you think Allah سبحانه وتعالى chose to punish the people of Nuh with the flood, and not with something else?

Under the supervision of your teacher or parent, build a small ark with your classmates or friends. Fill it with plastic people and animals. Then place it in an area where you can make a small flood and watch the ark float.

1. Prophet Nuh and his people lived in which present day country?
2. Why did Allah سبحانه وتعالى send Prophet Nuh to his people? What was his message?
3. What did Allah سبحانه وتعالى promise Nuh's people if they accepted Islam?
4. Name the four idols that Nuh's people worshipped. Explain why they worshiped the idols.
5. According to the Qur'an, which of Allah's blessings did Prophet Nuh point out to his people?
6. What did prophet Nuh's people say when they saw him building an ark, even though there was no river or sea around?
7. What was the punishment of worshipping false gods and refusing to accept the message of tawheed?

UNIT B CHAPTER 4 LESSON ONE

Surat Nuh (Noah) 1

Introduction

This surah was revealed in Makkah. It has 28 ayaat and mainly talks about the story of Prophet Nuh. Allah revealed this surah to Prophet Muhammad ﷺ to encourage him to be patient. In this surah, Allah سبحانه وتعالى tells us about the patience of Nuh, who called his people for over 900 years. Only a few of them followed Nuh and became believers.

In the surah Allah سبحانه وتعالى warns the kuffar of Makkah that they will be punished for their disbelief. Allah reminds them of the punishment of the people who rejected Nuh عليه السلام. They all were destroyed by the huge flood, and only Prophet Nuh and the believers were saved.

Allah Chooses Nuh as a Messenger to His People

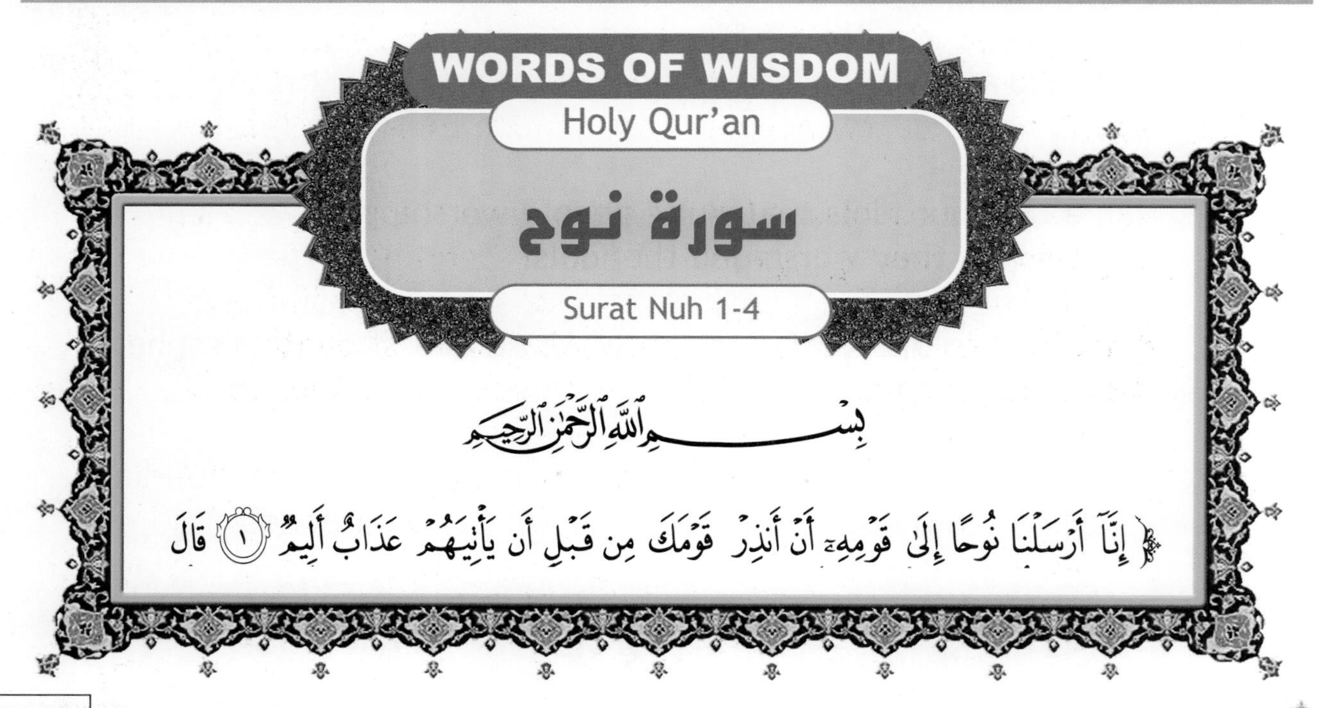

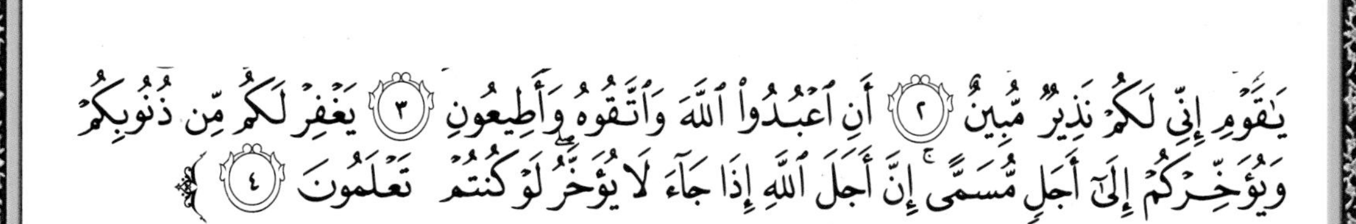

TRANSLITERATION

Inna arsalna nuhan ila qawmihi an anthir qawmaka min qabli an ya'tiyahum athabun aleem (71:1) Qala ya qawmi innee lakum natheerum mubeen (71:2) Ani 'abudoo Allaha wattaqoohu waatee'oon (71:3) Yaghfir lakum min thunoobikum wayu-akhkhirkum ila ajalim musamman inna ajal-Allahi itha ja'a la yu-akhkharu law kuntum ta'lamoon (71:4)

UNDERSTOOD MEANING

(71:1) I sent Nuh to his people, telling him to warn them before a painful punishment comes to them.
(71:2) He said, "My people, I am coming to you with a clear warning.
(71:3) If you worship Allah, fear Him and His punishment by staying away from disbelief and sin, and obey me.
(71:4) Then will forgive some of your sins, and will make your lives longer until your prewritten time of death. When death comes from Allah, it cannot be postponed, if only you knew.

Main Lessons

1 Prophets use encouragement and warning to help people keep on the straight path.

In this first section of the surah, Nuh uses both encouragement and warning to bring his people back to Islam. The encouragement is the promise of forgiveness and blessed, longer lives. The warning is the promise of punishment and destruction if they don't come to Islam. He commanded them to worship Allah ﷻ, do what they were supposed to do, and stay away from what Allah ﷻ forbade them.

2 Prophet Nuh was the first Messenger.

Prophet Nuh عليه السلام tried to guide his people to the straight path for over 900 years, without much success.

In one hadeeth reported in Al-Bukhari, Prophet Muhammad ﷺ said that Nuh was the first rasul (messenger) sent to Earth. He was the first messenger sent to disbelievers on Earth. Before his time, everyone was either a good or a bad Muslim, and no one worshipped idols. When his people started to worship idols instead of worshipping the One True God, Allah sent him as a messenger.

Hadeeth Shareef

عن أنس رضي الله عنه قال رسول الله ﷺ:

"أولُ نبيّ أُرسِلَ نوح."

رواه ابن عساكر والديلمي

Ibn Anas narrated that Prophet Muhammad ﷺ said:

"The first prophet to be sent as a messenger was Nuh."
(Reported Ibn Asakir & Ad-Daylami)

WORDS OF WISDOM

Holy Qur'an

سورة نوح

Surat Nuh 5-9

﴿ قَالَ رَبِّ إِنِّي دَعَوْتُ قَوْمِي لَيْلًا وَنَهَارًا ﴿٥﴾ فَلَمْ يَزِدْهُمْ دُعَاءِي إِلَّا فِرَارًا ﴿٦﴾ وَإِنِّي كُلَّمَا
دَعَوْتُهُمْ لِتَغْفِرَ لَهُمْ جَعَلُوٓا أَصَٰبِعَهُمْ فِيٓ ءَاذَانِهِمْ وَٱسْتَغْشَوْا ثِيَابَهُمْ وَأَصَرُّوا وَٱسْتَكْبَرُوا
ٱسْتِكْبَارًا ﴿٧﴾ ثُمَّ إِنِّي دَعَوْتُهُمْ جِهَارًا ﴿٨﴾ ثُمَّ إِنِّيٓ أَعْلَنتُ لَهُمْ وَأَسْرَرْتُ لَهُمْ إِسْرَارًا ﴿٩﴾ ﴾

TRANSLITERATION

Qala rabbi innee da'awtu qawmee laylaw-wanahara (71:5) Falam yazidhum du'a-ee illa firara (71:6) Wa-innee kullama da'awtuhum litaghfira lahum ja'aloo asabi'ahum fee athanihim wastaghshaw thiyabahum wa-asarroo wastakbaro-stikbara (71:7) Thumma innee da'awtuhum jihara (71:8) Thumma innee aa'lantu lahum wa asrartu lahum israra (71:9)

UNDERSTOOD MEANING

(71:5) He said, "Oh my Lord I have called my people night and day

(71:6) And all my calling did was to get them to run away faster from the truth.

(71:7) And whenever I called them so that they would believe and You would forgive them, they put their fingers in their ears and their clothes over their heads. And they insisted on disbelief and became very arrogant in rejecting Islam.

(71:8) Then I called them openly.

(71:9) Then after that I would call sometimes openly and sometimes individually.

Main Lessons

1 Prophet Nuh did his best to call his people back to Islam.

2 Prophet Nuh tried different ways to convince his people.

Notice that believers complain to Allah ﷻ only after they have done their very best. This is what Prophet Nuh did. He complained to Allah only after he had done all the things he must do. After hundreds of years of hard work, he felt that he had done everything. Then he complained to Allah ﷻ that he could not do more. Many people start complaining even before they try to do their jobs. Others quit soon after they start when they discover the difficulty of the task. Good believers start by asking for Allah's help and do their best to finish their tasks successfully. When they try their best and fail, they seek the help of the people around them.

The people of Nuh were very stubborn. They did not even want to hear what Prophet Nuh had to say.They put their fingers in their ears and their clothes over their heads to make sure they wouldn't hear anything. This did not cause Prophet Nuh to give up on them. He started calling people individually and in groups. Then he mixed calling to people openly, and then talking to them in private. So the meaning is that he was always trying different ways. When certain ways didn't seem to work, he would try other ways of calling them to Islam.

Healthy Habit

Always try to be patient, and keep trying even if something is difficult!

Many acts of disobedience to Allah ﷻ result in an increase in disease. Discuss this idea, and then pick a certain act of disobedience like drinking alcohol. Research the diseases that people can get because of this.

1. Why did Allah ﷻ send Nuh to his people?
2. What did Propht Nuh advise his people to do?
3. What did Prophet Nuh promise his people if they listened to him?
4. How did the people of Prophet Nuh behave when he talked to them? Why?
5. What are the ways Prophet Nuh used when he talked to them?

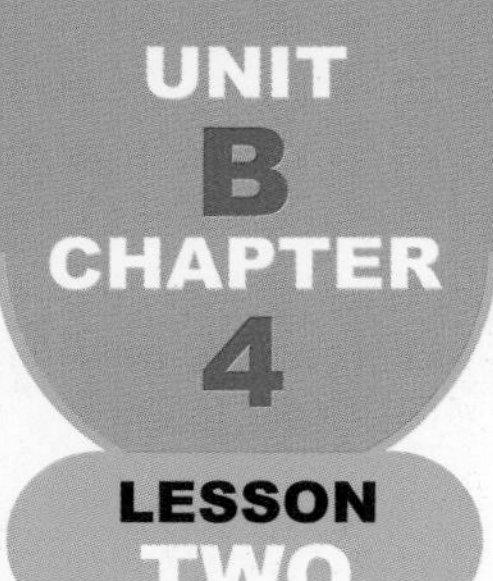

Surat Nuh (Noah) 2

Prophet Nuh Advises His People to Repent

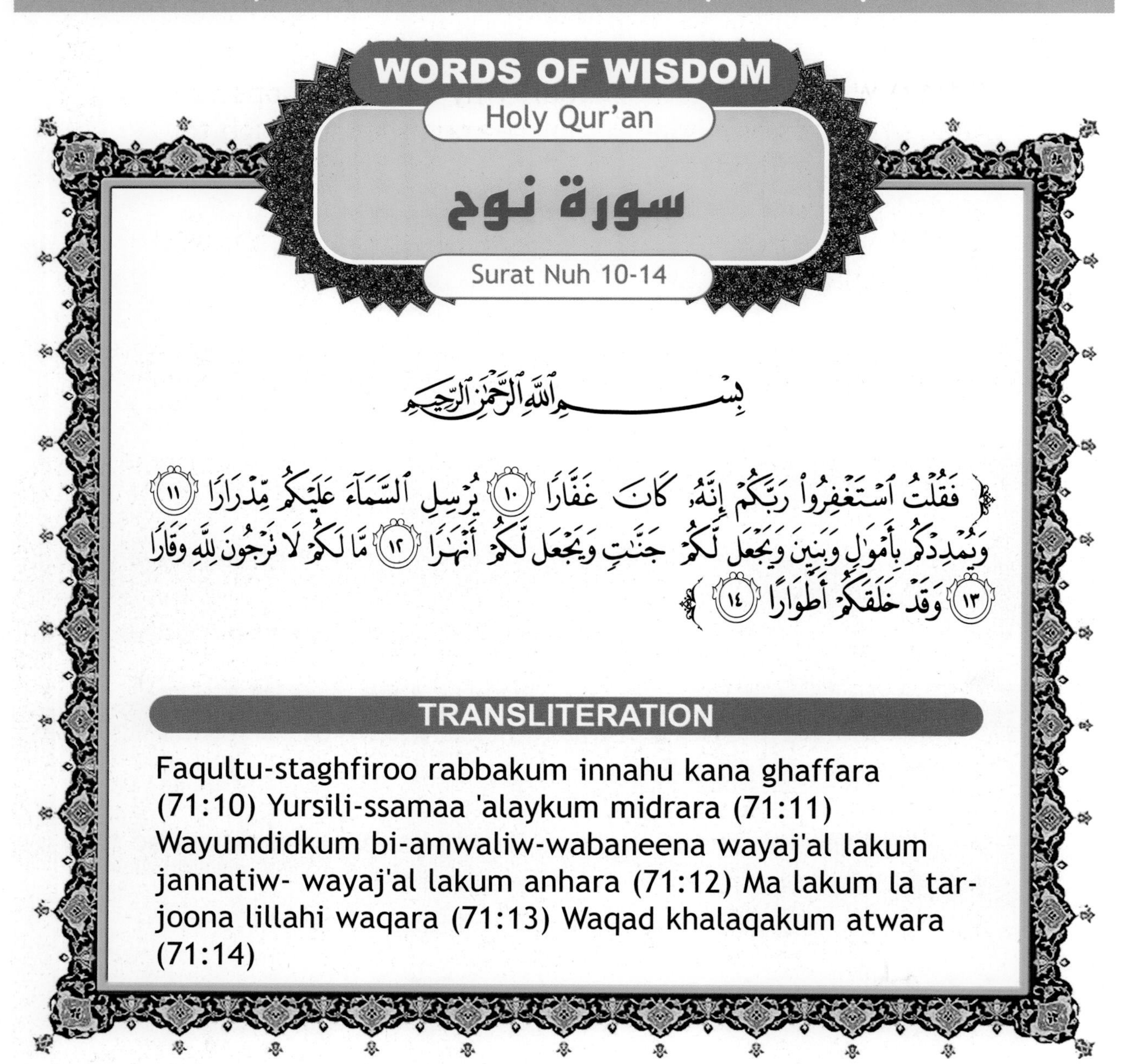

WORDS OF WISDOM

Holy Qur'an

سورة نوح

Surat Nuh 10-14

بِسْمِ اللَّهِ الرَّحْمَٰنِ الرَّحِيمِ

﴿ فَقُلْتُ اسْتَغْفِرُوا رَبَّكُمْ إِنَّهُ كَانَ غَفَّارًا ﴿١٠﴾ يُرْسِلِ السَّمَاءَ عَلَيْكُم مِّدْرَارًا ﴿١١﴾
وَيُمْدِدْكُم بِأَمْوَالٍ وَبَنِينَ وَيَجْعَل لَّكُمْ جَنَّاتٍ وَيَجْعَل لَّكُمْ أَنْهَارًا ﴿١٢﴾ مَّا لَكُمْ لَا تَرْجُونَ لِلَّهِ وَقَارًا
﴿١٣﴾ وَقَدْ خَلَقَكُمْ أَطْوَارًا ﴿١٤﴾ ﴾

TRANSLITERATION

Faqultu-staghfiroo rabbakum innahu kana ghaffara (71:10) Yursili-ssamaa 'alaykum midrara (71:11) Wayumdidkum bi-amwaliw-wabaneena wayaj'al lakum jannatiw- wayaj'al lakum anhara (71:12) Ma lakum la tar-joona lillahi waqara (71:13) Waqad khalaqakum atwara (71:14)

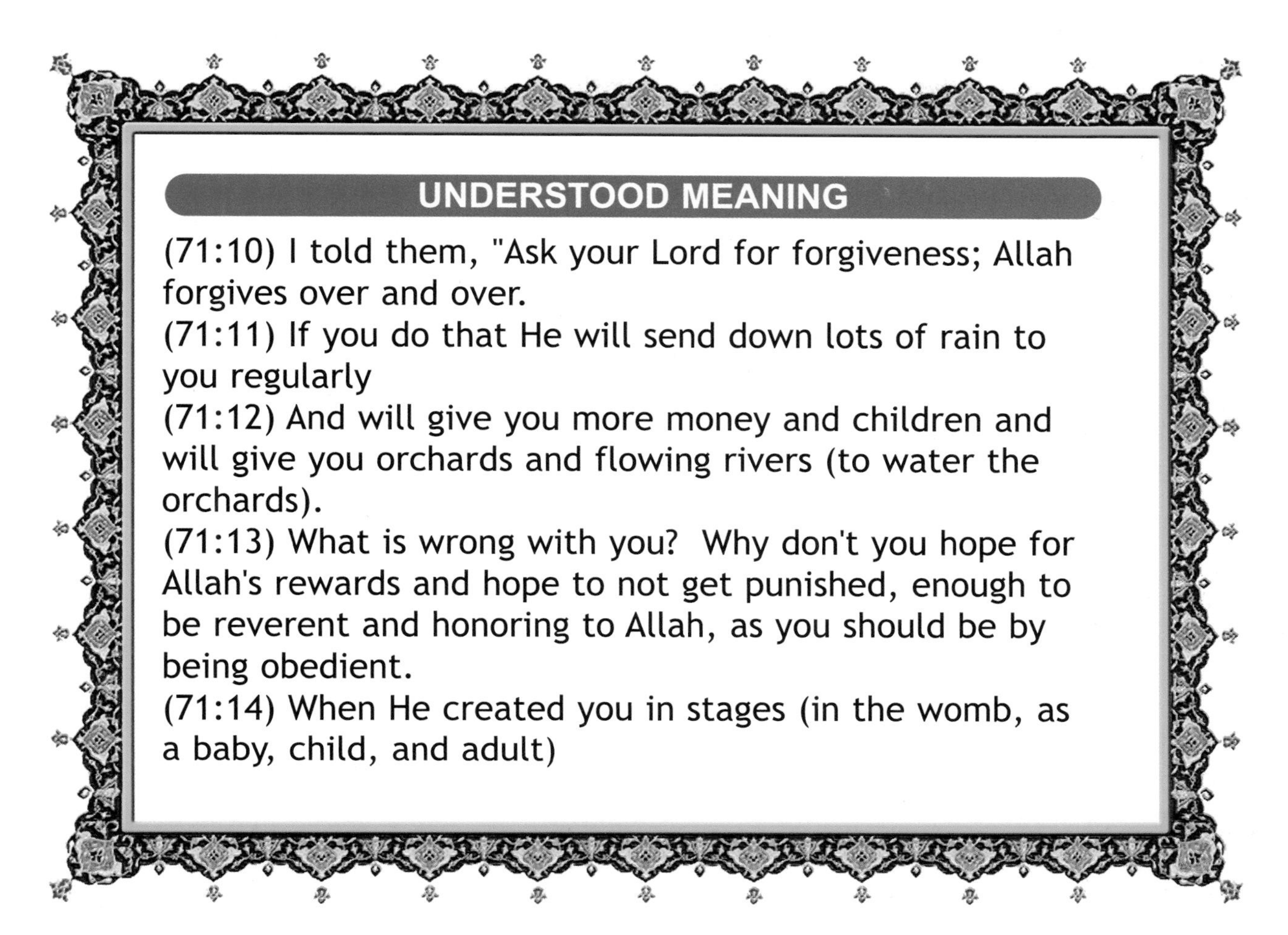

UNDERSTOOD MEANING

(71:10) I told them, "Ask your Lord for forgiveness; Allah forgives over and over.
(71:11) If you do that He will send down lots of rain to you regularly
(71:12) And will give you more money and children and will give you orchards and flowing rivers (to water the orchards).
(71:13) What is wrong with you? Why don't you hope for Allah's rewards and hope to not get punished, enough to be reverent and honoring to Allah, as you should be by being obedient.
(71:14) When He created you in stages (in the womb, as a baby, child, and adult)

Main Lessons

Istighfar is a Great Worship.

Seeking forgiveness of Allah is a very important thing. Many times we make mistakes without knowing. Ttherefore, we need to ask Allah to forgive us. Allah ﷻ is Al-Ghafoor, or All-Forgiving, and if we are sincere in our repentance He will forgive our sins. Prophet Muhammad used to do istighfar more than one hundred times every day. In these ayaat, Prophet Nuh teaches us that istighfar brings us all the blessings of Allah. It makes Allah ﷻ bless us with rain, food, money, children, and many other blessings.

STORYTIME

The second khaleefah, Omar ibn Al-Khattab رضي الله عنه , went out with the people to make the prayer for rain. This prayer is called صَلاةُ الاسْتِسْقاء Salat-ul-Istisqaa', the prayer of seeking rain. He stood up and spent the time only asking Allah for forgiveness. As he was leaving, the people said, "O leader of the believers, we didn't see you pray for rain." Then Khaleefah Omar read ayaat 10, 11, and 12 of Surat Nuh.

Healthy Habit

Always say Istighfar by saying:
"Astaghfir Allah,"
I ask Allah for forgiveness.

Du'aa دعـــــــاء

THE BEST ISTIGHFAR

عن شداد بن أوس قال: قال رسولُ اللهِ صلى الله عليه وسلم: سَيِّدُ الاسْتِغْفار أن تقول:

" اللهم أنت ربي لا إلهَ إلا أنتَ ، خلقتني وأنا عبدُكَ ، وأنا على عَهْدِكَ وَوَعْدِكَ ما استطَعْت ، أعوذ بِكَ من شر ما صنعت ، أبوءُ لك بنعْمَتِكَ عليَّ ، وأبوءُ بِذَنبي فاغفِرْ لي فإنه لا يغفِرُ الذُّنوبَ إلا أنْتَ"

رواه البخاري

Allahumma anta rabbi la ilaha illa unt, khalaqtani wa ana 'abduk, wa ana ala 'ahdika wa wa'dika mastata't, aboo'u laka bini'matika alayy, wa aboo'u bithanbi faghfir lee fa-innahu la yaghfiru-thunooba illa unt.

Shaddad Ibn Aws narrated that Rasulullah said: "The best of Istighfar is to say:

"O Allah, You are my Lord; there is no god but you. You created me, and I am your servant. And I am holding to my pledge and promise to worship you as much as I can. I acknowledge your blessings upon me. And I admit my sins, so forgive me, for no one can forgive sins except you."

Prophet Nuh Tells his People to Remember Allah's Gifts

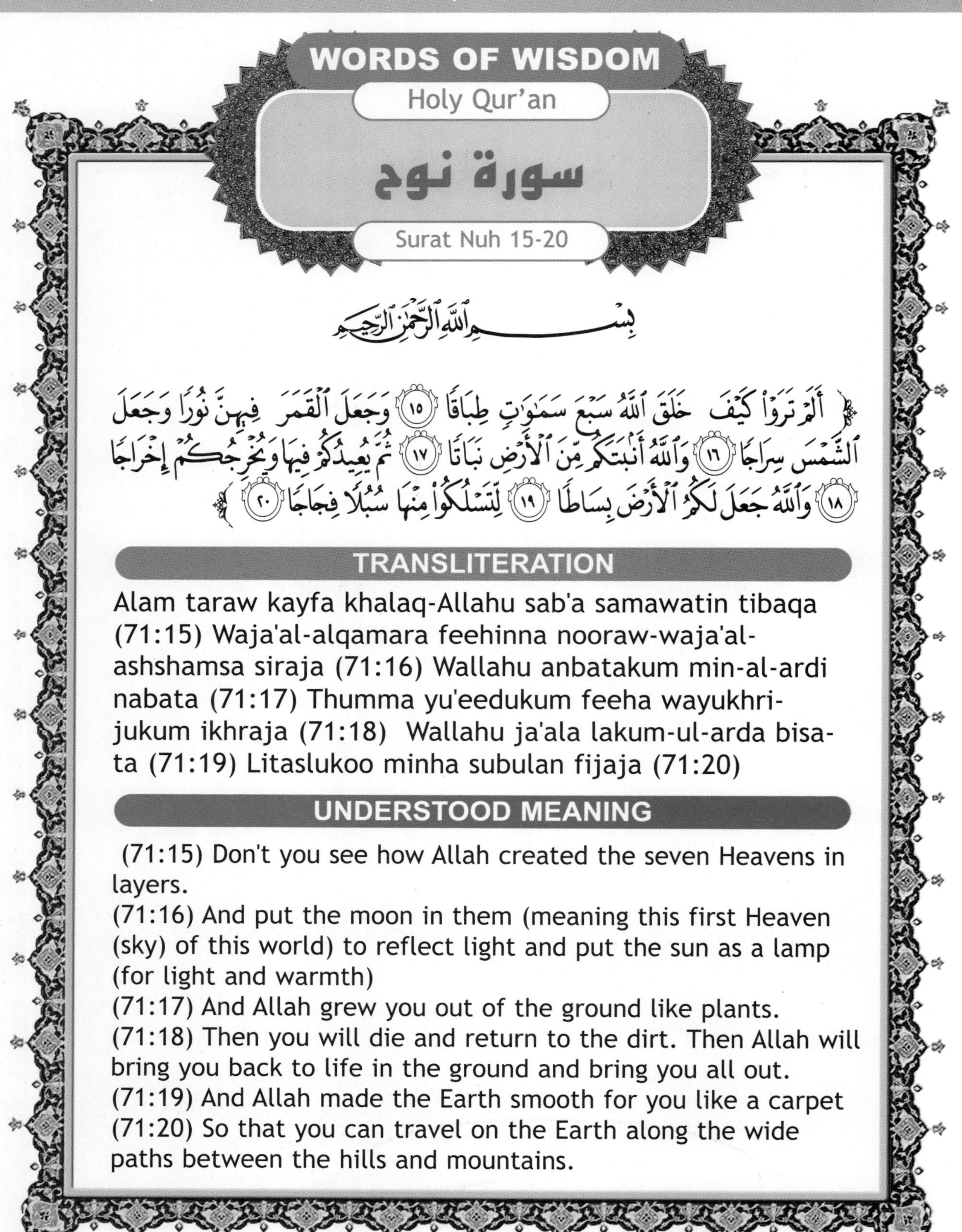

WORDS OF WISDOM

Holy Qur'an

سورة نوح

Surat Nuh 15-20

بِسْمِ اللَّهِ الرَّحْمَٰنِ الرَّحِيمِ

﴿ أَلَمْ تَرَوْا كَيْفَ خَلَقَ اللَّهُ سَبْعَ سَمَٰوَٰتٍ طِبَاقًا ﴿١٥﴾ وَجَعَلَ الْقَمَرَ فِيهِنَّ نُورًا وَجَعَلَ
الشَّمْسَ سِرَاجًا ﴿١٦﴾ وَاللَّهُ أَنۢبَتَكُم مِّنَ الْأَرْضِ نَبَاتًا ﴿١٧﴾ ثُمَّ يُعِيدُكُمْ فِيهَا وَيُخْرِجُكُمْ إِخْرَاجًا
﴿١٨﴾ وَاللَّهُ جَعَلَ لَكُمُ الْأَرْضَ بِسَاطًا ﴿١٩﴾ لِّتَسْلُكُوا مِنْهَا سُبُلًا فِجَاجًا ﴿٢٠﴾ ﴾

TRANSLITERATION

Alam taraw kayfa khalaq-Allahu sab'a samawatin tibaqa (71:15) Waja'al-alqamara feehinna nooraw-waja'al-ashshamsa siraja (71:16) Wallahu anbatakum min-al-ardi nabata (71:17) Thumma yu'eedukum feeha wayukhri-jukum ikhraja (71:18) Wallahu ja'ala lakum-ul-arda bisa-ta (71:19) Litaslukoo minha subulan fijaja (71:20)

UNDERSTOOD MEANING

(71:15) Don't you see how Allah created the seven Heavens in layers.
(71:16) And put the moon in them (meaning this first Heaven (sky) of this world) to reflect light and put the sun as a lamp (for light and warmth)
(71:17) And Allah grew you out of the ground like plants.
(71:18) Then you will die and return to the dirt. Then Allah will bring you back to life in the ground and bring you all out.
(71:19) And Allah made the Earth smooth for you like a carpet
(71:20) So that you can travel on the Earth along the wide paths between the hills and mountains.

Chapter Review

Healthy Habit

Always remember Allah's gifts and follow His guidance.

Why did Allah ﷻ liken humans to plants, rather than to animals, in ayah 17 of Surat Nuh?

1. What did Prophet Nuh mainly advise his people to do according to these ayaat?
2. What benefits would people gain if they made istighfar regularly?
3. Name four of the gifts Allah ﷻ gave to all people on Earth. Describe how each of these gifts is important to mankind.
4. Why is it important to remember and acknowledge the great gifts of Allah to mankind?

Surat Nuh (Noah) 3

The Bad Response of His People and How the Story Ended

WORDS OF WISDOM

Holy Qur'an

سورة نوح

Surat Nuh 21-28

بِسْمِ اللَّهِ الرَّحْمَٰنِ الرَّحِيمِ

﴿ قَالَ نُوحٌ رَّبِّ إِنَّهُمْ عَصَوْنِي وَاتَّبَعُوا مَن لَّمْ يَزِدْهُ مَالُهُ وَوَلَدُهُ إِلَّا خَسَارًا ﴿٢١﴾ وَمَكَرُوا
مَكْرًا كُبَّارًا ﴿٢٢﴾ وَقَالُوا لَا تَذَرُنَّ آلِهَتَكُمْ وَلَا تَذَرُنَّ وَدًّا وَلَا سُوَاعًا وَلَا يَغُوثَ وَيَعُوقَ
وَنَسْرًا ﴿٢٣﴾ وَقَدْ أَضَلُّوا كَثِيرًا وَلَا تَزِدِ الظَّالِمِينَ إِلَّا ضَلَالًا ﴿٢٤﴾ مِّمَّا خَطِيئَاتِهِمْ أُغْرِقُوا
فَأُدْخِلُوا نَارًا فَلَمْ يَجِدُوا لَهُم مِّن دُونِ اللَّهِ أَنصَارًا ﴿٢٥﴾ ﴾

TRANSLITERATION

Qala nuhur-rabbi innahum 'asawnee wattaba'oo mag-lam yazidhu-maluhu wawaladuhu illa khasara (71:21) Wamakaroo makran kubbara (71:22) Waqaloo la tatharun-na alihatakum wala tatharunna waddaw-wala suwa'aw wala-yaghootha waya'ooqa wanasra (71:23) Waqad adal-

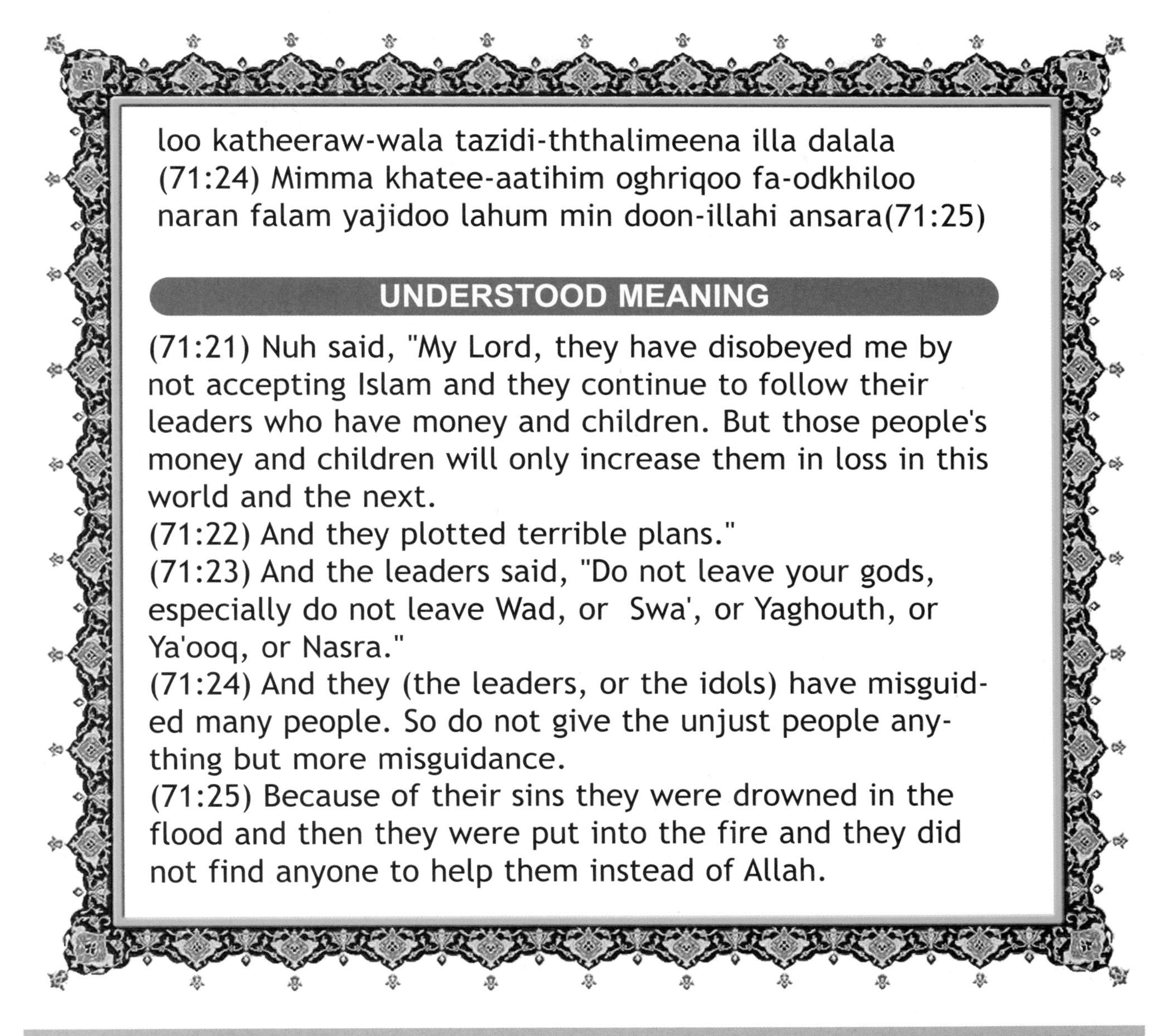
loo katheeraw-wala tazidi-ththalimeena illa dalala (71:24) Mimma khatee-aatihim oghriqoo fa-odkhiloo naran falam yajidoo lahum min doon-illahi ansara(71:25)

UNDERSTOOD MEANING

(71:21) Nuh said, "My Lord, they have disobeyed me by not accepting Islam and they continue to follow their leaders who have money and children. But those people's money and children will only increase them in loss in this world and the next.
(71:22) And they plotted terrible plans."
(71:23) And the leaders said, "Do not leave your gods, especially do not leave Wad, or Swa', or Yaghouth, or Ya'ooq, or Nasra."
(71:24) And they (the leaders, or the idols) have misguided many people. So do not give the unjust people anything but more misguidance.
(71:25) Because of their sins they were drowned in the flood and then they were put into the fire and they did not find anyone to help them instead of Allah.

Main Lessons

1 Money and power may make people arrogant and lead them to destruction.

The powerful and wealthy leaders of the people of Nuh refused to worship Allah and leave the idols. They told everybody to disobey Prophet Nuh and reject the true faith. Because they were wealthy and powerful, most people listened to them and disobeyed Nuh. So they all drowned in the flood and earned the punishment of Allah in the Hellfire. Prophet Nuh and his few modest and poor followers were saved in the ark and would be rewarded with Jannah.

2 How did idol worship start?

Wad, Suwaa', Yaghouth, Ya'ooq, and Nasra were good people from among Nuh's people. When they died, the people of Nuh became very sad. Shaytan came to them and suggested that they put up statues in their shapes to remember them. People later started to worship these statues. Allah sent Prophet Nuh to call people to the worship of Allah alone, and to stop worshipping the idols. The people did not obey Nuh, so Allah ﷻ punished the idol worshippers by the great flood. As a result of the flood, the statues were buried.

Years later the Shaytan directed people to their location and they dug them up. Therefore, idol worshipping continued in ancient lands and found its way to the Arabs. An Arabian man by the name of Amr Ibn Luhay brought idols for the first time to Al-Ka'bah in Makkah. Once he traveled to the region of Syria for business and borrowed a couple of idols, one of them called Hubal, from the people there. After that the people of Makkah started to worship idols. For this, the Messenger of Allah said he saw Amr Ibn Luhay dragging his intestines around Hell.

Healthy Habit

Avoid having statues at your home.

A town before a flood

The same town after a flood

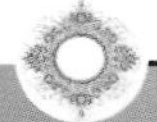

WORDS OF WISDOM

Holy Qur'an

سورة نوح

Surat Nuh 26-28

بِسْمِ ٱللَّهِ ٱلرَّحْمَٰنِ ٱلرَّحِيمِ

﴿ وَقَالَ نُوحٌ رَّبِّ لَا تَذَرْ عَلَى ٱلْأَرْضِ مِنَ ٱلْكَٰفِرِينَ دَيَّارًا ﴿٢٦﴾ إِنَّكَ إِن تَذَرْهُمْ يُضِلُّوا۟ عِبَادَكَ وَلَا يَلِدُوٓا۟ إِلَّا فَاجِرًا كَفَّارًا ﴿٢٧﴾ رَّبِّ ٱغْفِرْ لِى وَلِوَٰلِدَىَّ وَلِمَن دَخَلَ بَيْتِىَ مُؤْمِنًا وَلِلْمُؤْمِنِينَ وَٱلْمُؤْمِنَٰتِ وَلَا تَزِدِ ٱلظَّٰلِمِينَ إِلَّا تَبَارًۢا ﴿٢٨﴾ ﴾

TRANSLITERATION

Waqala nuhur-rabbi la tathar 'alal-ardi min-alkafireena dayyara (71:26) Innaka in tatharhum yudilloo 'ibadaka wala yalidoo illa fajiran kaffara (71:27) Rabbighfir lee waliwalidayya waliman dakhala baytiya mu'minaw-wa lil-mu'mineena walmu'minati wala tazidi-ththalimeena illa tabara (71:28)

UNDERSTOOD MEANING

(71:26) And Nuh said, "Oh my Lord, do not leave on the Earth a single household in which unbelievers live. (71:27) If you leave any of them, they will just misguide more of your servants and they will only have children, who will grow up disobedient and ungrateful to You. (71:28) Oh my Lord, forgive me and my parents and who-ever entered my house with faith. And all the believing men and believing women. And do not give anything to the oppressive people except destruction."

Chapter Review

1. Pick oppressive people throughout history and do some research to find how their lives ended.

2. Make a list of Muslims who need help in the world and spend some time praying for them.

3. Write a one-page report on the disaster of the tsunami, which took place in Southeast Asia in 2005, or the tragedy of New Orleans after Hurricane Katrina in 2005.

1. Why did the people of Nuh disobey their prophet?
2. What gods did the people of Nuh worship? What are their names?
3. Describe how the people of Prophet Nuh started worshipping their gods.
4. Can money and power be dangerous? Explain how.
5. What did Allah do to the people of Prophet Nuh in this life? What will Allah do to them in the next life?
6. What did Prophet Nuh ask Allah to do to his people?

Prophet Hud عليه السلام

CHAPTER FIVE

Pre-reading Questions

1. Who were the people of 'Aad?
2. What did the people of 'Aad Worship?
3. Whom did Allah choose as a prophet for 'Aad?
4. How did the people of 'Aad reject Prophet Hud?
5. How did Allah punish the disbelievers among the people of 'Aad?

Word Watch

Hud	هود
Aad	عاد
Iram	إرم
Ubar	أبَر

The People of 'Aad

Many years after Prophet Nuh عليه السلام, there lived a very industrious, hardworking people. They were the people of **'Aad** عاد. 'Aad was a King, and he was also the grandson of Prophet Nuh. The people of 'Aad lived in an ancient city called إرم **Iram**, a place in the south of present day Saudia Arabia, near the borders of Yemen and Oman. Allah blessed them with great wealth and they lived

life in peace and comfort. Allah gave them many blessings and made them very successful traders. They were very strong physically, and there was no disease in their society. The people of 'Aad built large and beautiful houses. On every hill they built a tower, and they were very proud of their beautiful buildings.

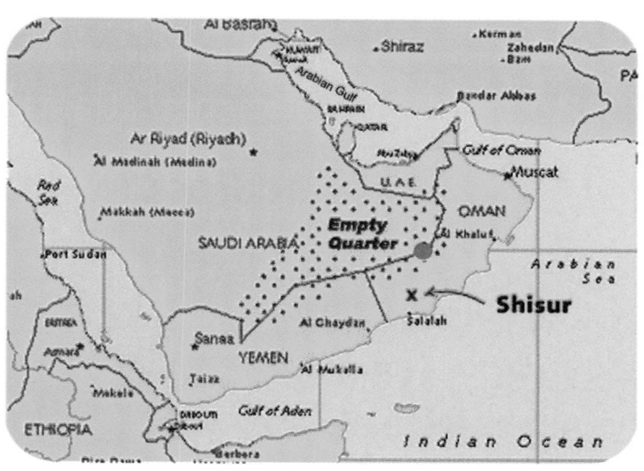

Allah is المغني Al-Mughni, The Giver of Wealth.

All money or wealth people have is from Allah.

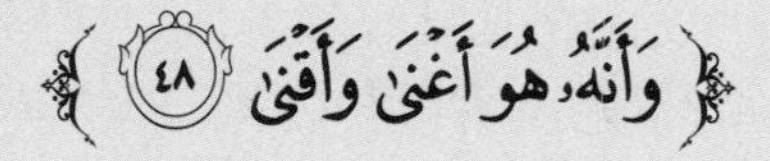

"And He is the One who gives wealth and belongings." [53:48]

The Ancient City of Ubar

UBAR-A wealthy incense trading post was said to be lost beneath the desert sands of Saudi Arabia. The Qur'an the holy book of the Muslims-said the people of Ubar were destroyed because they became corrupted by power and wealth. The city was said to have been swallowed up by the ground. With the help of space shuttle radar, ruins matching the story of Ubar were found-an incense-trading city that had collapsed into a giant sinkhole. While no one can say for sure if the ruins actually were Ubar (no inscription with the actual name of Ubar was found), there is a good chance the site represents at least some parts of the Ubar stories.

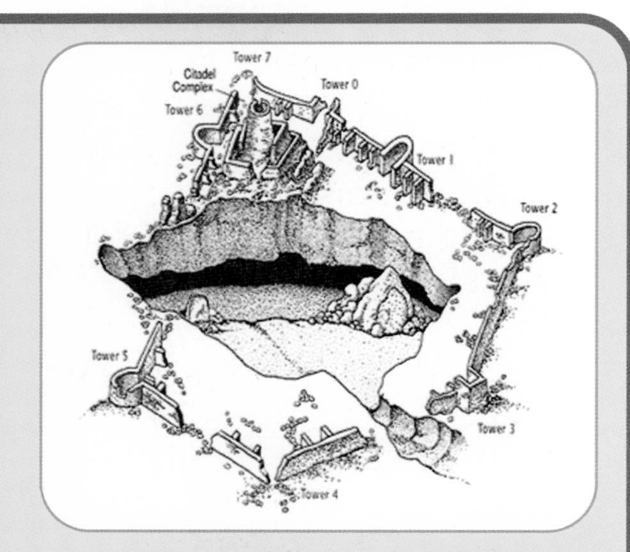

http://www.skeptic.com/atlantis/atlantis3.html

The People of 'Aad Worship Idols

Despite all of the blessings that Allah سبحانه وتعالى had granted them, the people of 'Aad did not believe in one Allah. Instead, they worshipped idols, which they carved out of stones. When anything good happened to them, they thanked their idols. Whenever they were in trouble, they prayed to those idols for help. Those people had forgotten all about Prophet Nuh and his message of worshipping one Allah, or tawheed. They forgot the awful punishment of Allah for worshipping false gods.

Allah Chooses Hud to Be a Prophet

Among the people of 'Aad lived a man named **Hud**. Allah سبحانه وتعالى chose him as His next prophet. He was from the tribe of 'Aad itself, and he was respected because of his noble family and his good manners. He was the great-grandson of Prophet Nuh عليه السلام. Hud was a very patient and kind man. When he received the command of Allah to teach His message, he immediately did so. He came to the people and said:

"O Brothers, why do you worship stones that you have carved yourself? The idols can not give you anything or take anything away from you. Allah has sent me to you."

Prophet Hud عليه السلام also said to his people:

"Allah has taught you all that you are able to do. He has also given you children and many animals. Therefore you should stop worshipping your false gods. Worship only Allah and obey His commands. Do well and do not commit sin and evil. Your Lord is only one, and He alone should be worshipped. He has created you, given you health and wealth, and made you a powerful nation."

Prophet Hud explained to them that the idols would only take them further away from Allah.

The Holy Qur'an says in Surat Hud:

وَإِلَىٰ عَادٍ أَخَاهُمۡ هُودٗاۚ قَالَ يَٰقَوۡمِ
ٱعۡبُدُواْ ٱللَّهَ مَا لَكُم مِّنۡ إِلَٰهٍ غَيۡرُهُۥٓۖ إِنۡ
أَنتُمۡ إِلَّا مُفۡتَرُونَ ﴿٥٠﴾
يَٰقَوۡمِ لَآ أَسۡـَٔلُكُمۡ عَلَيۡهِ أَجۡرًاۖ إِنۡ أَجۡرِيَ إِلَّا
عَلَى ٱلَّذِي فَطَرَنِيٓۚ أَفَلَا تَعۡقِلُونَ ﴿٥١﴾

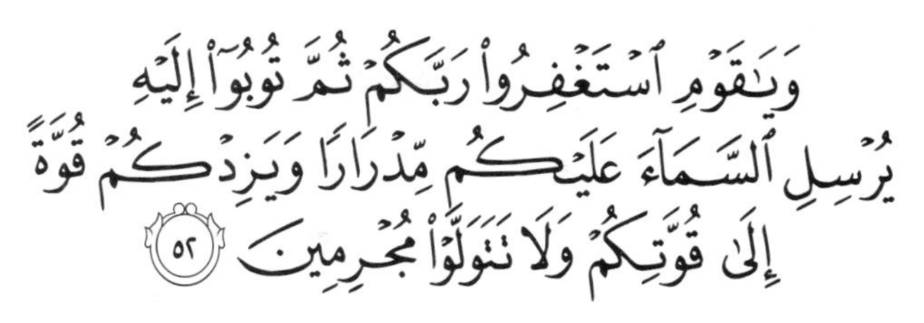

"And to the people of 'Aad, We sent their brother Hud. He said, "O my people! Worship Allah! You have no other Ilah (god) but Him, certainly, you do nothing but invent (lies)!" [11:50]

"O my people I ask of you no reward for this [Message]. My reward is only from Him Who created me (Allah). Won't you then understand?" [11:51]

"And O my people! Ask forgiveness of your Lord and then repent to Him. He will send you (from the sky) abundant rain, and add strength to your strength, so do not turn away as sinners." [11:52]

The People of 'Aad Reject Prophet Hud

Prophet Hud عليه السلام tried to explain to his people how everything they had was a blessing from Allah. In addition, Allah had made them Prophet Nuh's successors, and He had given them strength and power. The people of 'Aad rejected Prophet Hud's message and continued ridiculing him.

They said:
"We are not going to listen to you. We are not going to let our gods down, just because you tell us so. Who are you, anyway? You are nothing but a liar. If you are not a liar, then prove it."

Allah repeated their words in the Qur'an:

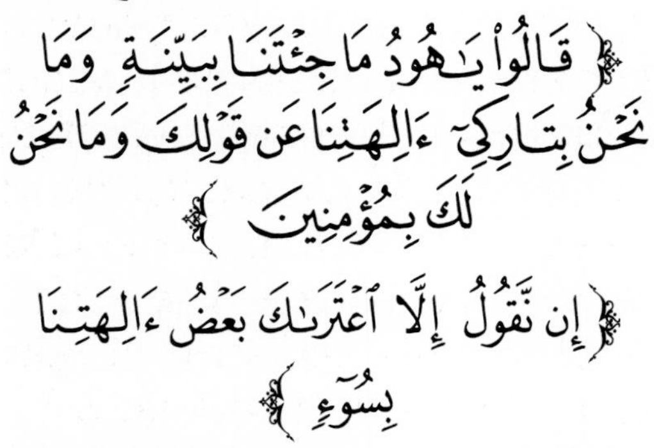

"0 Hud! No evidence have you brought us, and we shall not leave our gods at your command! And we don't believe in you.
All that we say is that some of our gods have touched you with madness." [Surat Hud11: 53-54]

Prophet Hud was very sad and disappointed when he heard this. He said to them, "Do you think the houses you have built will last forever? Remember that it is Allah Who has given you your fortunes."
Allah recounts in the Qur'an:

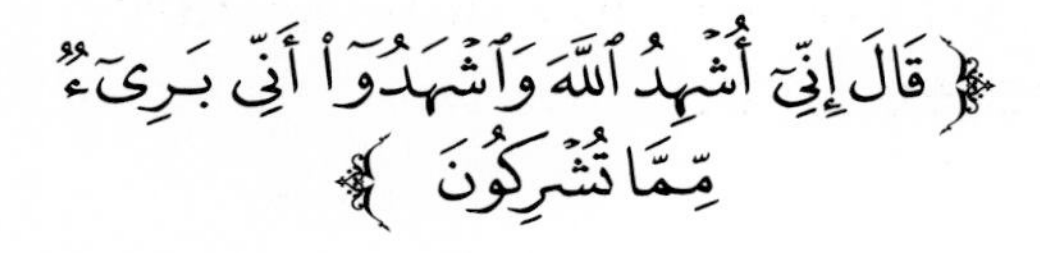

The city of Iram, which is now known as Ubar, was buried under the sands of the Empty Quarters for thousands of years. Scientists discovered the buried city in 1996.

He (Prophet Hud) said: "I call Allah to witness and bear you witness that I am innocent of your sin. You worship others with Him (Allah)."

﴿ مِن دُونِهِۦ فَكِيدُونِى جَمِيعًا ثُمَّ لَا تُنظِرُونِ ﴾

﴿ إِنِّى تَوَكَّلْتُ عَلَى ٱللَّهِ رَبِّى وَرَبِّكُم ۚ مَّا مِن دَآبَّةٍ إِلَّا هُوَ ءَاخِذٌۢ بِنَاصِيَتِهَآ ۚ إِنَّ رَبِّى عَلَىٰ صِرَٰطٍ مُّسْتَقِيمٍ ﴾

"So plot against me, all of you, and give me no breaks; I put my trust in Allah. He is my Lord and your Lord!" [11:55]

Despite Prophet Hud's warnings, the people of 'Aad went on worshipping their false gods. He was very disappointed. When he warned the people of 'Aad about the punishment of Allah, they challenged Prophet Hud. They didn't care. They told Hud to ask Allah to send them His punishment

The Qur'an quotes them as saying:

﴿ قَالُوٓا۟ أَجِئْتَنَا لِنَعْبُدَ ٱللَّهَ وَحْدَهُۥ وَنَذَرَ مَا كَانَ يَعْبُدُ ءَابَآؤُنَا فَأْتِنَا بِمَا تَعِدُنَآ إِن كُنتَ مِنَ ٱلصَّـٰدِقِينَ ﴾

"Then bring down [the punishment] on us that you have threatened, if you are truthful." [7:70]

Allah Punishes the Unbelievers

Shortly afterwards, a huge black cloud appeared in the sky above the people of 'Aad. When the unbelievers of 'Aad saw it, they said: "This cloud is surely going to bring us some refreshing rain."

But they were very much mistaken. Allah سبحانه وتعالى says in the Qur'an:

﴿ فَلَمَّا رَأَوْهُ عَارِضًا مُّسْتَقْبِلَ أَوْدِيَتِهِمْ قَالُوا۟ هَـٰذَا عَارِضٌ مُّمْطِرُنَا بَلْ هُوَ مَا ٱسْتَعْجَلْتُم بِهِۦ رِيحٌ فِيهَا عَذَابٌ أَلِيمٌ ﴾ ﴿ تُدَمِّرُ كُلَّ شَىْءٍۭ بِأَمْرِ رَبِّهَا فَأَصْبَحُوا۟ لَا يُرَىٰٓ إِلَّا مَسَـٰكِنُهُمْ كَذَٰلِكَ نَجْزِى ٱلْقَوْمَ ٱلْمُجْرِمِينَ ﴾

"Then when they saw it as a dense cloud coming towards their valleys, they said: 'This is a cloud bringing us rain!' Nay but it is that punishment which you were asking for! A wind wherein is a painful punishment! Destroying everything by the command of its Lord!" [46:24-25]

The clouds grew larger and larger as the wind howled louder and louder. At the first sign of the storm, Prophet Hud had gathered his followers and family and taken them to a safe place. The wind was full of dust and sand. It blew violently for eight continuous days. The people ran into their big houses and beautiful castles to hide. But nothing could save them from the punishment of Allah.

The wind swept everything away. The violent storm did not stop until the entire region was reduced to ruin. The unbelievers were destroyed and swallowed by the sands of the desert. Nothing was left except a few large stones, which were the remains of the houses and towers. Only Prophet Hud عليه السلام and his followers remained unharmed because they believed in Allah سبحانه وتعالى and obeyed Him.

Holy Qur’an

سورة القمر

Surat-ul-Qamar 18-22

﴿ كَذَّبَتْ عَادٌ فَكَيْفَ كَانَ عَذَابِي وَنُذُرِ ﴿١٨﴾ إِنَّا أَرْسَلْنَا عَلَيْهِمْ رِيحًا صَرْصَرًا فِي يَوْمِ نَحْسٍ مُّسْتَمِرٍّ ﴿١٩﴾ تَنزِعُ النَّاسَ كَأَنَّهُمْ أَعْجَازُ نَخْلٍ مُّنقَعِرٍ ﴿٢٠﴾ فَكَيْفَ كَانَ عَذَابِي وَنُذُرِ ﴿٢١﴾ وَلَقَدْ يَسَّرْنَا الْقُرْآنَ لِلذِّكْرِ فَهَلْ مِن مُّدَّكِرٍ ﴿٢٢﴾ ﴾

TRANSLITERATION

18. Kaththabat 'Aadun fakayfa kana 'athabee wanuthur
19. Inna arsalna 'alayhim reehan sarsaran fee yawmi nah-sim-mustamirr
20. Tanzi'u-nnasa ka'annahum a 'jazu nakhlim-munqa'ir
21. Fakayfa kana 'athabee wanuthur
22. Walaqad yassarnal-qur'ana liththikri fahal mim-mud-dakir

UNDERSTOOD MEANING

[54:18] 'Aad disbelieved, so how (great) was My punish-ment and My warning!
[54:19] Surely We sent on them a tornado in a day of continuous curse
[54:20] Tearing men away as if they were the trunks of hollow and torn up palm-trees.
[54:21] How (great) then was My punishment and My warning!
[54:22] And certainly We have made the Qur’an easy for remembrance, but is there anyone who will reflect?

People in Oman say this is the Tomb of Prophet Hud. It is located near the city of Salalah.

A Masjid in Oman

Musqat, the capital of Oman

The Country of Oman

Oman is a Muslim and Arab country in Asia. It is located in the southeastern corner of the Arabian Peninsula. Oman has a long Islamic history. During the eighth year after Hijrah, around 630 AD, Prophet Muhammad sent one of his Sahabah, Amr ibn Al-As, to invite Omanis to Islam. Omanis responded quickly and embraced the new faith. Some historians believe that the 'Aad, the people of Prophet Hud, used to live in Ubar in present Oman. Historians believe that Ubar is the same city of Iram which is mentioned in the Qur'an.

Country Facts

Capital: Muscat

Main Cities: Salalah, Nazwa, Suhar, Soor
Area: 212,500 sq km
Population: 3 million
People: Arab, Asian, African, Baluchi
Language: Arabic, English, Persian
Religion: Muslim
Currency: Omani Riyal

My Beautiful Muslim World

▲ *A beautiful village in Oman*

▲ *An oasis in Oman*

▲ *Inside a palace in Oman*

▲ *An area near Iram (or Ubar)*

Chapter Review

Do some online research about the city of Ubar. Write a journal entry on what you learned about the city of Ubar, and make a collage of pictures about it.

The people of 'Aad were big and tall. They were very strong. Why do you think Allah punished them by sending tornados to blow them around like hollow tree trunks?

1. What were the people of 'Aad famous for?
2. The people of 'Aad lived in what present-day country?
3. Why was Prophet Hud generally respected among his people?
4. What were the first few sentences Prophet Hud said to his people after he was chosen by Allah سبحانه وتعالى as his prophet?
5. According to the Holy Qur'an, what did Prophet Hud's people say when they heard his message? Why do you think they said that?
6. What was the punishment on the people of 'Aad?
7. Who was saved from the punishment?

Prophet Salih
عليه السلام

CHAPTER SIX

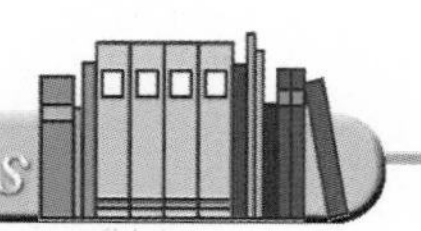

Pre-reading Questions

1. Who were the people of Thamood?
2. Who was Prophet Salih?
3. How did Thamood disobey Allah?
4. What was the miracle sent to Thamood?
5. What happened to the disbelievers?

Word Watch

Salih	صالِح
Thamood	ثَمود
Mada'in Salih	مَدائِن صالح
naqah	ناقة

The People of Thamood

Many years had passed since the punishment that befell the people of 'Aad. New generations came to succeed them. Among these were the people of **Thamood**. The people of Thamood ثمود were Arab tribes. They lived in a place now called مدائن صالح **Mada'in Salih**, in the northwestern part of

An ancient house in Mada'in Salih

Satellite picture of Arabia; Mada'in Salih is in the far Northwest of Saudi Arabia

Ancient houses in Mada'in Salih

present day Saudi Arabia. Mada'in Salih is an Arabic name that means "Towns of Salih."

Prophet Salih

The people of Thamood had beautiful gardens. They were blessed with beautiful springs, date palms, and trees which had plenty of fruit. They lived in huge houses that they carved out of massive red rocks in the mountains. Allah made them very skillful at carving. The people of Thamood were arrogant, and they oppressed the poor who lived among them.

The people of Thamood moved away from tawheed and started to worship idols. Therefore, Allah سبحانه وتعالى decided to send them a prophet from amongst themselves to guide them back to the right path. This prophet was صالح عليه السلام **Salih**. He was a well respected citizen of the people of Thamood. He came from a good family and was well known for his good character.

Thamood Rejects Allah's Message

"Worship only Allah," Prophet Salih عليه السلام told his people. "You have no other god but Allah, so you should do good. I am giving you good advice: You should believe what I say, for Allah has made me His Prophet." Allah سبحانه وتعالى reccounts in the Qur'an,

Prophet Salih told his people,
"Oh my people! Worship Allah, you have no other god but Him." [Surat Al-'A'raf 7:73]

▲ *Ancient houses in Mada'in Salih*

The people of Thamood did not listen to him. They said:

"O Salih! We wished you to be our chief, until you told us to leave our gods and worship your God Alone! We really doubt what you invite us to."

The rich and powerful of the tribe did not listen to Prophet Salih's message. However, many of the wise, poor and humble people followed him. The rich and powerful accused Prophet Salih of being a liar. They said:

"You are nothing but a man, just like any of us. If you are speaking the truth, then show us a proof that you are a prophet." [Surat Ash-Shu'ara' 26:154]

Healthy Habit

Always take the orders of Allah seriously whenever you learn about them; do whatever Allah ﷻ orders you to do promptly.

The Miracle of the Camel

Prophet Salih prayed to Allah سبحانه وتعالى to answer their request. Soon afterwards, a mountain moved and split. From it came a giant ناقة **naqah**, or she-camel, which was pregnant. This camel soon gave birth. Allah سبحانه وتعالى provided the Thamood people this miracle to prove that Salih was a Prophet. This was also a test from Allah سبحانه وتعالى for them, to see if they would obey His orders. Now they didn't have any excuses for not believing in Prophet Salih. The proof they asked for had been brought to them. Prophet Salih عليه السلام told them:

"O my people! This she-camel of Allah is a sign to you. Leave her to feed on Allah's Earth, and do not harm her, or a swift punishment will fall on you!" [11:64]

The she-camel and her young lived among Thamood. Allah ordered Prophet Salih to tell his people of the camel's rights. She would drink from the water of the well for one day, and leave it to them the second day:

"She has a right to drink (water), and you have a right to drink water, each on a day appointed." [Surat Ash-Shu'ara' 26:155]

"And tell them that the water is to be shared between her and them. Each one has the right to drink by turns." [54:28]

On the day the she-camel was to drink from the well, she would have enough milk for all the people of Thamood. They would milk her and fill all their containers. She was so big that when she would graze in the valley the sheep would flee and leave the way for her. The cattle would not come near the well on the day she would drink from it.

The people of Thamood were very amazed by this camel. Therefore, some of them believed in and followed Prophet Salih عليه السلام. It was clear that she was not a normal camel. She was a miracle from Allah سبحانه وتعالى and a blessed animal.

The disbelievers, however, were bothered by her a lot. This miracle proved that they were wrong and Salih was a true prophet. They began to accuse the camel of being a danger to their cattle and sheep. These unbelievers began to feel angry and started to feel hatred towards the she-camel and her young one. They could not bear to see them anymore.

Healthy Habit

Always listen to elders and teachers who teach you good things and give you wise advice.

Thamood Kill the Camel and Allah Punishes the Disbelievers

One day, the people of Thamood plotted to kill the camel. That way they could use the well every day. Nine men were appointed to kill the she-camel and her infant. While everyone was asleep, these men went out secretly to do the evil job.

The camel stood up as soon as she saw them, but they hit her on the neck, and she fell to the ground. First they slaughtered her. Then they slaughtered her calf. The next day, nobody saw the she-camel or her baby. The people searched and found them both dead. When Prophet Salih heard this, he become very angry.

Prophet Salih warned them saying:

> "Enjoy yourselves in your homes [no more than] three days. This is a promise that will not be belied!" [11:65]

This was a warning for them to repent to Allah ﷻ . Instead, the same nine men decided to kill Prophet Salih as well. They said, "Swear to one another that we shall make a secret night attack on him and his family. Afterwards, we will surely say to his near relatives that we do not know who attacked Salih." Allah ﷻ recounts in the Qur'an:

They said:

"We did not witness the destruction of his family, and we are telling the truth!" [27:48-49]

But Allah سبحانه وتعالى did not allow them to carry out their plot. As they were going to kill Prophet Salih, Allah showered rocks on them. The nine men were the first to die.

A second day passed after Prophet Salih's warning. Prophet Salih again warned the rest of his people of Allah's punishment that would befall them. The people of Thamood ignored him, and continued to worship their idols. Allah سبحانه وتعالى instructed Prophet Salih to leave the area with his family and followers.

On the third day, as the sun rose, a terrible earthquake shook the land. The earthquake destroyed everything. All the people were destroyed. The area was left barren as if nobody had lived there before! Prophet Salih عليه السلام and his followers were saved from this punishment. He turned away from the dead disbelievers saying:

"O my people! I have indeed delivered to you the message of my Lord, and have given you good advice but you do not like good advisers!" [7:79]

Holy Qur'an

سورة القمر

Surat-ul-Qamar 23-32

﴿ كَذَّبَتْ ثَمُودُ بِٱلنُّذُرِ ﴿٢٣﴾ فَقَالُوٓا۟ أَبَشَرًا مِّنَّا وَٰحِدًا نَّتَّبِعُهُۥٓ إِنَّآ إِذًا لَّفِى ضَلَٰلٍ وَسُعُرٍ ﴿٢٤﴾ أَءُلْقِىَ ٱلذِّكْرُ عَلَيْهِ مِنۢ بَيْنِنَا بَلْ هُوَ كَذَّابٌ أَشِرٌ ﴿٢٥﴾ سَيَعْلَمُونَ غَدًا مَّنِ ٱلْكَذَّابُ ٱلْأَشِرُ ﴿٢٦﴾ إِنَّا مُرْسِلُوا۟ ٱلنَّاقَةِ فِتْنَةً لَّهُمْ فَٱرْتَقِبْهُمْ وَٱصْطَبِرْ ﴿٢٧﴾ وَنَبِّئْهُمْ أَنَّ ٱلْمَآءَ قِسْمَةٌۢ بَيْنَهُمْ كُلُّ شِرْبٍ مُّحْتَضَرٌ ﴿٢٨﴾ فَنَادَوْا۟ صَاحِبَهُمْ فَتَعَاطَىٰ فَعَقَرَ ﴿٢٩﴾ فَكَيْفَ كَانَ عَذَابِى وَنُذُرِ ﴿٣٠﴾ إِنَّآ أَرْسَلْنَا عَلَيْهِمْ صَيْحَةً وَٰحِدَةً فَكَانُوا۟ كَهَشِيمِ ٱلْمُحْتَظِرِ ﴿٣١﴾ وَلَقَدْ يَسَّرْنَا ٱلْقُرْءَانَ لِلذِّكْرِ فَهَلْ مِن مُّدَّكِرٍ ﴿٣٢﴾ ﴾

TRANSLITERATION

23. Kaththabat thamoodu binnuthur
24. Faqaloo abasharam-minna wahidan-nattabi'uhu inna ithal-lafee dalaliw-wasu'ur
25. A'olqiyath-thikru 'alayhi mim-baynina bal huwa kaththabun ashir
26. Saya'lamoona ghadam-man-il-kaththab-ul-ashir
27. Inna mursilo-nnaqati fitnatal-lahum fartaqibhum wastabir
28. Wanabbi'hum annalma'a qismatum-baynahum kullu shir-bim-muhtadar
29. Fanadaw sahibahum fata'ata fa'aqar
30. Fakayfa kana 'athabee wanuthur
31. Inna arsalna 'alayhim sayhataw-wahidatan fakanoo kahasheem-ilmuhtathir
32. Walaqad yassarnal-qur'ana liththikri fahal mim-muddakir

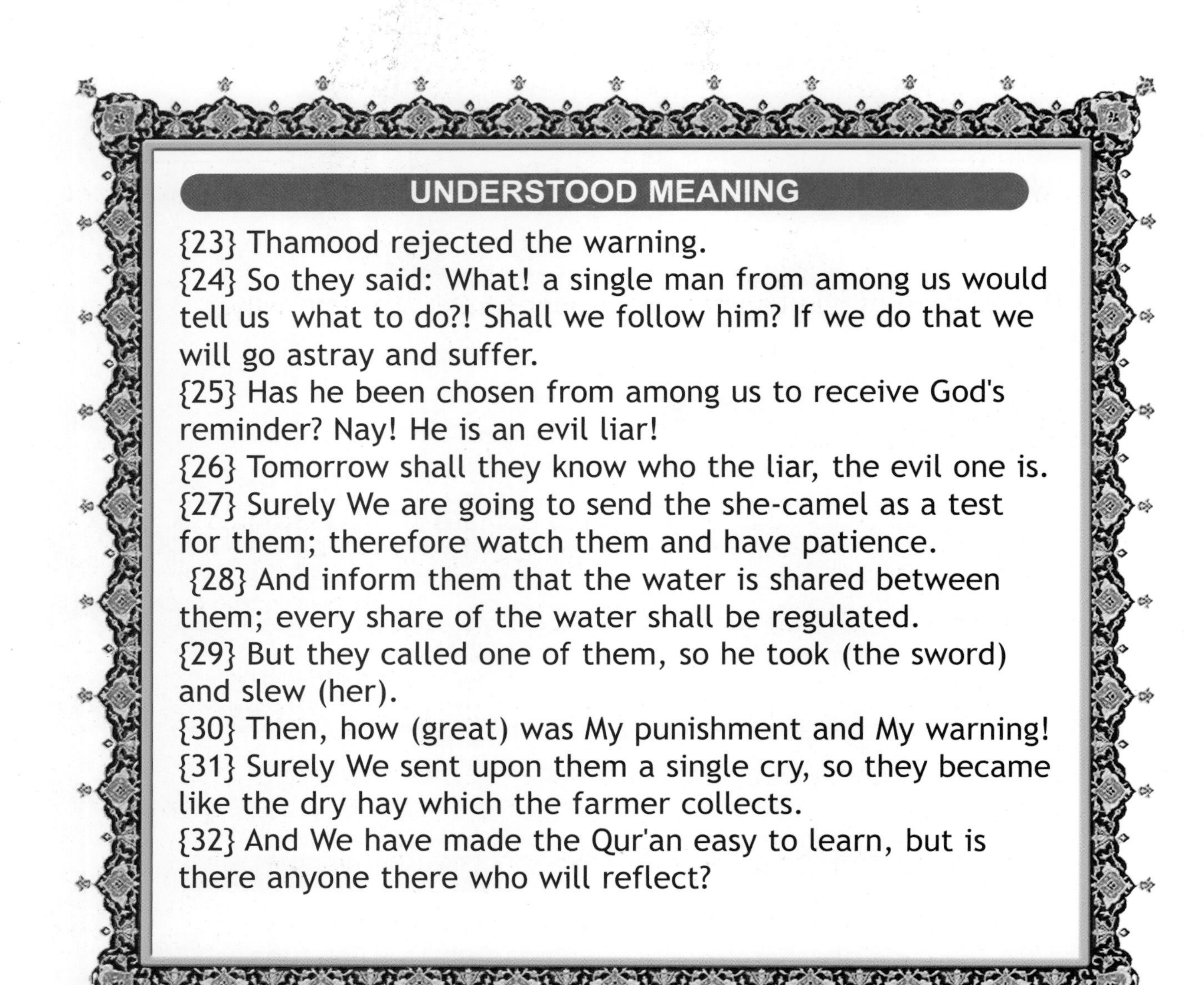

UNDERSTOOD MEANING

{23} Thamood rejected the warning.
{24} So they said: What! a single man from among us would tell us what to do?! Shall we follow him? If we do that we will go astray and suffer.
{25} Has he been chosen from among us to receive God's reminder? Nay! He is an evil liar!
{26} Tomorrow shall they know who the liar, the evil one is.
{27} Surely We are going to send the she-camel as a test for them; therefore watch them and have patience.
{28} And inform them that the water is shared between them; every share of the water shall be regulated.
{29} But they called one of them, so he took (the sword) and slew (her).
{30} Then, how (great) was My punishment and My warning!
{31} Surely We sent upon them a single cry, so they became like the dry hay which the farmer collects.
{32} And We have made the Qur'an easy to learn, but is there anyone there who will reflect?

Activity Time

Write a journal entry on a make-believe trip to Mada'in Salih in Saudi Arabia. Describe the place and your feelings about what the people of Thamood did to Prophet Salih and to themselves. You may browse the Internet for many pictures, movies, and information about Mada'in Salih.

Chapter Review

1. Why do you think the people of Prophet Salih were so rude and arrogant with him?

2. Did the miracle of the camel help Prophet Salih? Explain why.

1. The people of Thamood came after which people?
2. What were the people of Thamood famous for?
3. What did the people of Thamood worship?
4. Allah سبحانه وتعالى chose Salih as the prophet for the people of Thamood. According to the Qur'an, what was the first sentence Prophet Salih said to his people?
5. What did the people of Thamood request of Prophet Salih as proof of his prophecy?
6. What was the agreement, according to the Qur'an, regarding the female camel and her calf?
7. What did some of the disbelievers accuse the she-camel and her baby of? What did they do about it?
8. How many days did Prophet Salih give his people to repent to Allah سبحانه وتعالى ?
9. How did Allah سبحانه وتعالى protect Prophet Salih from the unbelievers?
10. What was the punishment for the disbelievers among the people of Thamood?

Madinah, general view.

Time Line

570 CE		595 CE	610 CE	610-622 CE	1
Prophet's Birth	Prophet's childhood	Marriage to Khadijah	Prophethood	The difficult times in Makkah	Hijr

MUSLIMS UNDER SIEGE

622 CE	2 A.H. 623 CE	3 A.H. 624 CE	5 A.H. 626 CE
Building Al-Masjid An-Nabawi and establishing brotherhood	The Battle of Badr	The Battle of Uhud	**The Battle of Al-Khandaq**

Searching for the Truth: The Journey of Salman Al-Farisi

Pre-reading Questions

1. Who was Salman Al-Farisi?
2. Do you know any stories about him?
3. Can you quote a hadeeth about this great man?

Word Watch

Salman the Persian سلمان الفارسي
Esfahan أصفهان

Salman Al-Farisi

Salman Al-Farisi was a great young man from Persia during the time of Prophet Muhammad. Persia is the old name for Iran. He was born in the city of **Esfahan.** Salman was not happy with what his people used to do because they were fire worshippers. Many of the Persian people were Magian, or Majoos, and they thought the fire was Allah ﷻ . Let us listen to the story of Salman Al-Farisi, or Salman the Persian, as he tells it.

I was a Persian boy from a tribe called Jian. My father was a leader of the village and

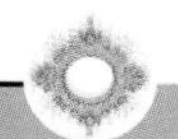

A Mosque in Esfahan, Iran

one of the richest people there. He loved me so much and always took care of me. My family used to worship fire. They raised me to serve the temple in the village, and I became the guardian of the fire that we worshipped. I was in charge of kindling it so that it would not die out.

The Curious Young Man

"One day I saw a church and heard Christians praying there. This aroused my curiosity. I knew nothing about Christianity. So I entered the church to see what the people did. Their prayer attracted me, and I thought about following their religion. I felt it was better than my Magian religion. I stayed there until sunset, and I asked the people in the church where their religion came from. They told me that it began in ancient Syria."

"When I returned home that night, my father asked me, 'Where were you all day?' I told him the whole story. My father became very worried when I told him that Christianity was better than our religion. He locked me up and shackled my legs to stop me from going to the church."

Looking for the True Faith

"I sent a message to some Christians asking them to help me. I managed to get rid of my shackles and escaped to Syria. When I arrived there, I asked about the most knowledgeable man in Christianity. The people there guided me to a monk. I told him that I wanted to become Christian, serve him, and worship with him. He agreed."

"Shortly afterwards, I discovered that he was a bad man. He received gold and silver as charity. Instead of giving it to the poor, he kept it for himself in seven sacks. This made me hate him very much. When he died, I told the people about his evil actions and showed them where he kept their gold and silver. They became very angry with him. They crucified his corpse and threw stones at it."

"The people selected a new and better monk. I loved him very much and spent a long time with him. He was a true and sincere worshipper of God. When he was about to die, I asked him whom I should follow after his death. He advised me to go to a man in Mosul, in northern Iraq. I went to Mosul and stayed with that monk until he died."

"Before the monk's death I asked him whom I should follow after him. He advised me to go to a man in Nasibeen. So I traveled to Nasibeen and stayed with the monk there until he died. On his death bed I asked him about whom I should follow after his death. He advised me to go to a man in Ammouriyyah, in present-day Turkey. I went there and met him. During my stay there I worked and owned a sheep and a number of cows."

The Promised Prophet

"The monk of Ammouriyyah was old and ill. When he was about to die, I asked him whom I should follow after him. He told me that there were no longer any followers of true Christianity. He sadly said, 'I don't know of a living person who follows the true religion of Jesus, the son of Mary, peace be upon him. However, to the best of my knowledge, in this era, a Messenger of God will appear in Arabia. He will come to a place of palm trees between two rocky lands. He will teach God's message to all peoples. After I die, stay here at my hut, and look for the traveling caravans from Arabia. Ask Arab merchants whether a prophet has appeared among them lately. If they answer "yes," then this is the one. Jesus, peace be upon

him, said he would come after him."

"There are signs that will tell you he is a prophet. Among his signs, you will see the Seal of Prophethood on his back, between his shoulders. He accepts and eats from gifts, and he does not eat from charity.'

Salman continued: "After the man died, I stayed in his hut and whenever a caravan passed by, I asked, 'What land do you come from?' Finally, one day, a caravan from Makkah came by, and when they told me that they were from the Hijaz, I asked, 'Has there appeared among you someone who says he is a prophet?"

"They replied, 'Yes, indeed!' I asked them to take me with them to the Arab land in return for the sheep and cows I had."

"When the caravan reached Makkah, the men betrayed me and sold me to a Jewish man there. The Jew then sold me to his cousin, who took me to his hometown, Yathrib. I saw there the palm trees and remembered the prophecy which the monk of Ammouriayah told me. Meanwhile, the Prophet ﷺ began his call in Makkah, but I knew nothing about him because I was a slave and very busy doing many things for my master."

Meeting Prophet Muhammad

"After the Prophet ﷺ migrated to Medinah, I wanted to see if he was a true prophet. So I went to him with some dates and offered it to him as sadaqah, or charity. He gave the dates to some of his companions, but he did not eat any. I became sure of the first sign of his prophecy. I again brought him some dates and offered them to him as a present. He ate from them and gave some to his companions. I became sure of the second sign of prophecy."

"One day I went to the Messenger in Al-Baqee', the graveyard of Madinah. I wanted to see if he had the Seal of Prophethood on his back. After he had buried a dead man, I offered him greetings. I then turned to his back, trying to see the Seal of Prophethood. He understood what I wanted and let me see it. When I saw the seal, I started kissing him and crying. The Messenger ﷺ asked me, 'What is the matter with you?' I told him the whole story. He was amazed by it and told me to retell it again to his companions."

Becoming a Muslim

Salman continued, "From that day on, I accepted Islam and stayed in Prophet Muhammad's company until the end."
Rasulullah helped Salman to regain his freedom and he became one of the great sahabah.
Rasulullah ﷺ was the kindest of all people in the whole world. He always took care of his companions and the people around him. Once he noticed that Salman felt like a stranger, being a Persian among Arabs in Madinah. So he declared to all people in Madinah:

سَلْمَان مِنْ آلِ البَيْتِ

Salman is part of my family

The Prophet indeed used to love and respect Salman because he was a true believer and great searcher for the truth. It was reported that the Prophet ﷺ one day put his hands on Salman and said, "If faith were high up in the stars, some men like that (pointing to Salman) would have attained it."

Story Time

When Salman Al-Farisi embraced Islam, the Prophet ﷺ established brotherhood between Salman and Abud-Dardaa', one of the kindest Sahabah. Salman went to stay with Abud-Dardaa' and found Ummud-Dardaa', his wife, dressed in shabby clothes. He asked her why she was dressed so poorly. She said, "Abud-Dardaa' is not interested in this dunya."

Then Abud-Dardaa' came and prepared a meal for Salman, but he didn't eat with him. Salman asked Abud-Dardaa' to join him, but Abu Ad-Dardaa' said, "I am fasting." (That was an optional fast). Salman then said, "I am not eating until you eat." So, Abud-Dardaa' ate. When it was midnight, Abud-Dardaa' got up to pray Qiyam-ul-Layl. Salman told him to sleep, and Abud-Darda' slept. When it was the last hour of the night, Salman told him to get up, and they both prayed together.

Salman told Abud-Dardaa', "Your Lord has a right on you, your body has a right on you, and your wife and family have rights on you; so you should repect the rights of all those who have a right on you." This means that the Muslim should not neglect the needs of his body and family.

Abud-Dardaa' came to the Prophet and told him the whole story. The Prophet ﷺ said, "Salman has spoken the truth."

(This story is reported in Saheeh-ul-Bukhari.)

Chapter Review

Draw a map of Iran and point out the cities of Tehran and Esfahan.

1. Islam is against racism. How can you prove that by using the story of Salman Al-Farisi?

2. Do you think Salman would have become a great Muslim if he had not been serious in his search for the truth? Explain your answer.

1. Where was Salman Al-Farisi from?
2. What was the thing Salman was searching for when he was young?
3. Why do think he was looking for that thing?
4. What religion did Salman follow before Islam?
5. What were the signs of prophethood he learned from the monk of Ammouriyyah?
6. Quote one Hadeeth about Salman.

All Arabia Attacked Madinah

CHAPTER
TWO

Pre-reading Questions

1. What is a trench?
2. Where did the Battle of the Trench happen?
3. Why were there many tribes in Arabia against the Muslims?

Word Watch

Ghazwat-ul-Khandaq	غزوة الخندق
Bani An-Nadeer	بني النضير
Huyayy Ibn Akhtab	حيي ابن الأخطب
Bani Qurayzah	بني قريظة
Madinah	المدينة

Introduction

In this chapter and the following one, you will learn about a very important part of the Seerah, or life story of Prophet Muhammad ﷺ. It is the story of غزوة الخندق **Ghazwat-ul-Khandaq**, or the Battle of the Trench, which happened during the month of Shawwal of the fifth year after Hijrah.

Evil Intentions

In a village north of **Madinah** there lived some tribes. When the Prophet ﷺ first came to the area he signed a goodwill agreement with them. Unfortunately, **Bani An-Nadeer**, one of these tribes, broke the agreement and tried to kill Prophet Muhammad ﷺ. They went against the advice of some of their wise elders, including Abdullah Ibn Salam, who believed in the Prophet and became a Muslim. Prophet Muhammad ﷺ ordered the tribe of Bani An-Nadeer to leave Madinah. Many of them left to a place called Khaybar. Others went farther north to Syria.

Some of the leaders of Bani An-Nadeer wanted to take revenge against the Muslims. They began to plan ways of raiding the Muslims in Madinah. **Huyayy ibn Akhtab**, the leader of Bani An-Nadeer, decided that the only way to defeat the Muslims was to do three things:

1. Have all the tribes in that part of Arabia unite to raid and destroy the Muslims in Madinah.
2. Have **Bani Quraythah**, another tribe in Madinah, break their treaty with the Muslims and turn against them.
3. Have Al-Munafiqeen, or the hypocrites, also turn against the Muslims in Madinah. These people had pretended to become Muslims but in reality they remained disbelievers.

Huyayy and twenty of his tribesmen went to Makkah to meet with the Quraysh and convince them to destroy the Muslims in Madinah once and for all. They promised the Quraysh that there would be many other tribes joining in the fight, including the Bani Quraythah بني قريظة . Bani Quraythah was a large tribe in Madinah. Huyayy also visited other tribes, including the tribe of Ghatafan, a huge tribe east of Madinah.

Quraysh Decide to Attack Madinah

The leaders of the Quraysh, Ghatafan, and other tribes decided to join in the plan. Many tribes of Arabia became involved in the fighting plan against the Muslims. They supplied men, weapons, and transportation for the fight. By the time the army was ready to march to Madinah, there were over ten thousand troops ready for battle.

When the Muslims in Madinah heard about the huge army marching towards them they began to panic. They had never fought an army that huge! The Prophet ﷺ quickly called a meeting to discuss what they should do.

Muslims Prepare to Defend Themselves

Madinah had natural protection around part of it because of many palm trees and areas of rocky land. Another part was protected by a wall made of the backs of houses built closely together. Only one large part still needed protection.

As you learned earlier, Salman Al-Farisi رضي الله عنه came from Persia, a land where they were very skilled in warfare. He came to the Prophet ﷺ with a very smart plan. He suggested that the Muslims should dig a khandaq, or a trench, on one side of the city.

Digging the Trench

Prophet Muhammad ﷺ agreed to Salman's brilliant plan and the Muslims began to work on the trench. Muslims were divided into different crews with different jobs. Everyone had a job to do. Even the Prophet ﷺ was working. He chose the hardest work of digging the trench.

Healthy Habit

Always work hard for your team and the Muslim community. Do that for the sake of Allah سبحانه وتعالى alone!

To keep their spirits up while working, the Prophet ﷺ lifted his voice and recited nasheeds:

By God, if not for Him,
we'd never have been guided,
nor given charity nor prayed.
So send down peace and make
firm our stand*.

The others fought against us
and when they wanted trouble, we resisted, we resisted.

The other men responded:
We are the ones who have
pledged ourselves to
Muhammad ﷺ, that we will
stay forever faithful in Islam.*

* In Arabic these words rhyme and make a nice sounding poem.

And then the Prophet ﷺ replied:

"O God, there's no real good living but in the next life; so bless the immigrants (Al-Muhajirun) and the supporters (Al-Ansar)."

One day while digging, the Prophet ﷺ struck a rock with his axe and sparks flew all over. The men working with him asked about the sparks. The Prophet ﷺ replied that those sparks meant that one day Islam would rule the lands of the Persians and the Byzantines. Those two empires were the super powers at that time. Salman the Persian was happy with this prophecy: Islam would reach his homeland, Persia. This good news gave the Muslims encouragement to work even harder. After six days of very hard work, the trench was completed.

The Huge Army Approaches Madinah

The huge enemy army reached Uhud hoping that they would meet the Muslims there again as they had two years before. When they did not find the Muslims there, the leaders of the enemy army led their men towards Madinah. Imagine how the Muslims must have felt when they saw the huge army marching towards their city. The Muslims could see thousands of men, horses, and camels, and they could hear the sounds of drums and war songs. The Muslims knew that if they lost the battle most of them would be killed and the rest would be slaves.

As the enemy army approached the city they prepared to attack. Suddenly, they noticed the huge trench surrounding the city. The enemy soldiers became confused at what they saw. They had never seen such a thing before! The trench was too wide for horses to jump and the archers hiding behind the trench could stop any men who tried to cross over.

The Enemies Get Confused

The battle took place during winter so it was very cold and winds blew hard at night. The Muslims were safe and warm inside their houses, while the enemy army only had flimsy tents to protect them. During the day the enemy army would try to come near the trench but they were driven back by the Muslim fighters and archers behind the trench. The plan was working very well for the Muslims.

The leaders of the enemy army realized that a siege would take a very long time. The Bani An-Nadeer leaders who came up with the plan to attack the Muslims started to get worried. They went to the leaders of Quraysh and other Arab tribes begging them to stay and keep up the attack against the Muslims. Huyayy promised the leaders he would get Bani Quraythah to attack the Muslims from inside Madinah. Rumors traveled around that Bani Quraythah, the allies of Muslims, might break their treaty with the Muslims. Also, the city of Madinah began running low on food and supplies. The Muslims started to panic.

DU'AA دعــــــاء

What do you say when you are about to do something hard?

اللهم لا سَهْلَ إلا ما جَعَلْتَهُ سَهلا وأنتَ تَجعَلُ الحَزْنَ إذا شِئْتَ سَهلا

Allahumma La Sahla illa ma ja'altahu Sahla wa anta taj'al-ul-hazna itha she'ta sahla.

Oh Allah, nothing becomes easy unless You make it easy, and You make the difficult thing easy.

WORDS OF WISDOM

Holy Qur'an

سورة الأحزاب

Surat Al-Ahzab 9-11

بِسْمِ اللَّهِ الرَّحْمَٰنِ الرَّحِيمِ

﴿ يَٰٓأَيُّهَا ٱلَّذِينَ ءَامَنُوا۟ ٱذْكُرُوا۟ نِعْمَةَ ٱللَّهِ عَلَيْكُمْ إِذْ جَآءَتْكُمْ جُنُودٌ فَأَرْسَلْنَا عَلَيْهِمْ رِيحًا وَجُنُودًا لَّمْ تَرَوْهَا ۚ وَكَانَ ٱللَّهُ بِمَا تَعْمَلُونَ بَصِيرًا ﴿٩﴾ إِذْ جَآءُوكُم مِّن فَوْقِكُمْ وَمِنْ أَسْفَلَ مِنكُمْ وَإِذْ زَاغَتِ ٱلْأَبْصَٰرُ وَبَلَغَتِ ٱلْقُلُوبُ ٱلْحَنَاجِرَ وَتَظُنُّونَ بِٱللَّهِ ٱلظُّنُونَا۠ ﴿١٠﴾ هُنَالِكَ ٱبْتُلِىَ ٱلْمُؤْمِنُونَ وَزُلْزِلُوا۟ زِلْزَالًا شَدِيدًا ﴿١١﴾ ﴾

TRANSLITERATION

9. Ya ayyuhal-latheena amano-thkuroo ni'matallahi 'alaykum ith ja'atkum junoodun fa'arsalna alayhim reehaw-wajunoodal-lam tarawh a waken-allahu bima ta'maloona baseera
10. Ith ja'ookum min fawqikum wamin asfala minkum wa-ith zaghat-il-absaru wabalaghat-il-quloob-ul-hanajira watathunnoona bill ah-ith-thunoona
11. Hunalik-abtuliyal-mu'minoona wazulziloo zilzalan shadeeda

UNDERSTOOD MEANING

[33:9] O you who believe! Remember the favor of Allah to you when armies came to you. We sent against them a strong wind and soldiers that you couldn't see, and Allah ever is Allah, of what you do, seeing.
[33:10] When they came upon you from above you and from below you, and when the eyes blurred [out of fear], and the hearts rose up to the throats, many of you began to have wrong thoughts of Allah.
[33:11] There the believers were tested and they were shaken severely.

Healthy Habits

1. Be positive, even when you are faced with negative situations.
2. Be creative, just like Salman the Persian!
3. Be patient, because Allah always protects His believers.

Draw the map of Saudi Arabia and show Makkah and Madinah on the map.

1. What was the name of the group who wanted to take revenge on the Muslims?
2. What was Bani An-Nadeer's plan to defeat the Muslims?
3. How did Bani Quraythah convince the Quraysh to join them?
4. What was Salman Al-Farisi's plan for defeating the disbelievers?
5. Why did Bani An-Nadeer want Bani Quraythah to join in the war against the Muslims?

Muslims Under Siege: The Battle of Al-Khandaq

CHAPTER THREE

Pre-reading Questions

1. What does trust mean to you?
2. How do you feel when you have been betrayed by someone?
3. Why is it important not to break a treaty?

Word Watch

Ka'b ibn Asad	كعب ابن أسد
Al-Aws	الأوس
Al-Khazraj	الخزرج
Nu'aym Ibn Mas'ood	نعيم ابن مسعود

The Betrayal of Bani Quraythah

Abu Sufyan, the leader of the Quraysh, sent Huyayy Ibn Akhtab secretly to meet with the chief of Bani Quraythah, **Ka'b ibn Asad.** Huyayy tried to convince Ka'b to attack the Muslims from the back when the time was right. He wanted the chief to break his treaty with Prophet Muhammad ﷺ and betray the Muslims.

Huyayy promised protection of Bani Quraythah from the Muslims. He also described how big his army was. Ka'b ibn Asad finally agreed to Huyayy's proposal. He thought that the Quraysh and the tribes had a bigger chance of destroying the Muslims. So he and the tribe of Bani Quraythah decided to support the Quraysh army.

The two leaders decided that Bani Quraythah would attack the Muslims from behind the city, on

the same day as the enemy would attack the trench.

Muslims Panic

The Prophet ﷺ and his companions quickly heard about the betrayal of Bani Quraythah. They were very shocked. The Muslims were successfully holding the enemy at the front of the city, and they depended on Bani Quraythah to protect the back. Now that Bani Quraythah was blocking Muslims from entering their neighborhood, the Muslims became worried. Leaders of **Al-Aws** and **Al-Khazraj**, the main tribes of Madinah, went to Bani Quraythah. They begged them to honor their treaty with the Muslims, but they refused. Bani Quraythah was warned that they would suffer a harsh punishment if they sided with the enemy. They insisted on their betrayal and began saying bad things about the Prophet ﷺ . They also announced that they no longer had a treaty with the Muslims. The leaders of Al-Aws and Al-Khazraj went and reported to the Prophet ﷺ what Bani Quraythah had declared. The Muslims were scared that the enemy army would be able to enter the city through the walls of Bani Quraythah.

To make things worse, Bani Quraythah cut off all food supplies to the Muslims. After a few days the Muslims began to feel the hunger.

DU'AA' دعـــــاء

When the Muslims were afraid of their enemies during the Battle of the Trench, they used to say this du'aa':

اللّهُمَّ اسْتُـرْ عَوْراتِنا وآمِنْ رَوْعاتِنا

Allahumma ustur awratina wa aamin raw'aatina

Oh, Allah, hide our weaknesses and grant us security!

The Enemy Prepares to Invade Madinah

The leaders of the enemy army were preparing to attack. The enemy soldiers began to dance and sing songs around their camps. They thought victory was not very far off. A small group of horsemen found a spot where the trench was narrow and attacked. Ali Ibn Abi Talib and other great Muslim fighters defeated them all. Every day, the enemies would throw arrows at Muslims across the trench. They hit and injured a few Muslims including Sa'd Ibn Mu'ath, one of the great Muslim leaders.

One day, the Prophet and the Sahabah were very busy attending to the attacks of the enemies. They couldn't even pray Asr prayer at the beginning of the appointed time, as they usually did. They could only pray it after sunset. Rasulullah was very angry that he and the Sahabah had missed the time of Salat Al-Asr.

The leaders of the enemy army planned to attack the city from the front and back. Abu Sufyan would lead the soldiers over the trench and Bani Quraythah would attack from the back of the city. The Muslims in Madinah became very fearful and worried. The hypocrites in the city tried to con-

vince people to run away but the Prophet and his companions remained very strong. They knew that even if they died they would win Paradise in the end!

Dividing the Enemy

During that difficult time, a man named **Nu'aym Ibn Mas'ood** from the tribe of Ghatafan came to the Prophet. He told him that he was becoming a Muslim but no one knew about it. He was a good friend to Bani Quraythah and to the Quraysh and the tribes. Nu'aym offered his help to Rasulullah. The Prophet asked him to help divide Bani Quraythah and the enemies.

He told Bani Quraythah they shouldn't attack the Muslims unless the tribes would promise to protect them even if they lost the war. He told them that the tribes were not serious about breaking into Madinah. The Quraysh, he said, most probably would go back to Makkah and leave them alone. So he told the leaders of the tribe of the Bani Quraythah tribe to ask the Quraysh to give some of their good fighters as a guarantee. Now Bani Quraythah began to hesitate about attacking the Muslims.

The Enemies become Confused

Then Nu'aym Ibn Mas'oud went to the enemy's army at the front of the city. He told Abu Sufyan that the Bani Quraythah had broken the deal and gone back to the Muslim side. "They are going to ask you for some of your men as hostages. Later they will give those men to Muhammad to prove that they are still with him," he said.

Abu Sufyan sent a message to Bani Quraythah to verify Nu'yam's story. He got a very cold response. Bani Quraythah answered, "We cannot fight this time. We also refuse to fight along with you unless you send us some wariors. You might return to your homelands and leave us defenseless." When the Quraysh and the tribes heard this they said, "By Allah ﷻ, Nu'aym was right."

The Quraysh then sent a message to Bani Quraythah telling them that they would not send any hostages, and they ordered them to go out to battle. When Bani Quraythah heard this they said, "Nu'aym spoke the truth."

Like Salman, Nu'aym had a great idea that helped the Muslims against their dangerous enemy. The Muslims had succeeded in dividing their enemies.

Nu'aym رضي الله عنه is my role model; he is my type of guy.

The Quraysh and the Tribes Lose the Battle

Meanwhile the Muslims spent their time praying to Allah ﷻ . The Prophet prayed, "Oh Allah, shelter us and protect us form all dangers." Allah ﷻ answered the prayer by sending down a violent storm and an army of angels against the enemy army. Their tents and equipment were turned upside down. The freezing cold wind crushed their high spirits. Soon, the enemy army began to withdraw. While all this was going on, the Muslims were safe and protected in their city. After a one month siege, the fight finally ended. The Muslims had succeeded in defeating the biggest army they had ever faced. Allah protected the Muslims and their city from harm. Only six Muslims, including Sa'd Ibn Muath, were martyred. On the other side, ten enemy soldiers were killed.

It was Allah's wisdom that very few people were killed in this battle. Allah ﷻ and the Muslims want people to be guided to Islam, not to be killed.

▲ *Trees of Madinah*

DU'AA دعـــــاء

When you are afraid of someone or something say:

بسْـــــم الله الذي لا يضُرُّ معَ اسْمِهِ شيءٌ في الأرضِ ولا في السَّـــماءِ،
وَهو السَّميعُ العَـليم

Bism-illah-il-lathi la yadhurru ma'-asmihi shay'un fil ardi wala fis-samaa'i wahuw-as wa-howa as-Samee'o al-Aleem

"In the name of God, by whose name nothing whatsoever whether in Heaven or on Earth, comes to harm; and it is He Who hears and knows all things."

Healthy Habits

1. Keep your promise.

2. Always pray to Allah ﷻ when faced with difficult situations.

Chapter Review

With your classmates, create a model of the Battle of the Trench. In the model, show Madinah, the trench, the enemy's army, and the Muslim army.

If you were an advisor to Muslims during the Battle of the Trench, what additional ideas would you offer to help in defending Madinah?

1. Why did Bani Qouraythah risk breaking the treaty and join the Quraysh and the other tribes in fighting the Muslims?
2. How were the Muslims depending on Bani QurKaythah to protect the city?
3. Who helped the Muslims to spread disunity among the enemy's army? What did he do?
4. How did Allah answer the prayers of the Muslims?

UNIT C
CHAPTER 4
LESSON ONE

Surat Al-Mursalat: The Winds 1

General Notes

Surat Al-Mursalat has fifty ayaat and was revealed in Makkah. Abdullah Ibn Mas'ood رضي الله عنه reported that Surat Al-Mursalat was revealed to Rasulullah while he was sitting in a cave in Mina near Makkah. The surah attracts our attention to Allah's great creations, the winds and other beautiful gifts made by Allah. The surah also talks about the Day of Judgment and the punishment of the disbelievers on that great day. Allah also gives the good news to believers, that they will win Jannah.

For your Information

Surat Al-Mursalat was one of the last suwar the Prophet ﷺ recited aloud in jama'ah prayer. Um Al-Fadl, (wife of Al-Abbas, the uncle of Rasulullah) said, "The Messenger of Allah, may Allah give him blessings and peace, led us in Maghrib Prayer. In the prayer he recited Al-Mursalat and that was the last Maghrib Prayer he performed with us before his death."

(Reported in Al-Bukhari and At-Tirmithi)

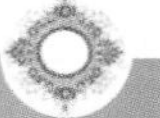

WORDS OF WISDOM

Holy Qur'an

سورة المرسلات

Surat Al-Mursalat 1-15

بِسْمِ ٱللَّهِ ٱلرَّحْمَٰنِ ٱلرَّحِيمِ

﴿ وَٱلْمُرْسَلَٰتِ عُرْفًا ﴿١﴾ فَٱلْعَٰصِفَٰتِ عَصْفًا ﴿٢﴾ وَٱلنَّٰشِرَٰتِ نَشْرًا ﴿٣﴾ فَٱلْفَٰرِقَٰتِ فَرْقًا ﴿٤﴾
فَٱلْمُلْقِيَٰتِ ذِكْرًا ﴿٥﴾ عُذْرًا أَوْ نُذْرًا ﴿٦﴾ إِنَّمَا تُوعَدُونَ لَوَٰقِعٌ ﴿٧﴾ فَإِذَا ٱلنُّجُومُ طُمِسَتْ ﴿٨﴾
وَإِذَا ٱلسَّمَآءُ فُرِجَتْ ﴿٩﴾ وَإِذَا ٱلْجِبَالُ نُسِفَتْ ﴿١٠﴾ وَإِذَا ٱلرُّسُلُ أُقِّتَتْ ﴿١١﴾ لِأَيِّ يَوْمٍ أُجِّلَتْ ﴿١٢﴾
لِيَوْمِ ٱلْفَصْلِ ﴿١٣﴾ وَمَآ أَدْرَىٰكَ مَا يَوْمُ ٱلْفَصْلِ ﴿١٤﴾ وَيْلٌ يَوْمَئِذٍ لِّلْمُكَذِّبِينَ ﴿١٥﴾ ﴾

TRANSLITERATION

Waalmursalati urfa (77:1) Fal-AAsifati 'asfa (77:2) Wn-nashirati nashra (77:3) Fal-fariqati farqa (77:4) Falmulqiyati thikra (77:5) 'Uthran aw nuthra (77:6) Innama too'adoona lawaqi' (77:7) Fa-itha-nnujoomu tumisat (77:8) Wa-itha-ssama'o furijat (77:9) Wa-ithaljibalu nusifat (77:10) Wa-itha-rrusulu oqqitat (77:11) Li-ayyi yawmin ojjilat (77:12) Liyawmil-fasl (77:13) Wama adraka ma yawmu alfasl (77:14) Wayluy- yawma-ithil-lil-mukaththibeen (77:15)

UNDERSTOOD MEANING

(77:1) I swear by the breeze which is sent, one (gust) after the other
(77:2) Then by the howling (winds)
(77:3) And I swear by (the winds) which scatter and direct the clouds
(77:4) Then by (the Qur'an) which separates truth from falsehood
(77:5) Then by (the messengers) who deliver this reminder
(77:6) As a delivery of the message of Allah or as a warning of Allah's punishment.
(77:7) Definitely, the (Day of Judgment) you are promised will happen
(77:8) It will happen when the light of the stars is gone
(77:9) And the sky is torn to pieces
(77:10) and when the mountains are quickly pulled up from their places.
(77:11) and when the messengers are gathered together for an appointment (in the Last Day.)
(77:12) For which day has this appointment been set?
(77:13) It is the Day of Judgment
(77:14) And how could you understand how terrible this day will be?
(77:15) A terrible punishment will fall on the disbelievers on the Day of Judgment.

Did You Know?

The word "wayl" is repeated many times in this surah and throughout the Qur'an. Arabs use this word when they want to threaten others with punishment. Here in this surah, Allah is threatening the kuffar with His great punishment in Hellfire. Prophet Muhammad also explained what the word wayl means:

> Al-Wayl is a canyon in Hell. The kuffar will fall for forty years before they reach the bottom of it. *(Al-Hakim, with a sound chain of narration).*

During this surah, Allah repeated the ayah:

> "A terrible punishment will fall on the disbelievers on the Day of Judgment, ten times." [Surat Al-Mursalat 77:15]

The reason for the repetition is that Allah wants to warn the disbelievers in a very alarming way. Allah wants to impress upon them to believe before His punishment befalls them.

UNIT
C
CHAPTER
4
LESSON
TWO

Surat Al-Mursalat: The Winds 2

Allah is the Creator of Man and Earth

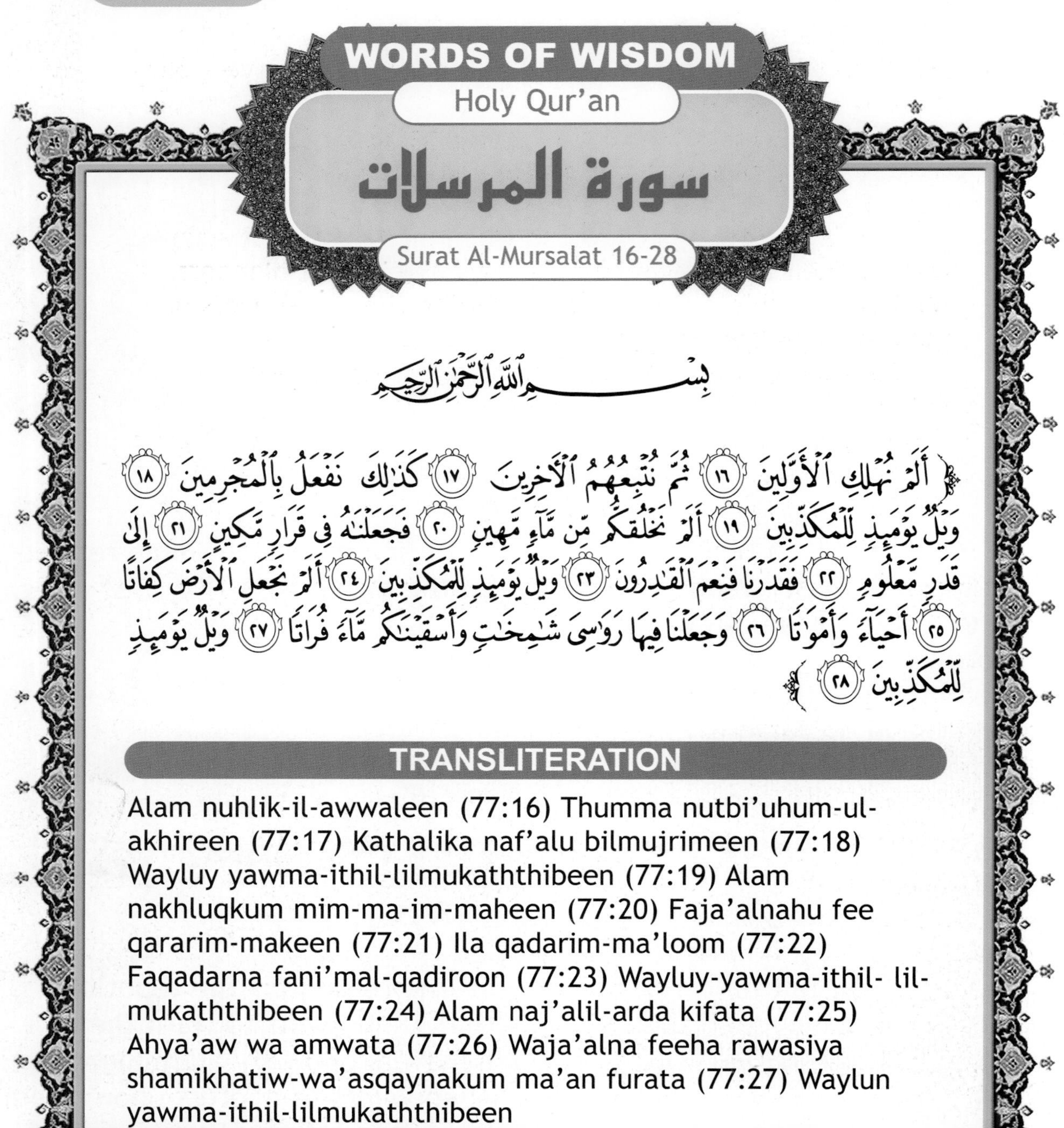

WORDS OF WISDOM

Holy Qur'an

سورة المرسلات

Surat Al-Mursalat 16-28

بسم الله الرحمن الرحيم

﴿ألم نهلك الأولين ﴿١٦﴾ ثم نتبعهم الآخرين ﴿١٧﴾ كذلك نفعل بالمجرمين ﴿١٨﴾ ويل يومئذ للمكذبين ﴿١٩﴾ ألم نخلقكم من ماء مهين ﴿٢٠﴾ فجعلناه في قرار مكين ﴿٢١﴾ إلى قدر معلوم ﴿٢٢﴾ فقدرنا فنعم القادرون ﴿٢٣﴾ ويل يومئذ للمكذبين ﴿٢٤﴾ ألم نجعل الأرض كفاتا ﴿٢٥﴾ أحياء وأمواتا ﴿٢٦﴾ وجعلنا فيها رواسي شامخات وأسقيناكم ماء فراتا ﴿٢٧﴾ ويل يومئذ للمكذبين ﴿٢٨﴾﴾

TRANSLITERATION

Alam nuhlik-il-awwaleen (77:16) Thumma nutbi'uhum-ul-akhireen (77:17) Kathalika naf'alu bilmujrimeen (77:18) Wayluy yawma-ithil-lilmukaththibeen (77:19) Alam nakhluqkum mim-ma-im-maheen (77:20) Faja'alnahu fee qararim-makeen (77:21) Ila qadarim-ma'loom (77:22) Faqadarna fani'mal-qadiroon (77:23) Wayluy-yawma-ithil- lil-mukaththibeen (77:24) Alam naj'alil-arda kifata (77:25) Ahya'aw wa amwata (77:26) Waja'alna feeha rawasiya shamikhatiw-wa'asqaynakum ma'an furata (77:27) Waylun yawma-ithil-lilmukaththibeen

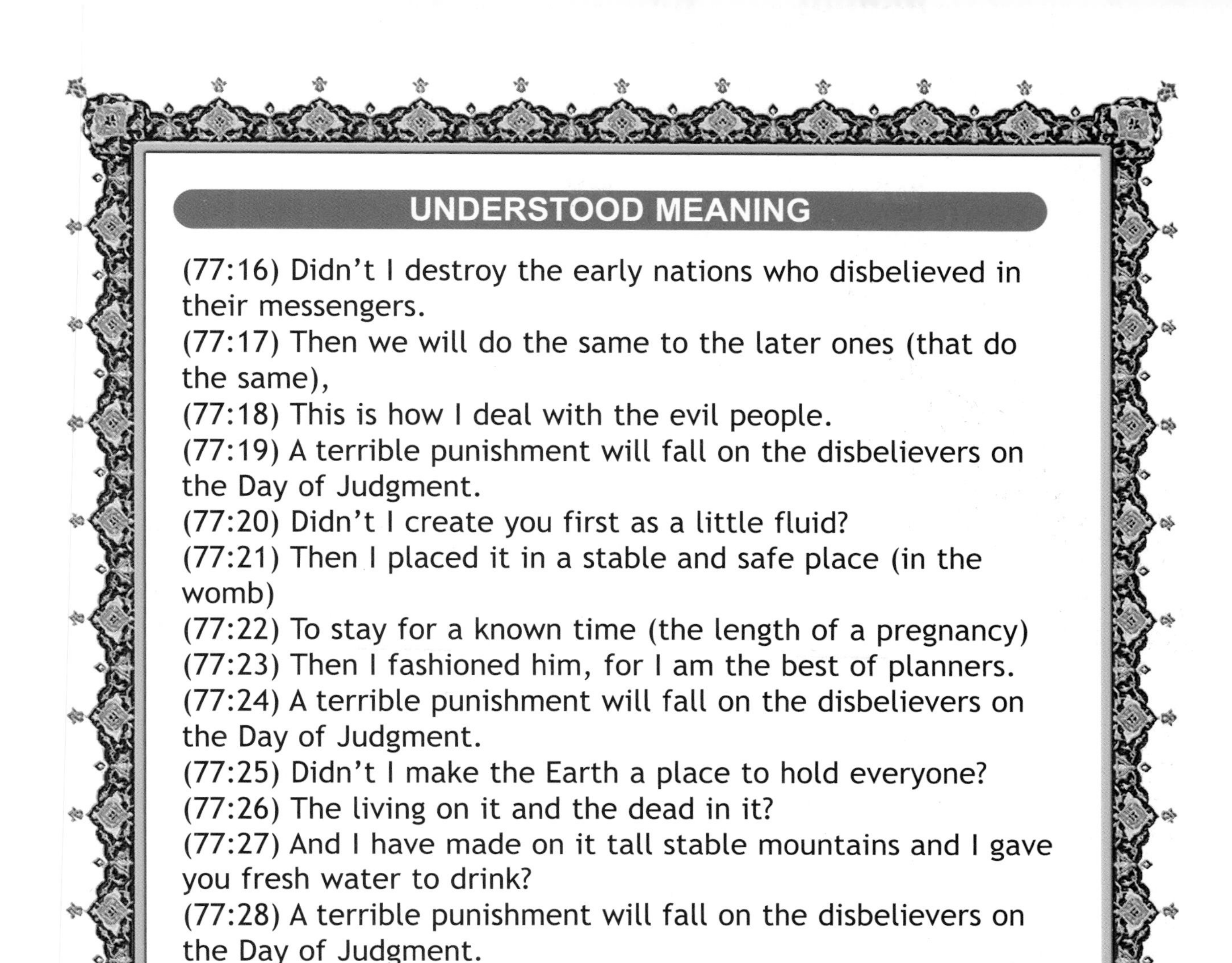

UNDERSTOOD MEANING

(77:16) Didn't I destroy the early nations who disbelieved in their messengers.
(77:17) Then we will do the same to the later ones (that do the same),
(77:18) This is how I deal with the evil people.
(77:19) A terrible punishment will fall on the disbelievers on the Day of Judgment.
(77:20) Didn't I create you first as a little fluid?
(77:21) Then I placed it in a stable and safe place (in the womb)
(77:22) To stay for a known time (the length of a pregnancy)
(77:23) Then I fashioned him, for I am the best of planners.
(77:24) A terrible punishment will fall on the disbelievers on the Day of Judgment.
(77:25) Didn't I make the Earth a place to hold everyone?
(77:26) The living on it and the dead in it?
(77:27) And I have made on it tall stable mountains and I gave you fresh water to drink?
(77:28) A terrible punishment will fall on the disbelievers on the Day of Judgment.

The mountain houses of the people of Thamoud. They were destroyed thousands of years ago when they refused to worship Allah alone and obey his Messenger Salih عليه السلام *. Their strong houses did not protect them against the punishment of Allah* ﷻ *.*

UNIT C CHAPTER 4 LESSON THREE

Surat Al-Mursalat: The Winds 3

The Punishment of the Disbelievers in Hell

WORDS OF WISDOM

Holy Qur'an

سورة المرسلات

Surat Al-Mursalat 29-40

بِسْمِ ٱللَّهِ ٱلرَّحْمَٰنِ ٱلرَّحِيمِ

﴿ ٱنطَلِقُوٓا۟ إِلَىٰ مَا كُنتُم بِهِۦ تُكَذِّبُونَ ﴿٢٩﴾ ٱنطَلِقُوٓا۟ إِلَىٰ ظِلٍّ ذِى ثَلَٰثِ شُعَبٍ ﴿٣٠﴾ لَّا ظَلِيلٍ
وَلَا يُغْنِى مِنَ ٱللَّهَبِ ﴿٣١﴾ إِنَّهَا تَرْمِى بِشَرَرٍ كَٱلْقَصْرِ ﴿٣٢﴾ كَأَنَّهُۥ جِمَٰلَتٌ صُفْرٌ ﴿٣٣﴾ وَيْلٌ
يَوْمَئِذٍ لِّلْمُكَذِّبِينَ ﴿٣٤﴾ هَٰذَا يَوْمُ لَا يَنطِقُونَ ﴿٣٥﴾ وَلَا يُؤْذَنُ لَهُمْ فَيَعْتَذِرُونَ ﴿٣٦﴾ وَيْلٌ يَوْمَئِذٍ
لِّلْمُكَذِّبِينَ ﴿٣٧﴾ هَٰذَا يَوْمُ ٱلْفَصْلِ جَمَعْنَٰكُمْ وَٱلْأَوَّلِينَ ﴿٣٨﴾ فَإِن كَانَ لَكُمْ كَيْدٌ فَكِيدُونِ ﴿٣٩﴾
وَيْلٌ يَوْمَئِذٍ لِّلْمُكَذِّبِينَ ﴿٤٠﴾ ﴾

TRANSLITERATION

Intaliqoo ila ma kuntum bihi tukaththiboon (77:29) Intaliqoo ila thillin thee thalathi shu'ab (77:30) La thaleeliw wala yughnee minallahab (77:31) Innaha tarmee bishararin kalqasr (77:32) Ka'annahu jimalatun sufr (77:33) Wayluy yawma-ithil-lilmukaththibeen (77:34) Hatha yawmu la yantiqoon (77:35) Wala yu'thanu lahum faya'tathiroon (77:36) Wayluy-yawma-ithil-lilmukaththibeen (77:37) Hatha yawm-ul-fasli jama'-nakum wal-awwaleen (77:38) Fa-in kana lakum kaydun fakee-doon (77:39) Wayluy-yawma-ithil lilmukaththibeen (77:40)

UNDERSTOOD MEANING

(77:29) On the Day of Judgment it will be said to them, "Go to the punishment you said was a lie (when Allah's messengers came to you with the warning)!"
(77:30) Go to the shade of three columns of black fiery smoke (from Hell).
(77:31) No, it is not going to shade you from the (heat of the sun over your heads) and it doesn't protect from the flames of Hell
(77:32) The flames in the smoke throw out big sparks like logs (or a fortress).
(77:33) They have the same color as the black camels with yellow highlights
(77:34) A terrible punishment will fall on the disbelievers in the Day of Judgment.
(77:35) On that day (after they have been judged) they will not be allowed to speak.
(77:36) And they will not be allowed to give any more excuses.
(77:37) A terrible punishment will fall on the disbelievers in the Day of Judgment.
(77:38) It will be said to them, "This is the Day of Judgment. You (the disbelievers) and the disbelievers of earlier nations are now collected together.
(77:39) So now if you have a plan you think will defeat Me (Allah), then try it."
(77:40) A terrible punishment will fall on the disbelievers in the Day of Judgment.

For Your Information

In these verses, Allah ﷻ uses several more techniques to warn and frighten the disbelievers.

1- He tells them what will be said to them on the Day of Judgment.

2- He warns them that they will not be allowed to talk their way out of their problem.

3- He says that they will be humiliated for their plotting against Islam.

UNIT C CHAPTER 4 LESSON FOUR

Surat Al-Mursalat: The Winds 4

Jannah, the Final Home of the Believers

▲ *Muslims praying inside a mosque in Delhi, India.*

Holy Qur'an

سورة المرسلات

Surat Al-Mursalat 41-44

﴿ إِنَّ الْمُتَّقِينَ فِي ظِلَالٍ وَعُيُونٍ ﴿٤١﴾ وَفَوَاكِهَ مِمَّا يَشْتَهُونَ ﴿٤٢﴾ كُلُوا وَاشْرَبُوا هَنِيئًا بِمَا كُنتُمْ تَعْمَلُونَ ﴿٤٣﴾ إِنَّا كَذَٰلِكَ نَجْزِي الْمُحْسِنِينَ ﴿٤٤﴾ ﴾

TRANSLITERATION

Inn-al-muttaqeena fee thilaliw wa'uyoon (77:41) Wafawakiha mimma yashtahoon (77:42) Kuloo washra-boo hanee-am bima kuntum ta'maloon (77:43) Inna kathalika najzil-muhsineen (77:44)

UNDERSTOOD MEANING

(77:41) Surely, the pious people will be in the shade of trees drinking from flowing springs,
(77:42) and [eating] fruits that they love to eat.
(77:43) Eat and drink and enjoy because of all the good deeds you used to do.
(77:44) This is how I reward the good doers.

UNIT C CHAPTER 4 LESSON FIVE

Surat Al-Mursalat: The Winds 5

More Warnings to the Disbelievers

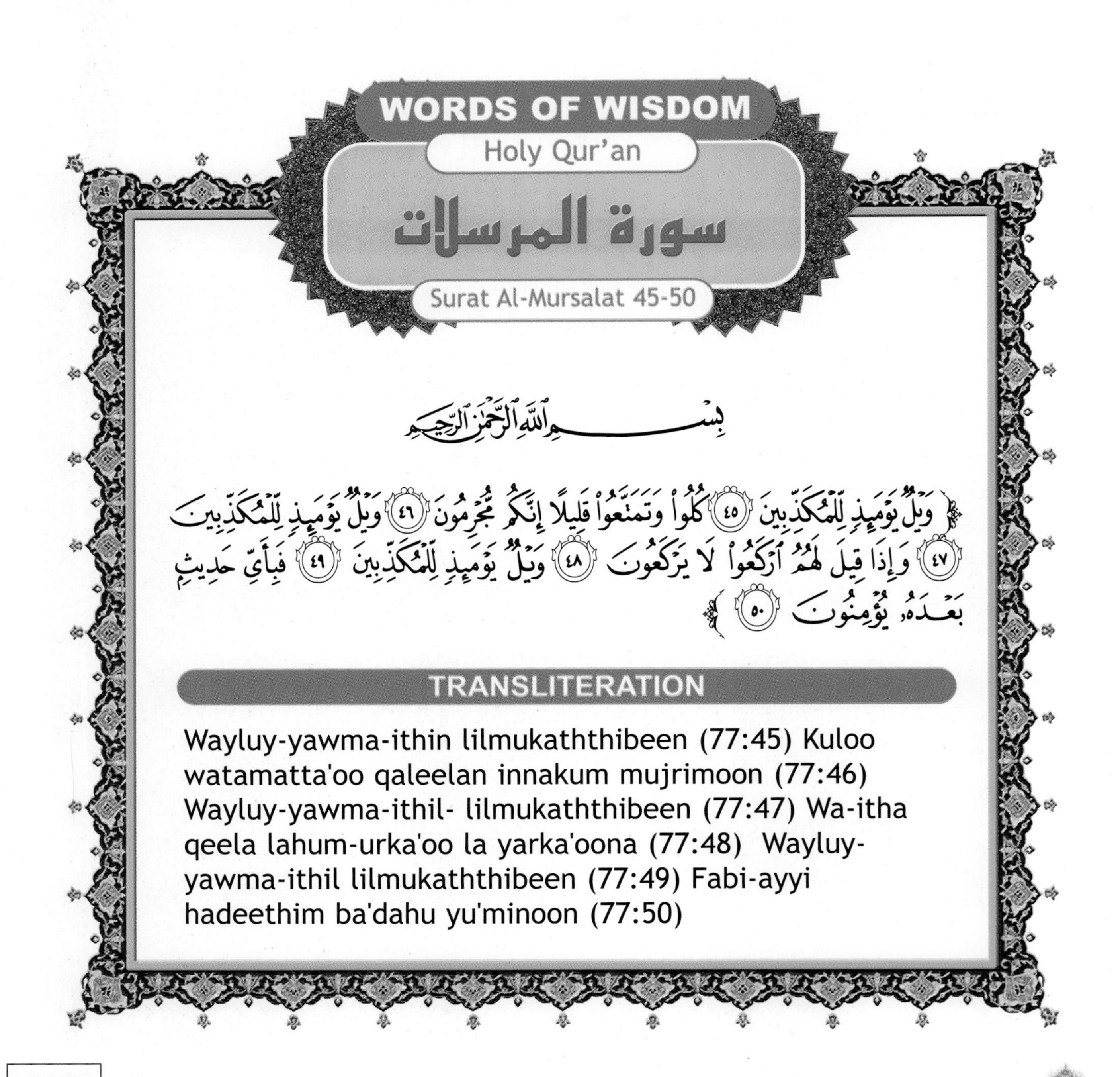

WORDS OF WISDOM

Holy Qur'an

سورة المرسلات

Surat Al-Mursalat 45-50

بِسْمِ اللَّهِ الرَّحْمَٰنِ الرَّحِيمِ

﴿ وَيْلٌ يَوْمَئِذٍ لِّلْمُكَذِّبِينَ ﴿٤٥﴾ كُلُوا وَتَمَتَّعُوا قَلِيلًا إِنَّكُم مُّجْرِمُونَ ﴿٤٦﴾ وَيْلٌ يَوْمَئِذٍ لِّلْمُكَذِّبِينَ ﴿٤٧﴾ وَإِذَا قِيلَ لَهُمُ ارْكَعُوا لَا يَرْكَعُونَ ﴿٤٨﴾ وَيْلٌ يَوْمَئِذٍ لِّلْمُكَذِّبِينَ ﴿٤٩﴾ فَبِأَيِّ حَدِيثٍ بَعْدَهُ يُؤْمِنُونَ ﴿٥٠﴾ ﴾

TRANSLITERATION

Wayluy-yawma-ithin lilmukaththibeen (77:45) Kuloo watamatta'oo qaleelan innakum mujrimoon (77:46) Wayluy-yawma-ithil- lilmukaththibeen (77:47) Wa-itha qeela lahum-urka'oo la yarka'oona (77:48) Wayluy-yawma-ithil lilmukaththibeen (77:49) Fabi-ayyi hadeethim ba'dahu yu'minoon (77:50)

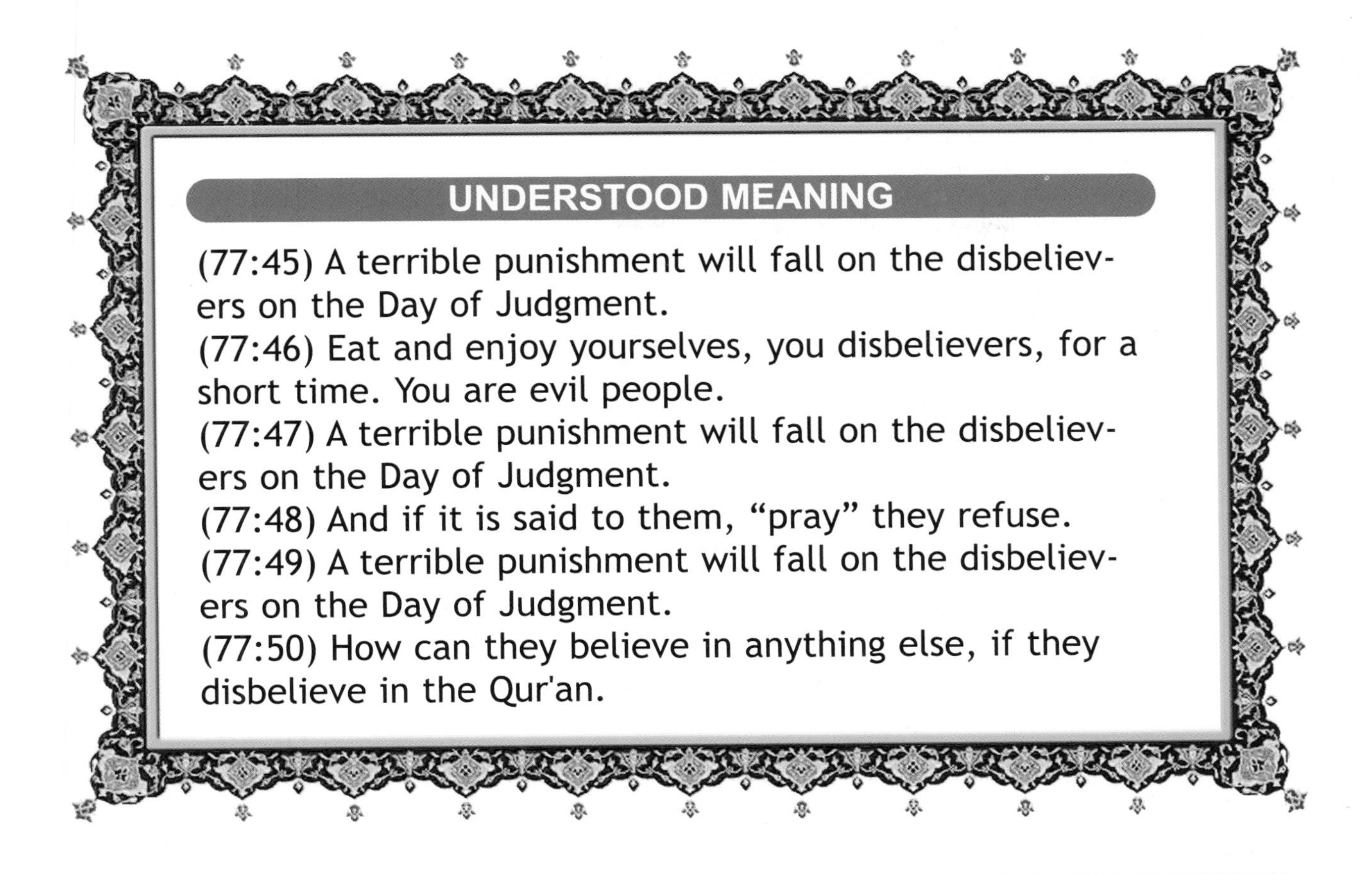

UNDERSTOOD MEANING

(77:45) A terrible punishment will fall on the disbelievers on the Day of Judgment.
(77:46) Eat and enjoy yourselves, you disbelievers, for a short time. You are evil people.
(77:47) A terrible punishment will fall on the disbelievers on the Day of Judgment.
(77:48) And if it is said to them, "pray" they refuse.
(77:49) A terrible punishment will fall on the disbelievers on the Day of Judgment.
(77:50) How can they believe in anything else, if they disbelieve in the Qur'an.

For Your Information

This section ended with three final ways of trying to shake the hearts of the kuffar:

1- Increasing the humiliation of the kuffar by comparing what will happen to them with what will happen to the believers on the Day of Judgment.

2- Warning them that they will be held accountable for all the enjoyment they think they have in this life.

3- Pointing out their madness by believing many things, like idols and witchcraft, while not believing in the Holy Qur'an, the real truth.

Make a list of all the different techniques Allah uses in this surah to scare the kuffar into reconsidering their position.

WORSHIP WITH HEART

Al Khushoo': The Heart of Worship

CHAPTER ONE

Pre-reading Questions

1. What is khushoo'?
2. Why is khushoo' important?
3. How can we achieve khushoo' during prayer and worship?

Word Watch

khushoo' خشوع

As Muslims, we pray five times a day. Salah is an important part of our daily lives. However, we need to take time and ask ourselves, "Are we performing our prayers properly?" In prayer, a person should experience **khushoo'**. In this lesson you will learn about khushoo' and its importance.

STORYTIME

Bilal was playing basketball with his friends. He was in the middle of shooting a three pointer, when suddenly, he heard his mother calling him. He did not know what his mother wanted, so he called a timeout and went to listen to his mother. As soon as he reached the door, Bilal's mother asked him, "Have you prayed Asr?" "No, I haven't," replied Bilal. Bilal could see the disappointment in her face as she said, "What are you waiting for Bilal?" "Can I pray after I finish the game? There is only one more quarter left," Bilal pleaded. "No, the game can wait. Go pray right now. You are about to miss the Asr prayer time," demanded his mother.

Bilal was upset because he wanted to finish the game. So he quickly went to the bathroom to make wudoo'. Without realizing it, Bilal skipped some of the steps of wudoo' because he was in such a hurry to finish. He was also in a hurry to pray so that he could return to the game. He began the prayer without saying "Allah Akbar" properly. His mind was not on the prayer; he was thinking of the game instead. He could hear the loud voices of his friends outside.

Bilal's mind was busy outside

the prayer, so he forgot to say the second surah after reading Al Fatihah. He swiftly went into rukoo' and prayed the rest of the prayer in a jumble of confusion. After he finished his prayer, he began wondering if his prayer was really valid. He tried to remember the surah he had recited in his prayer, but he couldn't! He could not even remember one surah he had recited! This is when Bilal realized that he had made a big mistake. He remembered some ayaat in the Qur'an that talk about khushoo'.

"Successful indeed are the believers," [23:1]

﴿ ٱلَّذِينَ هُمْ فِي صَلَاتِهِمْ خَٰشِعُونَ ﴾

"Those are humble in their prayers," [23:2]

﴿ وَٱلَّذِينَ هُمْ عَنِ ٱللَّغْوِ مُعْرِضُونَ ﴾

"And who avoid vain talk and actions." [23:3]

After remembering these ayaat, Bilal was angry with himself. He was sad he missed khushoo' during Salat Al-Asr because of a basket-ball game. Bilal decided that he was going to make his salah all over again, this time with proper khushoo'. Bilal realized his salah was more important than the bas-ketball game.

Understanding Khushoo'

Salah is one of the five pillars of Islam, and it is very important to every Muslim. A Muslim prays with his body, tongue and heart. Al-khushoo' means having your heart and mind thoughtful of Allah during salah, du'aa', or other kinds of worship. You feel khushoo' in your heart, and it gives you calm-ness, dignity, and humility before Allah.

What makes a person enjoy khushoo' is his love of Allah and his awareness that Allah is always watching. If your heart is busy with something else like games and entertainment, then you will miss khushoo'. And if khushoo' is not present in your salah, then your prayer isn't complete.

Rasulullah ﷺ has warned us that Shaytan tries always to ruin

our prayers. He distracts us during prayer by making us remember wordly matters. Shaytan is the number one enemy of Islam and Muslims. He promised to mislead and tempt the sons of Adam, saying,

"Then I will come to them from before them and behind them, from their right and from their left..." [7:17]

One of Shaytan's most important plots is to distract people from salah by all possible means. He takes away the joy of khushoo' during salah and worship. He wants the believers to lose the reward and the benefits of the salah.

Hadeeth Shareef

عن عثمان بن عفّان رضي الله عنه قال : سمعت رسول الله ﷺ :
" ما من امريء مسلم تَحْضُرُهُ صَلاة مكتوبة فيُحسِن وضوءَها وخُشُوعَها وركوعَها إلا كانتْ كفارة لما قبلها من الذنوب ، ما لم يؤتِ كبيرة وذلك الدهرَ كلَّه" رواه مسلم

Uthman Ibn Affan (R) narrated that he heard Rasulullah saying:

Any Muslim who observes an obligatory prayer perfecting the wudoo', the khushoo' and the rukoo, Allah will forgive his or her sins, except Al-Kaba'ir*, or the major sins, and that is forever.

(Reported in Muslim)

* Al-Kabair (major sins) can be only forgiven when the Muslim sincerely repents to Allah

Steps to Develop Khushoo' During Salah

1. Have complete awareness during salah.

During salah, you should empty your heart of any worldly matters that may distract you from prayer. Salah is not the time to think about a basketball game, a TV show, or the food that is cooking in the kitchen. Sometimes your thoughts may wander, but you should try your best to concentrate on your salah. An ayah in the Qur'an reminds us:

﴿وَمَا ٱلْحَيَوٰةُ ٱلدُّنْيَآ إِلَّا لَعِبٌ وَلَهْوٌ ۖ وَلَلدَّارُ ٱلْءَاخِرَةُ خَيْرٌ لِّلَّذِينَ يَتَّقُونَ ۗ أَفَلَا تَعْقِلُونَ﴾

"And the life of this world is nothing but play and joy. But far better is the Hereafter for those who fear Allah, don't you understand." [6:32]

So during salah, the only thing you should concentrate on is salah. If anything else comes to mind, try your best to block it out. Remember that Shaytan always tries to distract you. And you should not let Shaytan win!

2. Understand what you are saying during salah.

We say the entire salah in the Arabic language. Understanding what you are saying during salah is very important toward having proper khushoo'. If you understand what you recite, then you will be able to connect your heart with the words. You should memorize the meanings of the different words that are said during prayer. This includes Allahu Akbar, Subhana Rabiyal Atheem, Subhana Rabiyal Aala, the tasleem, and other words. Memorizing the meanings of surahs and du'aa' that you frequently say during Salah will help you develop khushoo'.

3. Feel Allah's greatness in your heart during salah.

We know that Allah سُبْحَانَهُ وَتَعَالَى is Al-Atheem (the Great). He owns and controls everything in this universe. He is Al-Muhaymin. We should then love, glorify, and fear Allah. Glorifying Allah سُبْحَانَهُ وَتَعَالَى helps us increase our khushoo' during salah.

4. Pray in a calm place.

We should always pray in a calm and peaceful place; a place that does not have much noise or Visual distractions. You should avoid praying in places where there is loud noise or a lot of people talking. Also, it is not a good idea to pray near the TV when it is on or near children who are playing or screaming.

Looking at the floor while in salah will help in developing khushoo'. Visual distraction usually makes us think about what we see, causing us to lose focus on the prayer. Therefore, we should always pray in a place that has no distracting movements or objects in front of us. Rasulullah ﷺ instructed us to look at the floor to where we place our heads in sujood. In this way we do not get distracted by things or movements around us.

5. Pray when you are relaxed.

Some people pray or worship Allah when they are tired or hungry, or need to use the bathroom. This is against the Sunnah of the Prophet. Rasulullah ﷺ instructed us to pray when we are comfortable and relaxed. When we are comfortable we can attain khushoo', but when we feel uncomfortable we lack khushoo'.

Finally, remember that khushoo' is the heart of your prayer and worship. If you lose focus and concentration during salah or worship, it will not be as good as Allah wants it to be. Allah, during the Day of Judgment, will ask us about the quality of our prayer. The Prophet Muhammad ﷺ said,

> "The first action for which a servant of Allah will be held accountable on the Day of Resurrection will be his prayers. If they are in order then he will have succeeded, but if they are lacking, then everything will be lacking."

Du'aa دعــــــاء

اللهمَّ إني أعوذ بكَ من عِـلْـم لا يَـنْـفَـعْ، ومِنْ
قَـلْـبٍ لا يخْـشَـعْ، ومن نفس لا تشبع،
ومن دَعْـوةٍ لا يُسْـتَجابُ لها

رواه مسلم

Allahumma inni a'oothu bika min ilmin la yanfa', wa min qalbin la yakhsha', wa min nafsin la tashba', wa min da'watin la yustajabu laha

O Alla,h I seek your protection from useless knowledge, a heart without khushoo', a body that doesn't get satisfied, and a du'aa that you do not answer.
(Reported in Muslim)

Healthy Habit

Always pray and worship with khushoo' in your heart.

Chapter Review

Find a story about khushoo' in prayer, and tell it to your family and class.

1. How can you tell if a person has khushoo' during prayer?
2. Shaytan doesn't want you to have khushoo' in your salah. Explain why.

1. What did Bilal do wrong in his salah?
2. What is the first action we are going to be judged on during the Day of Judgment?
3. Explain khushoo' and why it is important.
4. Who promised to try to take away khushoo' from the believers?
5. How can we develop khushoo' in our salah? Describe three ways to do that.

The Voluntary Prayers

CHAPTER
TWO

Pre-reading Questions

1. What is Salat-ut-Tatawwo'?
2. When do we pray extra prayers?

Word Watch

Salat-ul-Fard	صلاة الفَرْض
Salat-un-Nawafil	صلاة النوافِل
Salat-us-Sunnah	صَلاة السُنَّة
Salat-ut-Tatawwo'	صلاة التَطَوُّع

We all know the five obligatory prayers , or صلاة الفَرْض **Salat-ul-Fard,** that every Muslim must pray. Apart from the Fard prayers, there are صلاة النوافِل **Salat-un-Nawafil,** or extra prayers that we should also pray. These prayers are not obligatory, but Rasulullah ﷺ encouraged Muslims to pray them. Salat-un-Nawafil are comprised of two main types:

1. **Salat-us-Sunnah**
2. **Salat-ut-Tatawwo'**, or voluntary prayers.

صـــلاة الفرض
Salat-ul-Fard

صـــلاة النــوافــل
Salat-un-Nawafil

صـــلاة التطـــوع
Salat-ut-Tatawwo'

صـــلاة السـنــة
Salat-us-Sunnah

1 Sunnah Prayer صـلاة السنة :

Rasulullah ﷺ used to pray Sunnah prayers all the time. Regular Sunnah prayers have fixed times.

You learned earlier about Salat-us-Sunnah, and how the Prophet ﷺ used to do these all the time. He always encouraged Muslims to pray them on time. Read the following Hadeeth to learn the different Sunnah prayers and what rewards you get if you perform them regularly.

Hadeeth Shareef

عن أمِّ حَبيبَة رضيَ الله عَنْها قالتْ : قال رسولُ الله ﷺ :

" مَنْ صلّى في يوم وليلةٍ ثِنْتيْ عشْرة ركْعة تَطوُّعاً بُنِي له بهنَّ بيْتٌ في الجنّة: أربعاً قبل الظهر وركْعتين بعدها، ورَكْعتيْن بعد المغْرِب، ورَكْعتيْن بعْدَ العِشاء، ورَكْعتين قبل الغداة"

رواه مسلم وأبو داود وأحمد وابن ماجه

Ummu Habeebah narrated that Rasulullah ﷺ said:
"Whoever, during the course of one day and night, prays twelve voluntary rak'aat will have a house in Jannah built for him [or her]; four before Thuhr and two after it, two after Maghrib, two after Ishaa' and two before Fajr."

(Reported in Muslim, At-Tirmithi, Abu Dawood, Ahmad and Ibn Majah)

2 Salat-ut-Tatawwo' صلاة التطوع :

Rasulullah also used to pray voluntary prayers other than the Sunnah Ratibah.

He ﷺ encouraged Muslims to perform voluntary prayers as often as possible. Some scholars call them صلاة النفل Salat-un-Nafl, which means the same thing: voluntary or optional prayers.

While some of the prayers known as Salat-ut-Tatawwo' have fixed times, like Salat-ud-Duha, Salat-ul-Witr and Qiyam-ul-Layl, other voluntary prayers have no fixed time. You can pray almost at any time.

However, there are some times when you should avoid praying:

Wrong Times for Voluntary Prayers

1. After Salat Al-Fajr until the sun rises up a little.
2. The few minutes before the Athan of Salat Al-Thuhr.
3. After Salat-ul-Witr at night.
4. Between Salat Al-Asr and Maghrib.

Rasulullah taught us that during the Day of Judgment, Allah ﷻ will instruct al-mala'ikah, or the angels, to inspect the quality of our fard prayers. If a person missed some of his fard prayers or did not perform some the them well, Allah will ask the angels to add the voluntary prayers to his balance in order to help him out.

Healthy Habit

Always pray Salat-us-Sunnah and other voluntary prayers. Make sure you pray at least 12 rak'aat of Sunnah and other Nawafil to get a palace in Jannah.

Hadeeth Qudsi*

عن ابي هريرة رضي الله عنه أن رسول الله ﷺ قال:

"مَن عادى لي وليّاً فقد آذنْتُهُ بالحَرْب ، وما تقرَّبَ إليَّ عبدي بشيءٍ أحبَّ إليَّ ممّا افْترضْتُ عليه ، وما يزالُ عبْدي يتقرَّبُ إليَّ بالنوافِلِ حتّى أحبَّهُ ، فإذا أحْبَبْتُه كُنْتُ سمْعَهُ الذي يسْمَعُ بِه ، وبَصرَهُ الذي يُبْصِرُ بِه ، ويدَهُ التي يبْطِشُ بها ورجْلَهُ التي يمشي بها ، وإن سألني لأ عْطِينّه ولئن استعاذني لأعيذنّه"

رواه البخاري

Abu Hurayrah narrated that Rasulullah ﷺ said: Allah said,

"I will fight those who hurt my servants. The best worship I like my servant to do is the Fard prayers and worship. And my servant keeps doing the voluntary prayers until I love him. And when I love him, I will help him as he listens, as he sees, as he uses his hands, and as he walks with his feet. Additionally, whenever he asks me for something I will give it to him, and when he wants me to protect him against something I will protect him."

(Reported in Al-Bukhari)

* Hadeeth Qudsi is a special hadeeth whose meaning was sent from Allah to Prophet Muhammad, who in turn taught it to the sahabah.

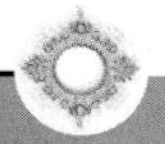

Chapter Review

Create a poster that shows Salat-us-Sunnah at different times, as well as some of the Salat-ut-Tatawwo'.

1. Explain the difference between Salat-ul-Fard and Salat-us-Sunnah.

2. Explain the difference between the Sunnah Ratibah and Salat-ut-Tatawwo'?

1. What is Salat-ut-Tatawwo'?
2. What is the Sunnah Ratibah?
3. What is the reward for praying Sunnah regularly?
4. Name three of Salat-ut-Tatawwo' that have fixed times.
5. List the times that are not good for Salat-ut-Tatawwo'.

CHAPTER THREE

Salat-ud-Duha

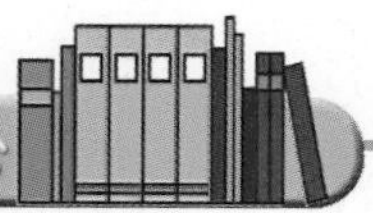

Pre-reading Questions

1. What is Salat-ud-Duha?
2. Is it a Fard prayer or a voluntary prayer?
3. How should we pray Salat-ud-Duha?

Salat-ud-Duha: Duha Prayer	صلاةُ الضُّحى
Sulama: Joint	سُـــلامى
Tasbeehah: Saying Subhan-Allah	تَسْبيحة
Tahmeedah: Saying Al-Hamdu-lillah	تحميدة
Tahleelah: Saying La-ilaha illallah	تهليلة

The Prophet ﷺ used to pray صلاة الضحى **Salat-ud-Duha** every day. It is one kind of Salat-ut-Tatawwo' that you learned about in the last chapter. Let's learn about this important voluntary prayer!

Zaid sees his father praying at around 9 o'clock in the morning. Zaid is puzzled because he doesn't understand why his dad is praying at this time. He knows that his father is not praying Salat-ul-Fajr, because it is too late for Fajr prayer, plus they prayed it together as a family.

Zaid: [wondering to himself]

Father: [finishes prayer and looks at Zaid's puzzled face]

Zaid: Baba, were you praying Thuhr early?

Father: [laughs] No, Zaid, I was praying Salat-ud-Duha.

Zaid: Salat-ud-Duha? That sounds like Thuhr.

Father: Salat-ud-Duha and Salat-uth-Thuhr are two different prayers.

Zaid: Wow! I've never heard of Salat-ud-Duha before.

Father: It's ok, Zaid. Every day we learn something new in life.

Zaid: So, when do you pray Salat-ud-Duha?

Father: We pray Salat-ud-Duha in the mid-morning. It is a voluntary prayer.

Zaid: Do we have to pray Salat-ud-Duha?

Father: Salat-ud-Duha is not Fard; it is an optional prayer. You don't have to do it, but if you want extra hasanat, you should.

Zaid: Baba, it is good to get extra hasanat! I want extra hasanat!

Father: [Laughing] Allah has made it very easy for us to get extra hasanat, because He is the most Merciful.

Zaid: How many rak'aat are in Salat-ud-Duha?

Father: Salat-ud-Duha can be prayed between 2 to 12 rak'aats. The Prophet ﷺ often used to pray 2 or 4 rak'aat.

Zaid: Wow that is the same number of rak'aat as Thuhr, Asr, and Isha.

Father: You are right, Zaid.

Zaid: Whenever I get a chance, I am going to pray Salat-ud-Duha, insha-Allah.

Father: Masha-Allah Zaid, that is very good.

Hadeeth Shareef

عن أبي هريرة رضي الله عنه قال: قال رسول الله ﷺ:

" مَنْ حافَظَ على شُفْعَةِ الضُّحى غُفِرَتْ لهُ ذنوبُهُ ولَوْ كانت مِثْلَ زَبَدِ البَحْرِ"

رواه أحمد وابن ماجه

Abu Hurayrah reported that the Prophet ﷺ said:
"Whoever regularly prays the two rak'aat of Duha his sins are forgiven even if they are as plentiful as the foam of the sea."
(Reported by Ahmad and Ibn Majah)

A Hadeeth and a Story

Once rasulullah told the Sahabah that there is a sadaqah due on each joint Allah placed in our bodies. You know that there are three hundred and sixty joints in a human being. So the Sahabah thought that they should offer three hundred and sixty sadaqah a day. They said, "Who can do such a thing, Messenger of Allah?" He replied, "To say Subhan-Allah is a sadaqah, to say Al-hamdu-Lillah is a sadaqah, to say la ilaha illa-Allah is a sadaqah, and advising others to do a good thing, or to avoid an evil behavior is a sadaqah." Then the Prophet ﷺ said, the two rak'aat of Duha equals all of that

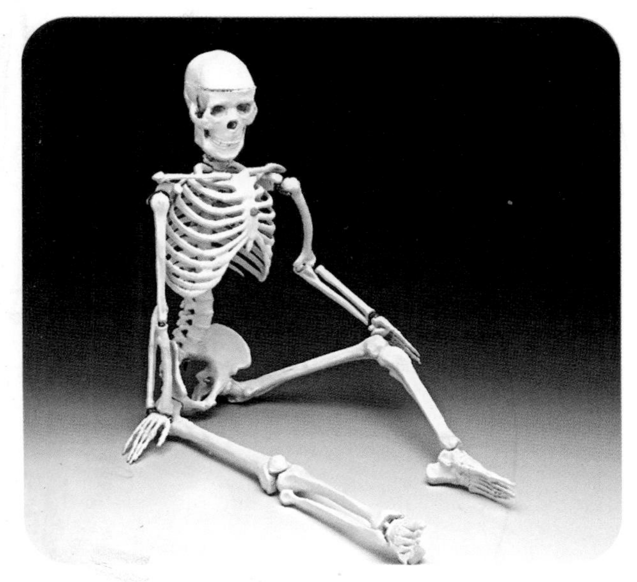

for you." Therefore, if you pray Salat-ud-Duha, you will be rewarded as though paying 360 sadaqah on all of the joints Allah created in your body.

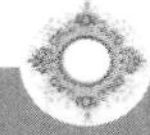

Healthy Habit

Pray Salat-ud-Duha every day if you can.

Allah named a Surah in the Qur'an "Ad-Duha." In the surah, He swore by Ad-Duha.

It must be an important time of day to worship Allah.

Chapter Review

Go out between 8 and 10 in the morning and see where in the sky the sun would be during the time of Salat-ud-Duha.

1. Why do you think only a few people pray Salat-ud-Duha?

2. What should we do to develop the habit of praying Duha regularly?

1. When is Salat-ud-Duha performed?
2. Is Salat-ud-Duha a Fard or a voluntary prayer?
3. How many rak'aat are there in Salat-ud-Duha? How many did the Prophet ﷺ perform?
4. What are the benefits of performing Salat-ud-Duha?

Salat-ul-Witr

CHAPTER FOUR

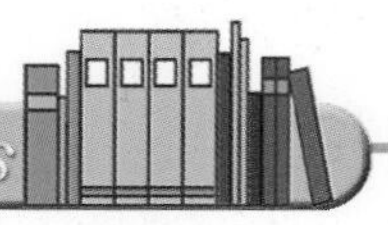

Pre-reading Questions

1. What is Salat-ul-Witr?
2. How should you perform it?
3. What is Du'aa'-ul-Qunoot?
4. Did rasulullah ﷺ keep on praying it every night?

Salat-ul-Witr صلاة الوِتْر
Du'aa'-ul-Qunoot دُعـاءُ القُنُـوت

Salt-ul-Witr is an important Tatawwo' prayer. Prophet Muhammad used to pray it every night. In this lesson, you will learn how you should perform this night-time Salah.

What is Salat-ul-Witr?

The word Witr وتر means one-of-a-kind, or odd. And that is why this particular prayer is called Witr, because it has an odd number of rak'aat, and no other prayer is like it.

Witr prayer is a Sunnah night-time prayer. The Prophet ﷺ usually performed Witr prayer after Ishaa' prayer. Usually, he would pray it later in the night after he had finished his Qiyam-ul-Layl prayer. He used to pray Witr in three rak'aat. However, sometimes he prayed one, five, seven, nine, and even eleven rak'aat.

Generally, Witr prayer consists of three rak'aat. It can be performed in one of the following manners:

1. Pray it like Salat-ul-Maghrib.
2. Pray it like Salat-ul-Maghrib but without the first Tashahhud. That is praying the three raka'at with only one tashahhud at the end.
3. Pray two rakaat first and make tasleem. Then pray the third rak'ah.

Du'aa-ul-Qunoot

What makes Salat-ul-Witr different from all other prayers is **Du'aa'-ul-Qunoot**. During the third rak'ah we say this special du'aa'. We can say Du'aa'-ul-Qunnot either before rukoo' or after rukoo'.

Let's learn that together:

Option 1

After reciting Surat-ul-Fatihah and another surah in the third rak'ah, you raise your hands up to the ears and say "Allahu Akbar" and make rukoo'. Then you straighten your back up, raise your hands up to your ears again and say "semi'allahu liman hamidah." Now you raise your hands palms up by your chest and recite the Du'aa'-ul-Qunoot. After finishing Du'aa'-ul-Qunoot, you make sujood and complete your prayer as you do in other regular prayers.

Option 2

After reciting Surat Al-Fatihah and another surah, you say Allahu Akbar. Then you refold your arms and recite Du'aa'-ul-Qunoot. After finishing Du'aa'-ul-Qunoot, you do Rukoo' and complete your prayer as you do in other regular prayers.

There are two ways to say Du'aa'-ul-Qunoot in Salat-ul-Witr:

Du'aa'-ul-Qunoot - 1

اللهمَّ اهْدِني فيمَنْ هَدَيْت

Allahumm-ahdinee fee man hadayt

O Allah, guide me among those whom You have guided

وَعافِني فيمَنْ عافَيْت

wa 'aafinee feeman 'aafait

and preserve me among those whom You have preserved

وَتَـوَلَّـنـي فيمن تَـوَلَّـيْت

Wa tawallanee feeman tawallayt
And protect me among those whom You have protected

وبـارِك لي فيما أعْطَـيْت

Wa baarik lee feema a'atayt,
And bless for me what You have given me

وَ قِـنـي شَـرَّ مـا قَـضَـيْت
waqinee sharra ma qadayt,
And guard me from the evil of that which You have commanded to happen,

فَـإنَّـك تَـقضي ولا يُـقْضى عليْك

Fa'innaka taqdee wala yuqda 'alayk,
for truly, it is You Who commands, and none imposes any command upon You.

إنَّـه لا يَـذِلُّ مَـنْ والَـيْـت

Innahu la yathillu man waalayt,
Indeed, never is he humiliated, whom You have supported

ولا يَـعِـزُّ مَـنْ عادَيْـت

wa la yaizzu man 'aadait
And never is he honored whom You take as an enemy

تباركْتَ ربي وتَـعـالَـيْت

tabarakta rabbana wa ta'alayt,
Our Lord, You are blessed and exalted

وصلى الله على النبي وعلى آله وصحبه وسلَّم

Wa sallallahu 'alannabiyyi wa 'aalihee wa sallam.
Allah's blessing and peace be upon the Prophet and his family.

(Reported in Ahmad)

Du'aa'-ul-Qunoot - 2

اللهمَّ إنـّا نَسْتَعينُكَ

Allaahumma innaa nasta 'eenuka
O Allah, we seek Your help

ونَسْتَغْفِرُك

wa nastaghfiruka
and we seek Your forgiveness.

ونؤمنُ بِكَ

wa nu'uminu bika
and we believe in You

ونَتَوَكَّلُ عليْك وَنثْني عليْكَ الخَيْره كله

wa natawakkalu 'alaika wa nuthnee 'alaikal khaira Kullah
And we depend upon You and give You all the praise

نَشْكُرُكَ ولا نكفُرك

Nashkuruka wa laa nakfuruka
We thank You, and we are not ungrateful to You,

ونخْلَعُ ونَتْركُ من يفجُرك

wa nakhla'u wa natruku man yaf juruk.
and we disown and shun those who disobey You.

اللهمَّ إياك نَعْبد

Allaahumma iyyaaka na'abudu
O Allah, You alone do we worship,

ولكَ نُصلّي ونَسْجد

walaka nusallee wa nasjudu
and to You we pray, and before You we prostrate ourselves,

وإلَيْكَ نسعى ونحفِد

wa ilaika nas'aa wa nahfidu,
and we hasten towards You and serve You

ونرجو رَحْمَتَكَ

wa narju rahmataka
and we hope for Your mercy,

وَنَخْشى عذابك

wa nakhsha 'athaabaka
and dread Your punishment

إن عَذابَك بِالكفّار مُلْحِق

inna 'athaabaka bil kuffaari mulhiq.
Surely, Your punishment shall overtake the disbelievers.

Rasulullah Prayed Witr Every Night:

Ali ibn Abi Talib رضي الله عنه said once:

"The Witr prayer is not obligatory as the other five prescribed prayers. But Rasulullah ﷺ kept on performing it all the time. He said 'Allah is Witr (one of a kind or singular) and loves what is Witr. So perform Witr prayer. O followers of Qur'an, observe Witr prayer.'"

Hadeeth Shareef

عن أبي هريرة رضي الله عنه قال : أوصاني خليلي بِثلاث ، لا أدَعَهُنَّ حتّى أموت: صَوْم ثَلاثَةِ أيام مِنْ كُلِّ شَهْر وَصَلاةِ الضُّحى ونَوْم عَلى وِتْر "

رواه البخاري ومسلم

Abu Hurayrah رضي الله عنه said:

"My beloved friend (Rasulullah ﷺ) enjoined upon me to do three things, and I will never stop doing them till I die; to fast three days of every month, to pray Salat-ud-Duha, and to pray Salat-ul-Witr before I sleep."

(Reported in Al-Bukhari and Muslim)

Healthy Habit

Always pray Witr prayer; do not sleep before performing this important salah.

Chapter Review

1. Practice Salat-ul-Witr along with your friends, in front of your teacher or parents.

2. Memorize at least one of the two du'aa's of qunoot you learned in this lesson.

How is Salat-ul-Witr different from Salat Al-Maghrib?

1. When is Witr prayer performed?
2. How many raka'at are in Witr prayer?
3. In how many ways can you perform Salat-ul-Witr? Describe two ways of performing it.
4. What is the name of the special du'aa you should say during Witr?
5. Say the du'aa you should say in Salat-ul-Witr.

Salat-ul-Musafir: The Traveler's Prayer

CHAPTER FIVE

Pre-reading Questions

1. What is Salat-ul-Musafir?
2. When and how do you shorten prayers?
3. When can you combine prayers?

Word Watch

Salat-ul-Musafir	صَلاةُ المُسَــــــافِـر
Qasr	قَصْـر
Jame'	جَمْـع

Main Idea

Allah ﷻ is merciful and kind. He made our religion easy to understand and implement. When we travel, we get tired and have less time to do things. We might not easily find a clean and peaceful place to pray in. Therefore, Allah allows Muslim travelers to shorten and combine some of their prayers. This lesson will help you understand the rules of **Salat-ul-Musafir**, the prayer of the traveler.

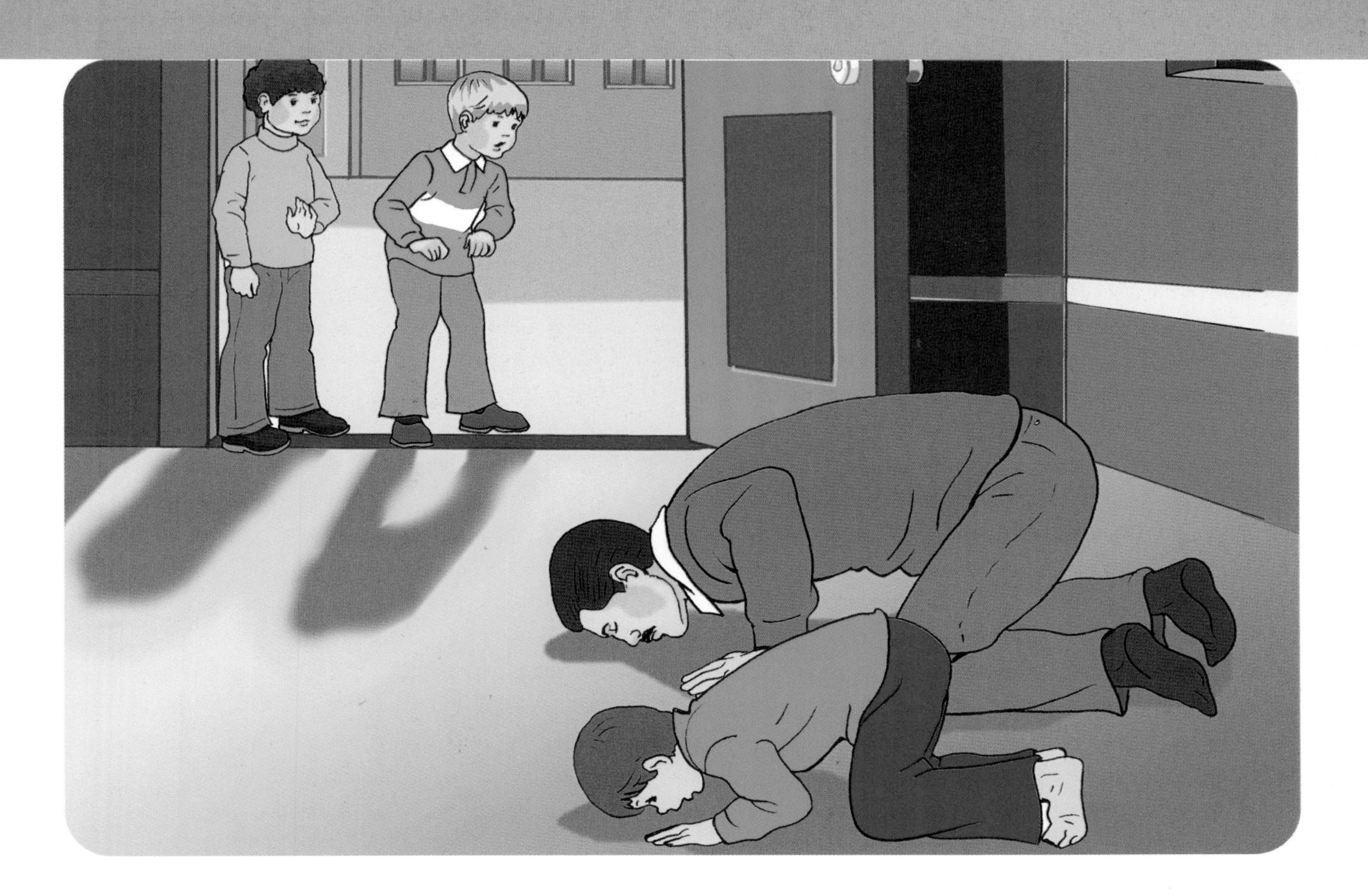

STORYTIME

Muhammad and his brother Hani were rushing to the prayer hall. They were playing outside and did not hear the athan. Muhammad and Hani were able to catch the last rak'ah, and they did not forget to make up the other three rak'aat of Thuhr Prayer.

"Alhamdulillah, we didn't miss the Jama'ah (group) prayer," Muhammad told his younger brother. "We still get the Jama'ah reward, right?" Hani asked. "Umm, I think so..insha'Allah."

As Muhammad tried to figure out the answer to his brother's question, he saw an unfamiliar man and his son walk into the prayer hall.

Muhammad said, "Hey Hani, have you seen those people before?" "No, maybe they are new in town," said Hani. "Yeah probably. Let's wait and introduce ourselves. I bet the boy is my age," Muhammad added.

So Muhammad and Hani sat and watched the father and son perform their prayers. The father and son ended their prayer after only two rak'aat.

"Muhammad! They only prayed two rak'aat! Thuhur prayer is four rak'aat!" Hani was amazed.

"Hmm..look. They are going back to pray again..." Muhammad said, relieved.

Indeed, the father and son prayed two more rak'aat. After they finished, Muhammad and Hani ran up to them.

"Assalamu Alaikum," Muhammad and Hani said together.

"Walaikum As-Salam,"

"My name is Muhammad, and this is my brother Hani."

"Nice to meet you, boys. I'm Dr. Mas'ood, and this is my son Omar." [He leaves them to talk.]

"Are you guys going to hang around for Asr Prayer?" Hani asked.

"Oh no, we need to leave soon. Besides, we already prayed Asr," Omar said. smiling.

"What?" Muhammad asked, surprised. "But wasn't that Thuhr you just prayed?"

"Yeah, we prayed both."

"At the same time?!"

"Yes, we shortened the Thuhr prayer from four raka'at to two, and Asr prayer from four raka'at to two and prayed them together."

"You can do that?" Muhammad and Hani replied together.

Omar laughed, "Yes, its called Salat-ul-Musafir."

WHAT IS SALAT-UL-MUSAFIR?

Allah makes worship and practicing Islam easy for Muslims. During travel, Allah allows travelers to shorten and combine their prayers. This is called Salat-ul-Musafir, which literally means, "the Traveler's Prayer," and is sometimes called "Salat-ul-Qasr," which means "the shortened prayer."

Qasr قصر : Shortening the Prayers:

Allah says in Al-Qur'an:

﴿ وَإِذَا ضَرَبْتُمْ فِي ٱلْأَرْضِ فَلَيْسَ عَلَيْكُمْ جُنَاحٌ أَن تَقْصُرُوا۟ مِنَ ٱلصَّلَوٰةِ ﴾

"When you travel through the Earth, there is no blame on you if you shorten your." salah [4:101]

Then, Allah ﷻ allows travelers to shorten the regular prayers. Rasulullah taught us that only the four rak'aat prayers may be shortened. These are Thuhr, Asr, and Ishaa' prayers. Fajr and Maghrib prayers cannot be shortened. Travelers still must pray Fajr in two rak'aat and Maghrib in three rak'aat.

What if we don't feel like the trip was burden enough to initiate a shortened and combined prayer?

What if we feel like we can pray the whole prayer without a problem? Omar ibn Al-Khatab was reported to have said:

"I wondered about why people shorten the salah ...and I mentioned this to the Prophet ﷺ and he said, 'This is a favor that Allah سُبحان الله has given to you, so accept his favor gratefully.'"

Indeed, the Prophet ﷺ always prayed Salat-ul-Musafir when traveling. Should we refuse to follow the great example of Rasulullah ﷺ?

According to the Qur'an and the sayings of the Prophet ﷺ, **Qasr** or shortening the prayer, may be applied during any kind of travel, be it long or short, rough or easy, traveling on camels or by airplane. A traveler may perform Salat-ul-Musafir the entire time he is on a journey and away from his home. For example, if Omar wants to go to New York to visit with relatives,

and it takes him 3 days to get there, he may pray Salat-ul-Musafir for those 3 days. Likewise, if the traveler stays at a certain place for a period of time, then he/she is permitted to pray Salat-ul-Musafir as long as the traveler is there. For example, if the journey took Omar 3 days to reach New York, and then he decided to stay in New York for 4 days, this would mean that he may perform Salat-ul- Musafir for the 4 days he's staying in New York, in addition to the other 3 days traveling back to his hometown.

If, however, Omar decides to reside [stay for good] in New York, he must resume praying the prayers in full.

Jame' جمع , or Combining the Prayers:

Travelers have the choice to pray the shortened prayer in its time or to join the shortened prayers. Let's learn how we can do that:

1. **Fajr Prayer:** We pray Fajr prayer in full, even during travel. We cannot combine Salat Al-Fajr, or Fajr prayer, with any other prayer. It's also recommended to pray the Sunnah of Fajr. That Sunnah is the only Sunnah which the Prophet kept praying during travel.

2. **Thuhr and Asr Prayers:** A Muslim traveler can shorten and combine Salat Al-Thuhr and Salat Al-Asr (Thuhr and Asr prayers) during travel. You can pray both prayers at Thuhr time or at Asr prayer time. For example, at Thuhr time, Omar would first pray Thuhr in 2 rak'aat. Right after finishing, he would get up, say iqamah again, and pray Asr in 2 rak'aat. If he chooses to combine the two prayers at Asr time, he can simply do the two shortened prayers in the same order.

3. **Magrib and Ishaa' Prayers:** The traveler can also do the same for Salat Al-Maghrib and Salat Al-Ishaa' (Maghrib and Ishaa' prayers). When the time of Maghrib would come, Omar would pray three rak'aat of Maghrib first and then he would pray the shortened Ishaa' prayers of 2 rak'aat right afterwards. What pattern have you noticed when shortening prayers? The prayers that have 4 raka'aat can be shortened to 2 rak'aat. The other prayers such as Fajr and Maghrib have fewer than 4, so these prayers should be prayed as usual.

A Muslim traveler can shorten the prayers without joining them if he or she wishes to do so. It's also recommended to pray Witr prayer after Isha', even during travel.

PRAYER	REGULAR	DURING TRAVEL
FAJR	2	2
THUHUR	4	2
ASR	4	2
MAGHRIB	3	3
ISHAA'	4	2

Athan and Iqamah for Salat-ul-Musafir

If there is a group of people traveling together and they all want to pray jama'ah prayer, then the athan and iqamah should be made. However, unlike the regular prayers, the athan and iqamah are performed a little differently. The athan is to be said only once for both of the combined prayers at a time. Nonetheless, each prayer must have a separate iqamah. For example, the mu'athin would make the athan once, perform the iqamah, and the imam would pray Maghrib (3 rak'aat). Then they would all get up and the mu'athin would make iqamah again and the imam would lead the Ishaa' prayer (2 rak'aat).

Sunnah Prayer

No Sunnah should be prayed between the two 'combined' salah. As a matter of fact, a traveler is not required to pray the Sunnah prayer. However, Rasulullah used to pray only the Sunnah of Fajr while traveling. Rasulullah, also, used to pray Witr during travel.

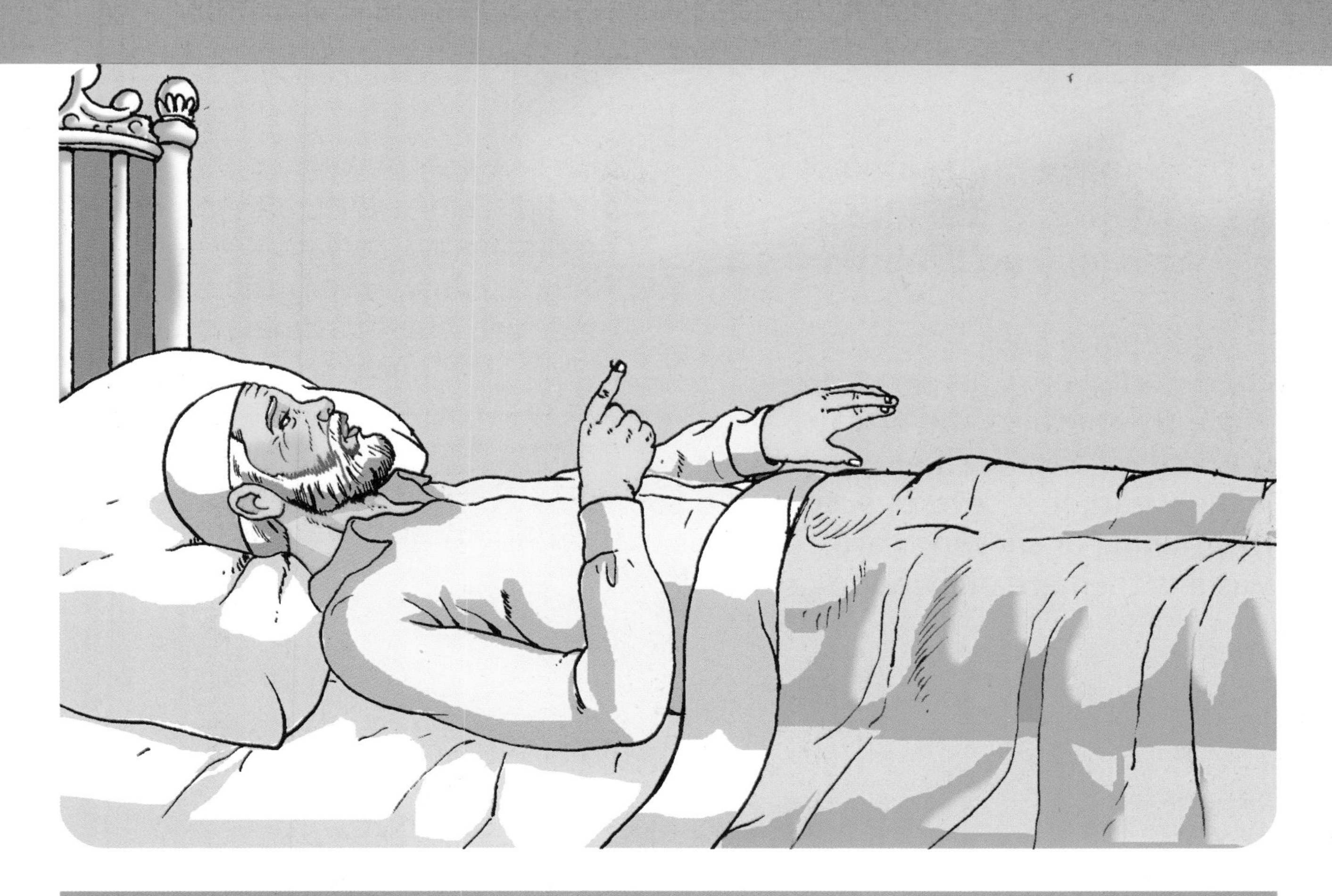

Other Exceptional Prayers

Prayer of the Sick

When a Muslim is ill, he or she might not be able to pray the same way as when he or she is healthy. He or she may not be able to stand, make rukoo' or sujood. Sometimes a sick person may not be able to even move. What should a sick person do? As you know, Allah is so merciful, and he wants us always to be happy and healthy. So He does not ask us to stand in prayer if we can't, or make rukoo' and sujood if it is painful or harmful. Once, Rasulullah was so sick that he could not stand in prayer, so he led the prayer sitting. Omar ibn Al-Khattab رضي الله عنه was dying and could not even sit during the prayer, so he prayed while he was lying down. Therefore, a sick person should pray the way he or she can. If praying the prayers becomes difficult, the sick person can combine Thuhr with Asr and Maghrib with Ishaa', but without shortening the prayers.

Combining Jama'ah Prayers in the Masjid due to Bad Weather

Sometimes your school might close during difficult weather. What do you think the masajid would do if the weather was bad? If the weather is severe, such as if it is raining or snowing hard, Muslims then are allowed to combine jama'ah prayers in the masjid. During difficult weather, the imam can do Jame' or join Thuhr and Asr or Maghrib and Ishaa' without shortening the prayer. The imam would join Thuhr and Asr at Thuhr time, and join Maghrib and Ishaa' at Maghrib time. This can only be done at the masjid, not at private homes.

1. Pretend that you and your classmates are traveling. Perform Qasr and Jame' for Thuhr and Asr prayers, and for Maghrib and Ishaa' prayers.

2. Pretend that you are, God forbid, sick, and can not stand or even sit. Do the prayer of Fajr while you are lying on a bed.

Chapter Review

1. Are you allowed to do Qasr and Jame' during travel even if you are not tired?
2. Since you are allowed to shorten your prayer during times of travel, are there other types of worship that are made easier for you during travel? What are they?

1. What does Salat-ul-Musafir mean?
2. What does Qasr mean?
3. What does Jame' mean?
4. What should you do if you are traveling and want to pray?
5. What are the prayers that you can shorten?
6. What are the prayers that you can join together?
7. Which Sunnah prayers should you pray while traveling?
8. What are the Sunnah prayers that Rasulullah ﷺ used to keep praying even during travel?
9. Describe what a sick person should do in the following situations:
   * He can not stand in prayer
   * She can not stand, or make rukoo' or sujood
   * She can not stand, or even sit
10. What can Muslims do if they want to pray jama'ah in the masjid during bad weather?

Appreciating Allah's Gifts

CHAPTER
SIX

Pre-reading Questions 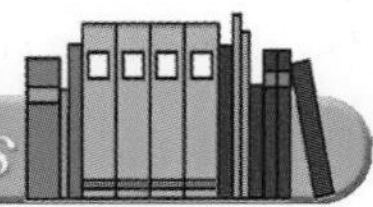

1. Who gave us everything we have?
2. What should we do for the One who gave us everything we have?
3. How can we be grateful to Allah?

Shukr: Gratitude شُكر
Ni'mah: Blessing نِعْمَة
Sujood-ush-Shukr: Prostration of Gratitude سُجودُ الشُّكْر
Ma'rib مأرِب
Saba': Sheba سبأ

الحَمْدُ لِلّه

Alhamdulillah

Can you think of how many times in a day you say this word? You say the word at least 17 times in a day! Just think about it. We say Alhamdullilahi Rab-il alameen every time we begin to recite Surat Al-Fatihah for prayer. But why do we say Alhamdullilah so many times?

Look around you. What do you see? You see the many gifts and treasures that Allah سبحانه وتعالى has blessed you with. Before you even look at other things, look at your self. Alhamdullilah, Allah سبحانه وتعالى has hopefully granted you good health. Hopefully, you can use your two legs to walk and your eyes to see. But these are just some of Allah's wonderful gifts. Allah's gifts are too numerous to count. They include anything that gives us happiness, delight, or comfort such as health, wealth, knowledge, family, and much more.

Holy Qur'an

﴿ وَإِن تَعُدُّوا۟ نِعْمَةَ ٱللَّهِ لَا تُحْصُوهَآ ۗ إِنَّ ٱللَّهَ لَغَفُورٌ رَّحِيمٌ ﴾

In Surat An-Nahl Allah says:

"If you tried to count the favors of Allah, you would never be able to number them; Allah is oft forgiving, most Merciful." [16:18]

How Should We Show Gratitude to Allah?

Sometimes we forget to appreciate the many gifts that Allah has blessed us with. How should we appreciate Allah's gifts? No matter how small the gift that Allah gives us, we must place great value on it and show our appreciation to the Giver. Yes, we need to look beyond just the gift and recognize the Giver, who is Allah ﷻ . We need to do this to express our gratitude and thankfulness toward our great Creator. Expressing gratitude to Allah is an act of worship known as عبادة الشكر Ibadat-ush-Shukr, or the worship of showing our gratitude to Allah. Here is how you show Allah your gratitude:

1. Have a Grateful Heart. You should acknowledge in your heart that everything you have is from Allah.

2. Have a Thankful Tongue. Say Alhamdulillah with your heart and tongue. Thanking Allah ﷻ with our tongues means expressing the thanks that our hearts feel. We thank Allah daily by saying Alhamdullilah for the blessings we receive from him, such as food, good health, and family. We also thank Allah ﷻ by our tongues when we say that the gifts and blessings we received are from Allah ﷻ .

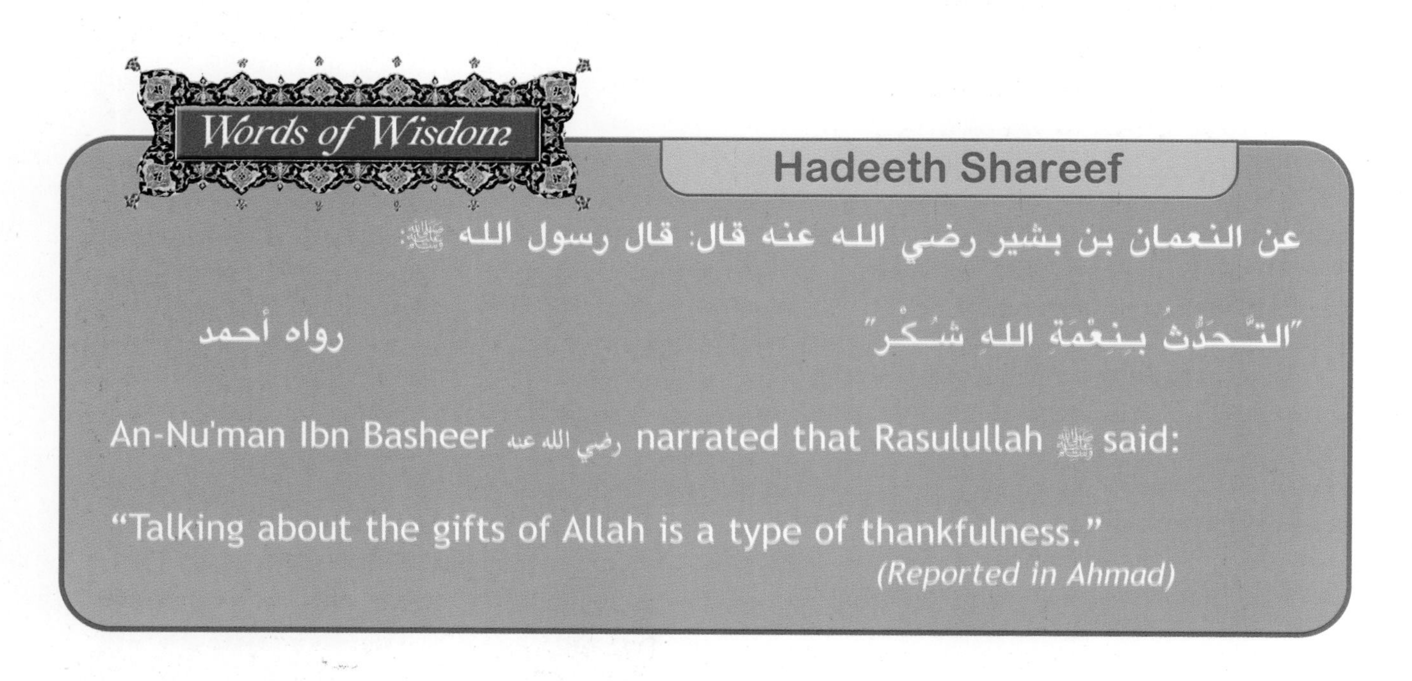

Holy Qur'an

﴿ وَأَمَّا بِنِعْمَةِ رَبِّكَ فَحَدِّثْ ﴾

"Make the favors of Allah on you known." [93:11]

3. Have a Grateful Body. The Prophet ﷺ sometimes used to stand up in prayer at night until his feet became swollen. Once he was asked why he did this, since all his past and future incorrect actions had been forgiven. He replied by saying, "Should I not be a thankful servant?" By physically tiring his body the Prophet ﷺ was showing great appreciation for what Allah had blessed him with. One other way to thank Allah is by doing سُجودُ الشُّكر **Sujood-ush-Shukr**. Whenever Allah gives you a favor you should make one sajdah, similar to the ones you do during regular salat. In the sajdah, you praise Allah and thank Him for what He did for you.

4. Obey Allah and avoid sins as much as you can.

5. Use the gifts He gave you in the right and halal way. For example, use your eyes to see only good and halal things, and avoid using your ears in hearing haram things.

6. Use and consume the gifts Allah gives you properly. Avoid wasting and neglecting these gifts. For example, Allah ﷻ gave you beautiful skin, so do not ruin it by applying tattoos or piercing it here and there.

7. Using your energy, time, and money that Allah gave you in serving Islam and helping others.

8. Give sadaqah and charity, if you can, to needy people.

9. If people gives you something or helps you in a situation, you should thank them and be kind to them. Rasulullah ﷺ said:

" من لا يشكُر الناسَ لا يشكر الله "

رواه أحمد

"The one who does not thank people [when they do favors for him or her, he or she is not thankful to Allah."

(Reported in Ahmad)

Shukr or Gratitude Brings You More Gifts and Blessings

Allah ﷻ loves His servants who acknowledge His blessings and show Him their gratitude. He even gives them more gifts and blessings if they are grateful. Allah ﷻ says in Al-Qur'an:

﴿ وَإِذْ تَأَذَّنَ رَبُّكُمْ لَئِن شَكَرْتُمْ لَأَزِيدَنَّكُمْ ۖ وَلَئِن كَفَرْتُمْ إِنَّ عَذَابِي لَشَدِيدٌ ﴾

"And remember! Your Lord declared 'If you are grateful, I will surely give you more, and if you are ungrateful; truly My punishment is terrible indeed.'" [Surat Ibraheem 14:7]

DU'AA

دعـــــاء

عن عبد الله بن غنّام رضي الله عنه قال: قال رسـول الله صلّى الله عليه وسلّم:

من قال حين يصبح:

"اللهمَّ ما أصبَحَ بي مِنْ نِعْمَةٍ فَمِنْكَ وَحْدَكَ لا شَريكَ لك، فلَكَ الحمدُ ولكَ الشُّكْرُ"

فقد أدّى شُكْرَ يَومِه ومَنْ قال مِثْلَ ذلك حين يُمْسي فقد أدّى شُكْرَ ليلته.

رواه أبو داود

Abdullah Ibn Ghannam reported that Rasulullah ﷺ said: "He who says in the morning " Allahumma ma 'asbaha bi min ni'matin famin-ka wahdaka la shareeka lak falak-lhamdu walaka-shukr."

Which means: "O Allah, whatever gift I received in the morning is from You Alone, so my praise and thanks are due to You. Whoever ever says this has rendered his day's gratitude, and he who says the same thing at night has rendered his night's grati-tudes.

Reported in Abu Dawood

Ma'rib in Yemen

STORYTIME

Ungrateful Attitude Leads to Loss of Allah's Gifts

In the Qur'an, there is a story about a people who were a very prosperous nation. They were called **Saba'** or the Nation of **Sheba**. They used to live in the area of **Ma'rib**, in Yemen. They had a great dam called Sadd Ma'rib. The dam was two miles long and 120 feet high. They were very rich and enjoyed a great water supply. The whole area flourished with fruit gardens, and it was free from insects. The climate was very pleasant. It was a happy country, enjoying canals and roads, and gardens to the right and left.

Each of the twelve towns of Saba' had its own prophet of Allah. Each of the prophets called their people to correct their belief in Allah ﷻ and obey Him. But the people became arrogant in their wealth, their skills, and the great work of their fathers and grandfathers. Sadly, they forgot to praise and worship Allah ﷻ for all that He had given them. They went astray. So Allah punished them with a mighty flood that destroyed their dam. Then they lost everything: their dam, their gardens, and their fields. The people of Saba' went from wealth to poverty.

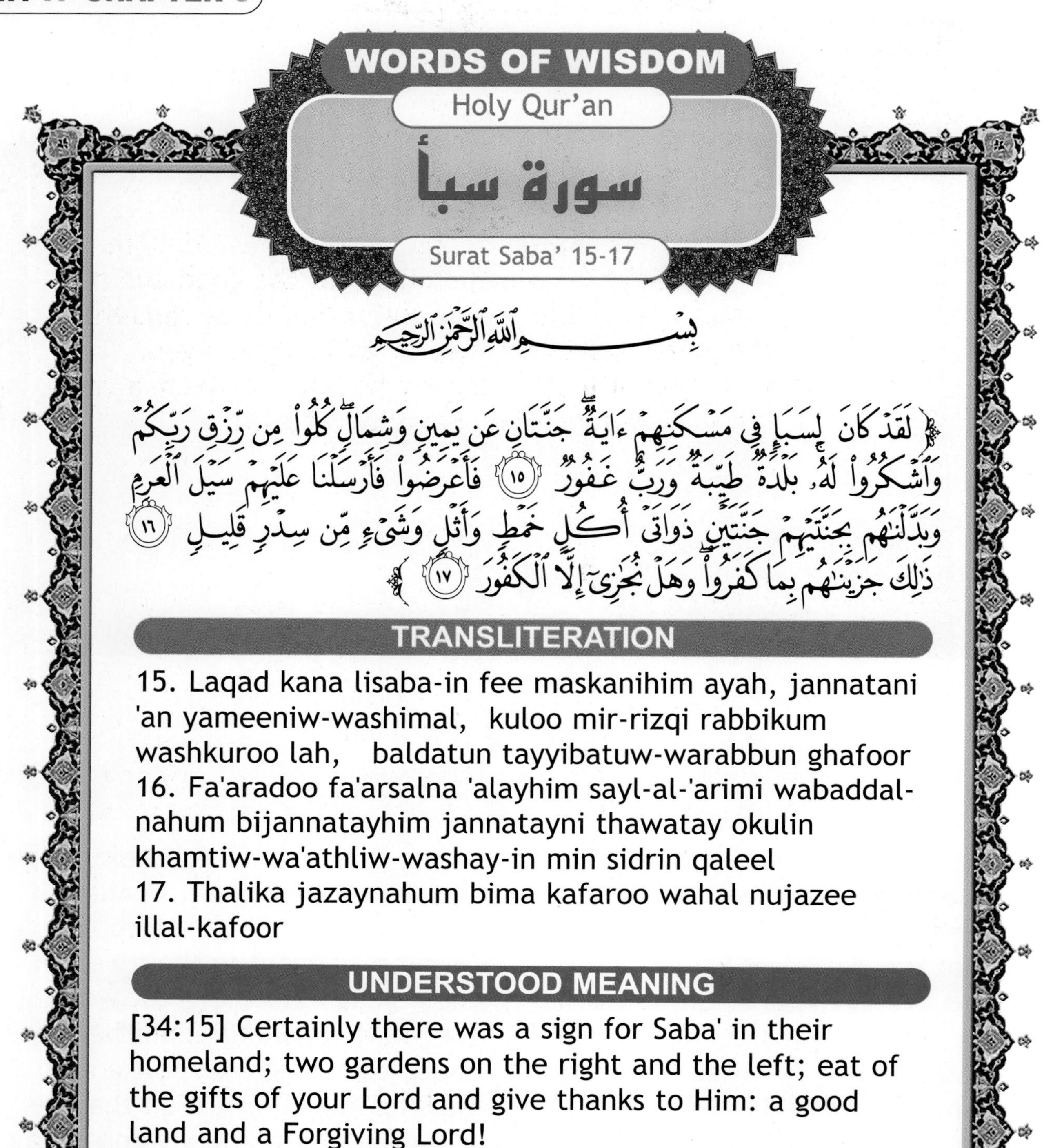

WORDS OF WISDOM

Holy Qur'an

سورة سبأ

Surat Saba' 15-17

بِسۡمِ ٱللَّهِ ٱلرَّحۡمَٰنِ ٱلرَّحِيمِ

﴿لَقَدۡ كَانَ لِسَبَإٖ فِي مَسۡكَنِهِمۡ ءَايَةٞۖ جَنَّتَانِ عَن يَمِينٖ وَشِمَالٖۖ كُلُواْ مِن رِّزۡقِ رَبِّكُمۡ
وَٱشۡكُرُواْ لَهُۥۚ بَلۡدَةٞ طَيِّبَةٞ وَرَبٌّ غَفُورٞ ١٥ فَأَعۡرَضُواْ فَأَرۡسَلۡنَا عَلَيۡهِمۡ سَيۡلَ ٱلۡعَرِمِ
وَبَدَّلۡنَٰهُم بِجَنَّتَيۡهِمۡ جَنَّتَيۡنِ ذَوَاتَيۡ أُكُلٍ خَمۡطٖ وَأَثۡلٖ وَشَيۡءٖ مِّن سِدۡرٖ قَلِيلٖ ١٦
ذَٰلِكَ جَزَيۡنَٰهُم بِمَا كَفَرُواْۖ وَهَلۡ نُجَٰزِيٓ إِلَّا ٱلۡكَفُورَ ١٧﴾

TRANSLITERATION

15. Laqad kana lisaba-in fee maskanihim ayah, jannatani 'an yameeniw-washimal, kuloo mir-rizqi rabbikum washkuroo lah, baldatun tayyibatuw-warabbun ghafoor
16. Fa'aradoo fa'arsalna 'alayhim sayl-al-'arimi wabaddal-nahum bijannatayhim jannatayni thawatay okulin khamtiw-wa'athliw-washay-in min sidrin qaleel
17. Thalika jazaynahum bima kafaroo wahal nujazee illal-kafoor

UNDERSTOOD MEANING

[34:15] Certainly there was a sign for Saba' in their homeland; two gardens on the right and the left; eat of the gifts of your Lord and give thanks to Him: a good land and a Forgiving Lord!
[34:16] But they disobeyed, so We sent upon them a flood, and in place of their two gardens We gave to them two gardens producing bitter fruit and (growing) tamarind and a few lote-trees.
[34:17] This is how We rewarded them because they disbelieved; and We only punish the ungrateful.

Chapter Review

Healthy Habits

1. Always remember that Allah سبحانه وتعالى is the One who has given you everything in your life.
2. Always have a thankful heart toward Allah.
3. Always say Alhamdullilah for the good and bad things in your life. If you suffer bad days, remember the many more good days Allah has given you.
4. Do not look at those who have more than you, but look at those who have less than you.

Make a chart of the many things that Allah سبحانه وتعالى has blessed you with. Then make an effort to thank Allah for all the blessings in your life.

1. How many times in a day do we say the word Alhamdullilah?
2. How can we thank Allah سبحانه وتعالى by our hearts?
3. How can we thank Allah سبحانه وتعالى by our tongues?
4. Say one du'aa' for thanking Allah.
5. Name three other ways that we can thank Allah for the blessings He has provided us with. Give an example for each one.
6. Why did Allah سبحانه وتعالى take away the wealth of the people of Saba'?

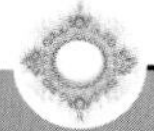

Sujood-ush-Shukr

CHAPTER SEVEN

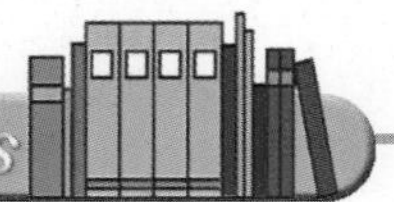

Pre-reading Questions

1. How important is it to appreciate Allah's Gifts?
2. What should we do when something good happens to us?
3. What is Sujood-us-Shukr?

Word Watch

sujood-ush-Shukr سُجود الشكر

There are certain types of sujood that are done outside of regular prayer. One of them is **sujood-ush-shukr** سُجود الشكر . Lets learn together what it is.

One day Bilal and Sarah came home and found their mother very worried. She did not even smile at them as she usually does.

Bilal: What is wrong Mom? Why you are so sad?

Mother: Don't worry about me, let me fix you your meal.

Sarah: Please Mom, tell us what is happening.

Mother: All right, I will let you

know after you eat your meal.

Bilal: Okay, Mom, if you insist.

Bilal and Sarah ate their food, washed and brushed their teeth, and then ran to their mother.

Sarah: Tell us now, Mom.

Mother: Your father called me a while ago, and he told me that the company he is working for is losing money. They might lay off a number of employees, including your father.

Bilal: So, Dad might loss his job?

Mother: I hope not.

Sarah: That is sad, I pray to Allah to help the company so no one will be laid off.

All: Ameen.

Bilal: Boy, this sounds scary. I never worried about that before. If this happens, Allah forbid, we will be poor.

Sarah: We won't be able to buy the things we like!

Bilal: ...and we won't be able to go on vacations.

Mother: Stop saying that. Just make du'aa', and ask Allah to let your father keep his job.

Sarah and Bilal continued making du'aa' for their father. In the evening, their father came home and everyone in the house came running around him.

Bilal: What happened Dad?

Sarah: Tell us, Dad!

Father: I don't know yet. We will know by tomorrow, insha'Allah. Don't worry. We will accept whatever Allah chooses for us. He will take care of us, insha'Allah.

Mother: May Allah ﷻ help us. I am going to fix your dinner.

Father: I want to pray Salat Al-Asr now.

The family spent the evening thinking and talking about the problem. In the morning, everybody prayed Fajr. Bilal and his father prayed Fajr in the masjid. Sarah and her mom prayed Fajr together at home. They all made du'aa and asked Allah ﷻ to keep dad on his job. Mr. Mahmood went to work, while Sarah and Bilal went to school.

After school, Bilal and Sarah ran home. The moment they got into their house they asked their mother about their father. Their mom said that Mr. Mahmood told her that he didn't learn anything new yet. After

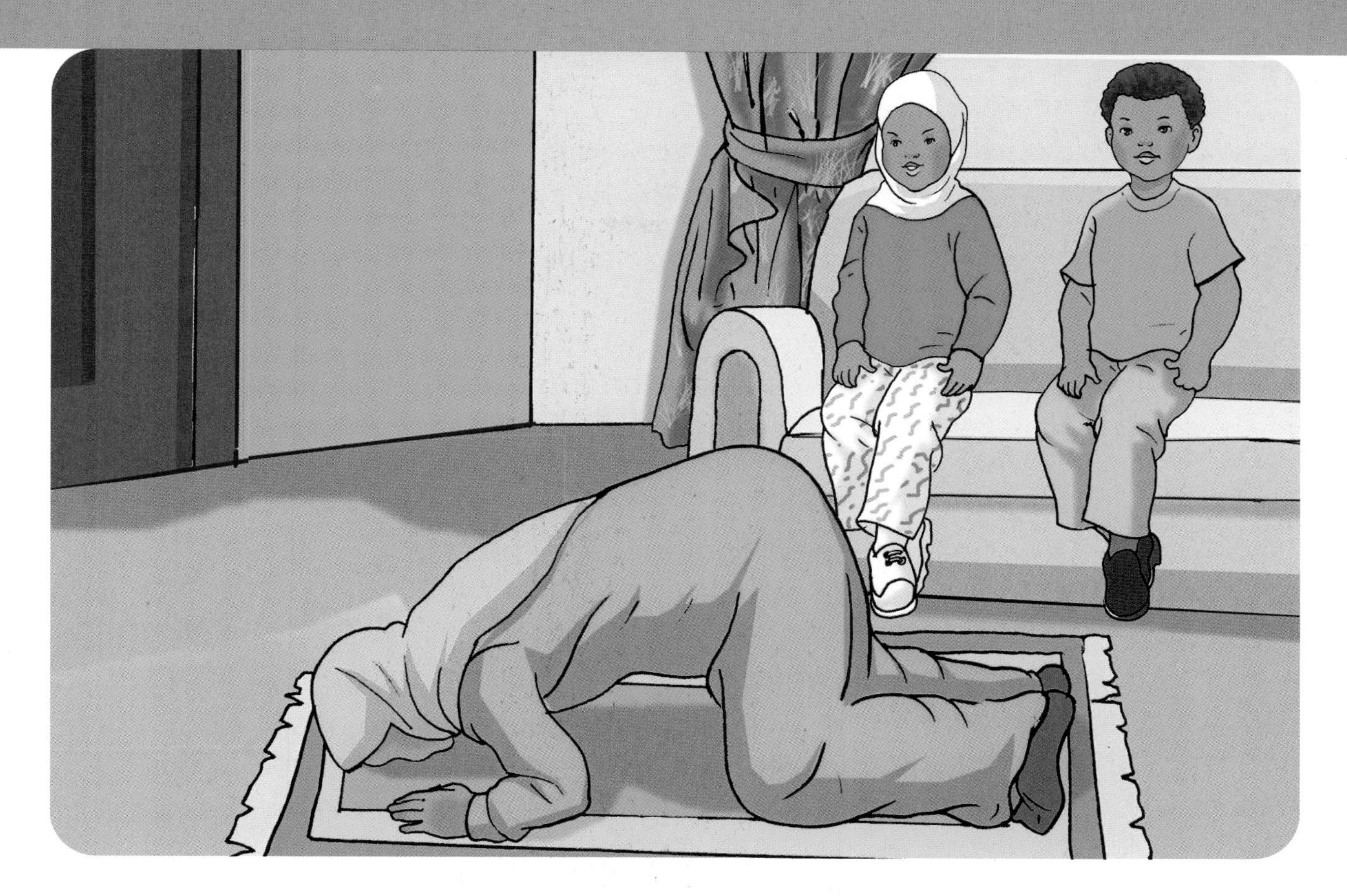

a while the phone rang. Mrs. Mahmood answered. Her husband was the caller. Bilal and Sarah listened impatiently.

"Alhamdulillah, congratulations. We will be waiting for you," Mama said happily.

Bilal and Sarah started jumping and laughing. They knew that their father had not lost his job. Mama told them the good news about their father's job. She told them that the company changed their plans and did not fire anyone. Then mama went on and made sujood. Bilal and Sarah looked at each other. Mama took a while in sujood, and then she raised her head.

Bilal: What did you do, Mama?

Mama: I made Sujood-ush-Shukr.

Sarah: What is that?

Mama: The Prophet ﷺ used to make sujood-ush-Shukr whenever something good happened to him. This is one way to thank Allah for His favors. Alhamdulillah, Allah kept your dad's job, so I wanted to thank Him by making sujood-ush-Shukr.

Thanking Allah for His Blessings

Think about the times that you are very happy:

- Grandparents coming to visit
- Getting a good grade on a test
- Fasting the whole month of Ramadan
- Day of Eid
- Going to a nice place for a vacation
- Getting a new baby sister or brother
- First day of school

For all these occasions in which you were happy, did you ever stop and think about the source of your happiness? Yes, seeing your grandparents, getting a good grade, and enjoying Eid. are reasons for you to be happy. However, who permitted these occasions to happen? Who is the One Who made all these things happen? Allah ﷻ is the source of all happiness. Everything that is good in our lives comes from Allah ﷻ . How can we thank Allah for the good in our lives? One way is to do sujood-ush-Shukur, which is what the Prophet ﷺ used to do.

How to Perform Sujood-ush-Shukr

Go into sujood-ush-Shukr without saying AllahuAkbar. Say “subhana rabiy-al-'ala” like you would say during regular sujood. You can also thank Allah ﷻ and praise Him for the favors He gave to you. When you finish, you raise your head, and no tasleem is needed. You do not need wudu to perform Sujood-ush-Shukr, but it is better to do it with wudu.

Holy Qur'an

﴿ وَإِذْ تَأَذَّنَ رَبُّكُمْ لَئِن شَكَرْتُمْ لَأَزِيدَنَّكُمْ وَلَئِن كَفَرْتُمْ إِنَّ عَذَابِي لَشَدِيدٌ ﴾

And remember! Your Lord declared (publicly), "If you are grateful, I will grant you more (gifts and favors); but if you show ingratitude, truly My punishment is terrible indeed." [14:7]

Hadeeth Shareef

عن أبي بكرة الأسلمي رضي الله عنه أن النبي ﷺ "كان إذا أتاه أمرٌ يسُرُّهُ أو بُشِّرَ بِهِ خَرَّ ساجداً للهِ تباركَ وتعالي"

رواه ابن ماجه وأبو داود والترمذي

Abu Bakrah Al-Aslamiy narrated that when something good happened to the Prophet ﷺ, or when he received good news, he would make sujood, thanking Allah for it.

(Reported by Ibn Majah, Abu Dawood and At-Tirmithi)

Healthy Habit

Always do sujood-ush-Shukr whenever something good happens to you or to the Muslims.

Did You Know

When Allah helped Prophet Muhammad win over the kuffar of Makkah in the 8th year after Al-Hijrah, he entered Makkah riding on his camel. Rasulullah did not brag or make a victory yell. Instead, he performed sujood-ush-Shukr on the back of his camel.

STORYTIME

Once a servant of Allah ﷾ was making du'aa' thanking Allah ﷾ for His endless gifts. He said:

" يا رَبِّ لكَ الحَمْدُ كما يَنْبَغي لِجَلال وَجْهِكَ وعَظيم سُلْطانِك"

Ya Rabbi lak-al-Hamdu kama yanbaghee lijalali wajhika wa atheemi sultanik

"O my Lord, I praise You as your majestic face and grand power should be praised."

The angels became confused. They never heard anyone praise Allah ﷾ this way before. Therefore, they did not know how many hasanat this servant of Allah should get. His praise of Allah ﷾ was so great and open ended. Therefore, they went up to the Heavens and asked Allah how they should record these hasanat. Allah ﷾ then ordered the angels to write the praise of that servant exactly as he said it. Allah ﷾ promised to reward the man very generously when he meets him on the Day of Judgment.

(This is a Hadeeth narrated by Ibn Omar and reported in Ibn Majah)

Chapter Review

Practice sujood-ush-Shukr with your classmates.

How does being a thankful person make you a better person?

1. What is sujood-ush-Shukr?
2. How do you perform it?
3. When do we perform it? List some reasons.
4. Is wudu required for sujood-ush-Shukr?
5. Write a du'aa you like in which you thank and praise Allah سبحانه وتعالى for His gifts.

ISLAMIC CHARACTER

Forgiveness

CHAPTER ONE

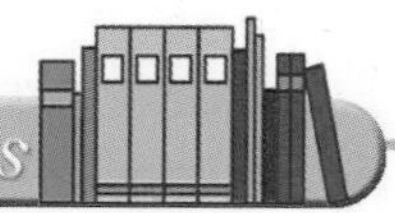

Pre-reading Questions

1. Does everyone make mistakes?
2. How should we behave when others hurt our feelings?
3. Who is the really strong person?

Those who forgive are good people. God loves those who are good.

The Holy Qur'an

There is no revenge as complete as forgiveness.

Josh Billings

Turn to forgiveness and enjoin good, and turn aside from the ignorant.

The Holy Qur'an

Everyone Makes Mistakes

Sometimes people wrong others, and this happens to everybody. At times they are small offenses that are easy to forgive. Sometimes people make bigger mistakes that are hard to forgive but you still forgive them. Other times, some mistakes seem too big to be forgiven. It isn't always easy to forgive someone who has wrongfully harmed us. In fact, it is very hard for us, sometimes, to forgive. This is probably because of our anger and pride. We may decide to seek revenge and attack back. The problem here is that our reaction to the mistakes of others can be bad and not Islamic. When you forgive, you avoid unIslamic reactions and behavior. You also show a very important Islamic characteristic: patience.

Before you let Shaytan destroy your relations with others, think harder. Ask yourself the following questions:

- Isn't the person who hurt you a human being?
- Isn't it a fact that humans do good things, but they also make mistakes sometimes as well?
- Aren't you the same?
- Don't you like people to forgive you when you commit offenses against them?
- Don't you like them to remember that you were good to them many more times in the past?

The right answer to these questions, in most cases, is YES. Listen to Ibn Rajab, a great Muslim scholar:

> "No one is free of mistakes, therefore, the fair person forgives the few mistakes of a person because of the many other good things he has done did in the past."

Look at the following table. Suppose Amir is one of your friends, and he called you a name today and hurt your feelings. Should you end your relationship with him just because of that? Of course you talk to him about his mistake, but you continue to take him as your brother in Islam. You should look at the good things he does and the favors he did for you in the past. You will figure out that he did far more good things than bad deeds. Then you forgive him and keep his friendship. Also, there might have been a time before when you wronged him and he forgave you.

The Balance Table

	Amir's Mistakes		Amir's Good Deeds
1	Called me a name today	1	Prays regularly
2		2	Fasts Ramadan
3		3	Generally, he is good to me
4		4	Helps me in math
5		5	Brought me a gift last month

Healthy Habit

Always be balanced in evaluating other people. When they make mistakes, remember their good deeds, too.

Control your Anger: This Makes You Stronger

Forgiving someone doesn't mean you can't fight back, it just means you don't want to fight back. We should forgive anyone who hurt us by mistake, even when we have the power to take revenge. By avoiding anger you are also avoiding conflict.

Holy Qur'an

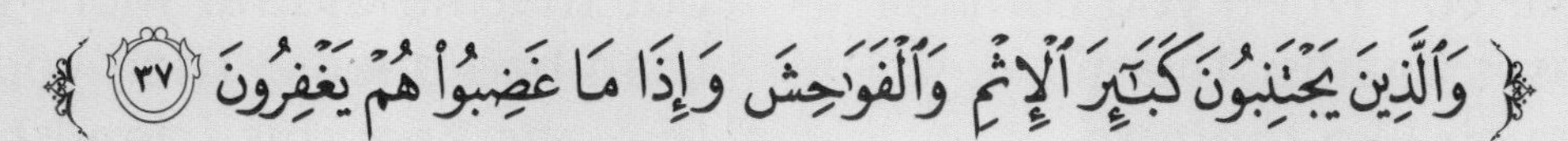

(Allah is pleased with) those who avoid great sins and shameful acts, and even while they are angry they forgive. [42:37]

Hadeeth Shareef

عن أبي هريرة رضي الله عنه قال : قال رسول الله ﷺ:

" ليسَ الشَّديدُ بالصُّرَعَة، إنما الشَّديدُ الذي يملِكُ نفسه عِندَ الغضَب "

رواه البخاري ومسلم

Abu Hurayrah narrated that Rasulullah ﷺ said:

"The powerful one is not the one who bullies others. Rather, the truly powerful one is he who can control himself while angry."

(Reported by Al-Bukhari and Muslim)

Healthy
Habit

Always control your anger!

Be a Forgiver: it Makes You a Winner

The real success is when you win Allah's pleasure and His rewards. Forgiving others enables you to do that.

If two Muslim brothers or sisters quarrel, they both have up to three days to forgive each other and resume their normal relations. The one who forgives first and greets the other will gain the greater reward from Allah ﷻ . Forgiving each other, even forgiving one's enemies, is one of the most important Islamic virtues. In the Qur'an, Allah ﷻ told the believers to return the bad treatment of others with treatment which is superior.

WORDS OF WISDOM

Holy Qur'an

سورة فصلت

Surat Fussilat 34-36

بِسْمِ ٱللَّهِ ٱلرَّحْمَٰنِ ٱلرَّحِيمِ

﴿ وَلَا تَسْتَوِى ٱلْحَسَنَةُ وَلَا ٱلسَّيِّئَةُ ۚ ٱدْفَعْ بِٱلَّتِى هِىَ أَحْسَنُ فَإِذَا ٱلَّذِى بَيْنَكَ وَبَيْنَهُۥ
عَدَٰوَةٌ كَأَنَّهُۥ وَلِىٌّ حَمِيمٌ ﴿٣٤﴾ وَمَا يُلَقَّىٰهَآ إِلَّا ٱلَّذِينَ صَبَرُوا۟ وَمَا يُلَقَّىٰهَآ إِلَّا ذُو
حَظٍّ عَظِيمٍ ﴿٣٥﴾ وَإِمَّا يَنزَغَنَّكَ مِنَ ٱلشَّيْطَٰنِ نَزْغٌ فَٱسْتَعِذْ بِٱللَّهِ ۖ إِنَّهُۥ هُوَ ٱلسَّمِيعُ
ٱلْعَلِيمُ ﴿٣٦﴾ ﴾

TRANSLITERATION

34. Wala tastawil-hasanatu walas-sayyi-atu idfa' billatee hiya ahsan, fa-ithallathee baynaka wabaynahu 'adawatun kaannahu waliyyun h ameem
35. Wama yulaqqaha illallatheena sabaroo wama yulaqqaha illa thoo haththin 'ath eem
36. Wa-imma yanzaghannaka min-ash-shaytani nazghun fasta'ith billahi innahu huwassamee'ul-aleem

UNDERSTOOD MEANING

[41:34] The good and the evil are not alike. Push evil away with the best manners. Then your enemy will become like your close friend.
[41:35] And none will acquire this great character-trait except those who are patient and those who are greatly blessed (by Allah).
[41:36] And if the whispers of Shaytan should cause you to do evil, seek refuge in Allah; surely He is the All Hearing, the All Knowing.

Hadeeth Shareef

عن أنس بن مالك رضي الله عنه قال: قال رسول الله ﷺ :
لا تباغضوا ولا تحاسدوا ولا تدابروا وكونوا عباد الله إخوانا، ولا يحلّ
لمسلم أن يهجر أخاه فوق ثلاث ليال ... وخيرهما الذي يبدأ بالسلام ”

رواه البخاري ومسلم

Anas Ibn Malik narrated that Rasoolullah ﷺ said:

"Do not hate each other, do not be jealous of each other and do not abandon each other. O servants of Allah, be as brothers. It is forbidden that a Muslim should abandon his brother for more than three days, and the better of them is he who repairs their relationship and greets the other first."

(Reported by Al-Bukhari and Muslim)

Rasulullah ﷺ Was a Great Forgiver

Forgiveness is a quality that Prophet Muhammad ﷺ demonstrated throughout his life. A great example of his forgiveness is his journey to the people of At-Ta'if. Prophet Muhammad ﷺ went to At-Ta'if to teach Islam. The people of At-Ta'if refused to accept Islam. But still, the people of At-Ta'if would not leave him alone. They made their children and slaves throw stones at him, and they continued to do that for three miles. His body was covered with wounds. Allah sent the Angel Jibreel to ask Prophet Muhammad if he wanted Allah to crush the people of At-Ta'if in between two mountains there. Prophet Muhammad ﷺ refused, and instead he asked Allah to forgive them with the hope that the next generation to grow up at At-Ta'if would accept Islam. Fifteen years later, the people of At-Ta'if became Muslims, exactly as Rasulullah had hoped. The kind forgiveness of Allah and His Prophet worked.

Forgiveness is a wonderful way of exercising patience. Forgiving someone lets you avoid unIslamic reactions and behavior such as anger, cursing, and backbiting. Forgiveness lets us avoid conflict while teaching us responsibility. At the same time, we are obeying Allah's order and following the example of Prophet Muhammad ﷺ.

Allah Loves to Forgive

DU'AA

دعــــــــاء

عن عائشة رضي الله عنها: قال رسول الله صلّى الله عليه وسـلم قولي :

" اللهم إنّك عفوٌّ تحب العفو فاعفُ عني "

رواه أحمـــد

Ai'sha reported that Rasulullah taught her a du'aa to say in Laylat-ul Qadr. It says:

"Oh Allah, you are the most forgiving One: You love to forgive, so forgive me."

Allah ﷻ is the most forgiving. His forgiveness overtakes His punishment and anger. We can see the importance of forgiveness through Asmaa' Allah Al-Husna (the Beautiful Names of Allah). Many of His names are related to His great forgiveness.

During every prayer we recite

بسم الله الرحمن الرحيم

Bismillah-ir-Rahman-ir-Rahim

"The Forgiving." This name is mentioned more than 70 times in the Holy Qur'an.

"The Most Beneficent." This name is mentioned 115 times, making it the name most often repeated in the Holy Qur'an.

"The Most Merciful." This name is mentioned 57 times in the Holy Qur'an.

Is Any Crime Too Big to Be Forgiven?

A person committed 99 murders. He went to a scholar and said to him, "I have committed 99 murders. Is there any chance of being forgiven?" The scholar replied, "Of course not." The man got angry and killed the scholar. However, his heart was restless and he went to another scholar. He said, "I have committed 100 murders. Is there a chance of being forgiven?" The scholar replied, "Yes, it is possible. Go to the next town and be in the company of good people." So the man set out to the town of good people, but he died during the journey. A person passing by saw two angels arguing over his body. The angel from Hell said, "His body belongs to me, as he has not done any good in his life." The angel from Heaven said, "His body belongs to me for he had repented and was on his way to be with the good people." The passer-by suggested measuring the distance of the man's body from both the town he left and the town of the good people. This was done. The man was found to be closer to the town of good people, and for that reason the man was admitted into Heaven.

Healthy Habit

Try always to forgive people who wronged you.

Why?

1. Allah ﷻ orders us to!
2. It's following the example of Prophet Muhammad ﷺ !
3. It allows us to keeps friendships!
4. It keeps anger from growing inside us!
5. It prevents larger conflicts!

Story Time

Bilal came home angry. He rushed to his room and jumped on his bed crying. His mom went to see what was wrong.

Mom: Honey, what is wrong, why are you crying?
Bilal: Nothing!
Mom: Oh, don't say that. You are crying. Something must have gone wrong.
Bilal: Amir!
Mom: What is wrong with him?
Bilal: He said a very bad thing to me. He called me bad names!
Mom: Oh, that is too bad. Why did he do that?
Bilal: I don't know!
Mom: Did you do anything bad to him?
Bilal: No, I just didn't play ping pong with him at school. I played with Zaid instead.
Mom: Oh, now I understand. Amir got jealous, then became angry at you. He could not control his anger, so he did this awful thing. A'oothu billihi mina-Shaytani-Rajeem.
Bilal: I will never speak to him again!
Mom: Bilal, do not make Shaytan laugh at you.
Bilal: How is that?
Mom: Shaytan always tries his best to make Muslims fight and hate each other.
Bilal: But he hurt me so badly. The other boys laughed at me, too.
Mom: I understand he made a bad

mistake. He was in a weak moment so Shaytan could make him fall in his trap. Let me tell you a good story about Bilal ibn Rabah (Radi-Allahu-anhu). Bilal ibn Rabah and Abu Tharr Al-Ghifari were friends. Both of them were great companions of Rasulullah. One day Abu Tharr got angry with Bilal, so he said to Bilal in an insulting way, "You are just a son of a black woman."

Bilal: Really, did he say that?

Mom: Yes, unfortunately.

Bilal: What did Bilal Radi-Allahu-anhu do?

Mom: He went to the Rasulullah and complained.

Bilal: What did Rasulullah do?

Mom: He called Abu Tharr Al-Ghifari and asked him, "Bilal told me you called him a name. Did you do that?" Abu Tharr did not lie. He said, " Yes, Rasulullah I did." The Prophet then told Abu Tharr that Muslims do not do what he just did. Only ignorant and racist people say those kind of things. Rasulullah said, "Abu Tharr you still have some pagan manners." Abu Tharr was very sorry at that point. He lay on the floor of the masjid and called on Bilal to put his foot on his face in retribution.

Bilal: Really? Why did he do that?

Mom: He wanted to purify his heart and teach himself a lesson. He did not want to act like the racists and disbelievers.

Bilal: What did Bilal (Radi-Allahu Anhu) do?

Mom: What do you think he did? What would you do if you were in his place?

Bilal: Tough question, Mom! But I wouldn't step on my Muslim brother's face.

Mom: Good boy! Bilal refused to do that and immediately forgave Abu Tharr Al-Ghifari.

Bilal: Oh! Great manners! Bilal is my hero. I'm proud that my name is Bilal. Thank you for giving me this name.

DU'AA

دعـــــاء

" اللهم اغفرلي ولأخي / أختي "

Allahumma Igfir Li Wa Li-Akhi / Okhti

"O My Lord, forgive me and my brother (sister)."

Chapter Review

Write a play with your classmates the subject of this lesson, and act it out in class.

Why do you think Shaytan always pushes us to have fights with others?

1. What should be your first reaction when someone hurts your feelings?
2. Why does it make you stronger when someone wrongs you?
3. What did Allah tell us to do to those who wrong us?
4. Quote a Hadeeth of the Prophet that tells us what to do when we experience problems with our Muslim brothers and sisters.
5. List three things we should do when we have a problem with our friends.
6. List three things we must not do when we have a problem with our friends.

Respect: A Pillar of Good Muslim Character

CHAPTER TWO

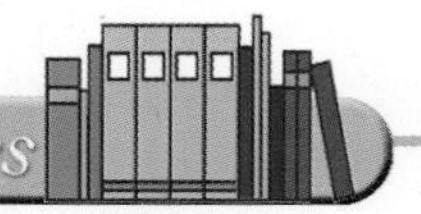

1. What does respect mean?
2. Whom should we respect?

Word Watch

ihtiram (Respect) إحترام

How Do You Like Others to Treat You?

Everyone likes others to give him or her special regard and attention. This is exactly the meaning of respect. Respect shows that you care about people's feelings and well being.

No one likes to receive impolite or disrespectful treatment from others. It is especially bad when older and recognized people are disrespected by those who are younger than they are.

In this chapter, you will learn about the importance of respecting humanity, parents, teachers, elders, oneself, others, and the environment around us.

UNIT E CHAPTER 2 LESSON ONE

Respecting Humanity

Pre-reading Questions

1. Who created human beings?
2. How does the Creator treat human beings?
3. How should we respect humanity?

Word Watch

taqwa (piety) تقوى

Human beings come in different shapes, colors and sizes. Your friend may look completely different from you, but you are more alike than you think. How could this be? Although we might look very different in our outward appearances, every human being in this world is the creation of Allah سبحانه وتعالى . Allah does not set apart anyone because of the color of their skin or where they are from. Allah tells us in the Qur'an that He does not differentiate between people except according to "taqwa."

Holy Qur'an

﴿ يَا أَيُّهَا النَّاسُ إِنَّا خَلَقْنَاكُم مِّن ذَكَرٍ وَأُنثَىٰ وَجَعَلْنَاكُمْ شُعُوبًا وَقَبَائِلَ لِتَعَارَفُوا إِنَّ أَكْرَمَكُمْ عِندَ اللَّهِ أَتْقَاكُمْ إِنَّ اللَّهَ عَلِيمٌ خَبِيرٌ ﴾

"O mankind! We created You from a single (pair) of a male and a female, and made you into nations and tribes, that you may know each other (Not that you may despise each other). Verily the most honored among you in the sight of Allah is (he who is) the most righteous among you." [49:13]

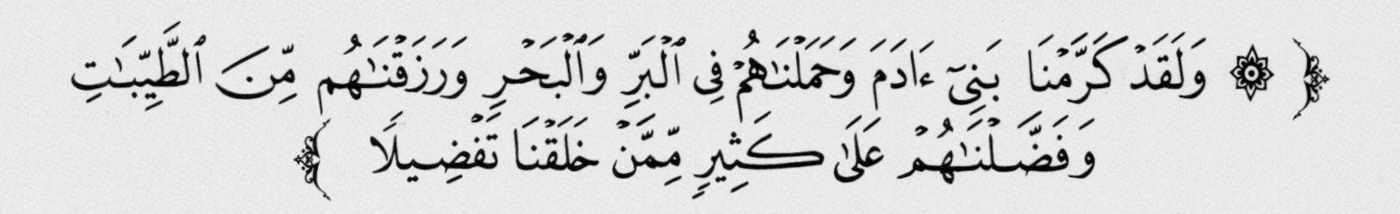
﴿ وَلَقَدْ كَرَّمْنَا بَنِي آدَمَ وَحَمَلْنَاهُمْ فِي الْبَرِّ وَالْبَحْرِ وَرَزَقْنَاهُم مِّنَ الطَّيِّبَاتِ وَفَضَّلْنَاهُمْ عَلَىٰ كَثِيرٍ مِّمَّنْ خَلَقْنَا تَفْضِيلًا ﴾

"We have indeed honored the Children of Adam, and provided for them means of transportation on land and sea, and given them wholesome food and favored them over the greater part of Our creation." [17:70]

This shows that Allah ﷻ blessed and honored humans and made them His best and most favored creation. All humans share these blessings of Allah and the high place He gave them on Earth.

Whether some people are black or white, males or females, Muslim, Jewish, or Christian, all are children of Adam. Therefore, they are all human beings and deserve to be respected for their humanity.

Respecting and loving Allah ﷻ means that one has to appreciate His creation. Since human beings are Allah's creation, like everything else in this world, we have to respect His creation. In the eyes of Islam all human beings are equal and deserve respect.

A great example of respect towards humanity is shown by the Prophet Muhammad ﷺ. Rasulullah and a group of the sahabah were sitting somewhere in Madinah. Suddenly, a funeral of a Jewish man passed by. The Prophet ﷺ immediately stood up and showed respect for the dead person. One of the sahabah asked the Prophet ﷺ why he stood for the funeral of a Jewish person. The Prophet then answered, "Well, he is a human being."

You might ask, "What if a person or a group of people disbelieve in Allah ﷻ and do evil things. Should we still respect them?" The answer to this question can be found in the following short story.

STORYTIME

A Jewish man who hated the Prophet ﷺ used to throw stones at him and say bad words to him. The Prophet ﷺ was very patient towards the Jewish man. After some time the Prophet noticed the absence of the Jewish man. He did not come out of his house for many days. The Prophet ﷺ then got worried and went to ask about the man. He found out the man was sick and in bad condition. Out of kindness and respect, the Prophet ﷺ went to visit the Jewish man. After the visit, the Jewish man became humbled and embarrassed by the kindness of the Prophet ﷺ and embraced Islam.

Chapter Review

The 99 Names of Allah

Allah is **المُحيي Al-Muhyee: The Giver of Life**

Allah ﷻ gave life to all humanity.

Healthy Habit

Always respect other humans, regardless of their color, culture, religion, or gender. If they mistreat you, show them your good behavior. This often makes them respect you and correct their behavior.

1. What is respect?
2. Why do we need to respect other human beings?
3. Which of Allah's creations is held above the rest?
4. What does the story of the Prophet and the Jewish man teach us?

UNIT E CHAPTER 2 LESSON TWO

Respecting Parents

Pre-reading Questions

1. Whom should you respect most among the people around you?
2. How should we respect our parents?
3. What are the things that we should avoid with our parents?

Respect for Parents

In Islam, every day is Mother's and Father's Day. We should love, respect, and appreciate our parents every day throughout the year. Parents have the right to demand respect. They deserve respect and appreciation from their children. Parents are very important to us and we must treat them with great respect and admiration. We must listen to them with great respect, talk to them with great respect, look at them with great respect, and touch them with great respect. It is not enough to love your parents; you must highly respect, admire, and be very humble toward them. The Qur'an says:

Holy Qur'an

﴿ وَقَضَىٰ رَبُّكَ أَلَّا تَعْبُدُوٓا۟ إِلَّآ إِيَّاهُ وَبِٱلْوَٰلِدَيْنِ إِحْسَٰنًا ۚ إِمَّا يَبْلُغَنَّ عِندَكَ ٱلْكِبَرَ
أَحَدُهُمَآ أَوْ كِلَاهُمَا فَلَا تَقُل لَّهُمَآ أُفٍّ وَلَا تَنْهَرْهُمَا وَقُل لَّهُمَا قَوْلًا كَرِيمًا ﴿٢٣﴾
وَٱخْفِضْ لَهُمَا جَنَاحَ ٱلذُّلِّ مِنَ ٱلرَّحْمَةِ وَقُل رَّبِّ ٱرْحَمْهُمَا كَمَا رَبَّيَانِى صَغِيرًا ﴾

"Your Lord has commanded that you worship none except Him, and (that you show) kindness to parents. If one of them or both of them attain old age with you, do not say "Uff" to them nor repulse them, but speak kindly to them and be humble to them through mercy and say: My Lord! Have mercy on them both as they cared for me when I was young." [17:23 - 24] Surat Al-'israa'

Appreciation and respect for parents is mentioned in the Qur'an 11 times. In every example, Allah reminds children to appreciate the care and love they received from their parents. Allah سبحانه وتعالى gets angry at us for just showing the slightest signs of impatience or anger with our parents. Imagine how angry Allah would be if we did worse than that. Allah dislikes it when children raise their voices to their parents, or disobey them.

STORYTIME

Abdullah ibn Awn was a great Tabe'i, or student of the Sahabah. Once his mother called him from the other room, so he answered her with a low voice out of respect. His mother did not hear him well, so she called him again. Abdullah now raised his voice to make her hear him better. After doing that, Abdullah felt bad because he did not like to raise his voice over the voice of his mother. He thought that he had comitted a sin. So he offered a big sadaqah to wipe out his mistake.

Parents Sacrifice a Lot When Raising Their Children

Parents go through a lot of trouble to care for and raise their children from the time they are born until they become adults. And despite all of the hard work, parents still love and protect their children. No matter how kind or obedient a child may be, he can never truly repay his parents for their love and patience. Abdullah ibn Umar, a leading scholar among the Prophet's companions, once saw a man from Yemen carrying his mother on his back and going around Al-Ka'bah in his tawaf during Hajj. Rather than complaining, the man was happy. The man looked at Abdullah Ibn Omar and asked him whether by doing this he had paid back his debt to his mother. Ibn Omar said, "No. You have not even paid back one twinge of her labor pain when she gave birth to you."

Respecting Mothers

We should show respect to both our fathers and mothers. But mothers are given a special type of kindness and respect in Islam. Mothers experience a lot of pain and hardship during pregnancy and the delivery of their children. And as the child grows up, it is the mother who spends most of her time caring for him or her.

STORYTIME

It was narrated by Abu Hurrayrah that a man came to the Prophet ﷺ and asked him, “Who is most deserving of my good friendship?" The Prophet ﷺ answered, "Your mother."
The man asked again, "Then who?" "Your mother," the Prophet ﷺ replied.
The man asked again, "Then who?" "Your mother," the Prophet ﷺ replied for the third time.
The man asked again, "Then who?" "Then your father, then the closest to you in kinship, and then others," Rasulullah replied for the fourth and last time.

Role Play

Khalid: Baba, can I go to Isma'eel's house to play with his new game?
Baba: Hamzah, today we have plans to visit Uncle Ahmad.
Khalid: But, Baba, Isma'eel got this really, really cool game.
Baba: You can go tomorrow after school, insha'Allah.
Khalid: [sounding impatient and mad] No, I want to go today. I can't wait until tomorrow.
Baba: Hamzah, when I tell you something you should listen and understand. I know you want to go play the game, but today is not a good day.

Khalid: I am sorry Baba. It's just that I really can't wait to play the game. But inshaAllah I can go tomorrow.

The 99 Names of Allah

Allah is البَـــر Al-Bar: The Giver of Compassion

Allah ﷻ gives all people His love and compassion

Hadeeth Shareef

قال رسول الله ﷺ:

" أطِعْ أبـَــــاك "

Rasulullah ﷺ said:

"Obey your father."

Healthy Habits

To show respect and kindness to parents, always practice the following habits:

- Listen to them in an obedient and patient manner.
- Speak to them in a soft and respectful voice.
- Obey them when they tell you to do something, as long as it is not haram or against Islam.
- Show your love to them through kind actions and words.
- Help them around the house by washing dishes, vacuuming, and doing other chores.
- Make du'aa for them whether they are alive or dead.
- Help your mother in the house and carry grocery bags for her during shopping.

Make a list of the things that your parents do at home to make your life comfortable. You will discover that they are doing a lot of things without your help. Then, pick three items out of the list that you feel you can help your parents do on a continuous basis.

Discuss the difference between the life of a boy who is kind to his parents and another who is disobedient and impolite with them. Who is happier in life, and why?

1. Why should every day be Mother's and Father's Day?
2. Why is it important to respect parents?
3. What is the hadeeth about being close to our mothers?
4. The hadeeth in the lesson says that we should have a close friendship with our mothers? Why is this the case?

UNIT E
CHAPTER 2
LESSON THREE

Respecting Teachers

Pre-reading Questions

1. How important are our teachers? Why?
2. Who was the best teacher for all Muslims?
3. What do our teachers do for us?
4. How should we treat our teachers?

If you can read this, thank a teacher.

Anonymous

Word Watch

Mu'allim (Teacher)	معلم
Mu'allimoon (Teachers)	معلمون
Mu'allima	معلمة
Mu'allimat	معلمات

Can you remember your first grade teacher? Most people can never forget the names and the faces of their teachers. That is because teachers are very important in our lives. They teach us how to read, write, and become better people.

Do you remember who was the first person to teach you Surat Al-Fatihah? Imagine the number of times that you recite Al-Fatihah in a day. Every time you recite Al-Fatihah, that teacher will get hasanat.

Teachers love teaching their students, and they are happy when their students succeed in life. Teachers deserve a lot of respect, appreciation, and love from their students.

Early Muslim teachers and scholars used to travel on their camels for months through the deserts and mountains to learn Qur'an, hadeeth, math and science from their teachers. They used to offer their teachers all the respect and admiration they deserved.

The companions of the Prophet ﷺ are our best examples of great, respectful students. They all loved their great teacher, Rasulullah, and they loved to learn from him all the time. They used to listen to him carefully and obey his orders. They learned by heart most of what he taught them. They implemented his advice and recommenda-tions without delay. They used to refrain from talking in his presence without his permission. When they were permitted to talk, they spoke softly and never raised their voice above the voice of rasulullah. When they wanted to leave, they asked his permission first. They were truly respectful students.

Imam Abu Haneefah used to avoid extending his feet in the direction of his teacher's house. Muslim khaleefahs used to instruct their children to be humble and obedient to their teachers.

Did You Know?

After your parents, your teachers do the most to teach you and help you grow. Shaytan tries his best to make us dislike our teachers so we will not learn very well.

Hadeeth Shareef

عن أبي أمامة الباهلي رضي الله عنه قال: قال رسول الله ﷺ :
"إنَّ الله وملائكتَهُ وأهلُ السماواتِ والأرْضِين حتّى النمْلة في جُحرِها وحتى الحوتَ لَيُصلّون على معلّم الناس الخَيْر" رواه الترمذي

Abu Umamah Al-Bahuli narrated that Rasulullah ﷺ said:

"Allah, His angels, those in Heavens and on Earth, even the ant in its nest and the fish, [all of these] pray for the one who teaches people what is good."
(Reported by At-Tirmithi)

Healthy Habits

1. Greet your teachers with "Assalamu Alaykum" whenever you see them.
2. In class, you should raise your hand before you talk.
3. When the teacher is teaching, do not interrupt.
4. Do the work that your teacher assigns you.

WHY GOD CREATED TEACHERS.

When God created teachers,
He gave us special friends
To help us understand His world
And truly comprehend
The beauty and the wonder
Of everything we see,
And become a better person
With each discovery.
When God created teachers,
He gave us special guides
To show us ways in which to grow
So we can all decide
How to live and how to do
What's right instead of wrong,
To lead us so that we can lead
And learn how to be strong.
Why God created teachers,
In His wisdom and His grace,
Was to help us learn to make our world
A better, wiser place.

Author: Unknown

Chapter Review

- Write a paragraph about how much you appreciate your teacher.
- Make a nice card for your teachers to show how much you appreciate them.
- One of your classmates makes fun of his teacher and is disrespectful to her. Discuss or write what you would do.

1. Why are teachers very important in every society?
2. How should we give our respect to teachers?
3. What did the Prophet ﷺ say about teachers?

UNIT E CHAPTER 2

LESSON FOUR

Respecting Elders

Pre-reading Questions

1. How should we treat our elders?

Imagine that you are sitting down in a chair waiting to get into the doctor's office and an older lady enters the room. There are no seats available for her to sit on. Would you pretend that you did not see her walk in or would you get up and offer her your chair? A good person would get up from the chair and invite the old lady to sit down. Respecting elders in Islam is very important because elderly people have a lot of knowledge and wisdom. They have lived for a long time and learned many many things.

Have you noticed how your grandparents know a lot of things, but at the same time they need help picking up heavy things? When people become old they lose their physical ability to do many things you can easily do now. Their eyes may not see as well as yours. When they walk for a long time they become tired. One day you will become like them, inshaAllah, and need the help of those who are younger than you.

Old people not only need the help of younger ones but they deserve their respect too. You can learn a lot of good things from your elders. They can teach you many things from their long experience in life. Unwise children think that old people are boring, while smart children sit and listen carefully to what the wise and old people say. Older people often have interesting stories to tell filled with information and experiences they have gained in their lives. They can give great ideas and warn you against many harmful things or actions. One good tip can make you succeed in life or save you from falling into a big problem. Islam emphasizes respect for the elderly. The Prophet Muhammad ﷺ said:

Hadeeth Shareef

عن ابن عباس رضي الله عنه قال : قال رسول الله ﷺ :

" ليسَ منا من لَم يَرحَم صَغيرَنا ويُوَقِّر كَبيرَنا "

رواه التّرمذي وأبو داود

Ibn Abbas narrated that Rasulullah ﷺ said:

"He is not one of us who does not have kindness for our young and respect for our old."

(Reported by Abu Daud and Tirmidhi)

In another Hadeeth, Rasulullah ﷺ promises any young person who is kind to an elderly person that Allah ﷻ will in turn send him someone who will be kind to him when he becomes old. So, if you respect the elderly now, Allah ﷻ will guide the young people to respect you when you become older, insha'Allah.

Respecting Elders

When you respect your elders you care about how they feel. You believe that their ideas, thoughts, and feelings are important.

This means you should:

* listen to them when they talk even if you think what they are saying is boring.
* not talk back to them in an impolite manner.
* greet them with "Assalamu Alaikum" when you see them.
* answer your grandparents and elders when they ask a question.

When they pass away, you can also show respect to any Muslim who has passed away by making du'aa for them and asking Allah ﷻ to forgive them. You can show respect to them by donating something for the sake of Allah ﷻ in their name. They would be happy to receive such nice gifts from you.

Allah ﷻ wants all young and old Muslims to be respectful to each other. When you show respect to others, Allah ﷻ loves you, and all His creation loves you too.

Good Reasons to Respect Elders

1. Showing sincere respect to your elders pleases Allah and makes Him love you.
2. The people with the best manners are the closest to Prophet Muhammad ﷺ in the Hereafter in Jannah.
3. Showing respect to elders means they will respect you too.
4. Your family and friends love to be with you because you respect their feelings.

Healthy Habits

* Greet your elders when you see them.
* Never talk back to elders in a rude way.
* When you see an older person carrying heavy things or needing help, then you should help him or her.

Test Yourself

Scenario; (What if?)	What would you do?
You see an older person struggling to carry grocery bags.	
Your grandfather has a hard time reading the newspaper without his glasses.	
There are no empty seats on the bus, and an older person enters the bus.	

1. How can raising your voice over older people be disrespectful?
2. What will other people think of you when you show respect to your elders?

1. Why do elders deserve respect?
2. Mention a hadeeth about respecting elders.
3. What kind of changes do people go through as they age?
4. List four ways you can show respect to others?

UNIT
E
CHAPTER
2
LESSON
FIVE

Respecting Others

Pre-reading Questions

1. How important is respecting others?
2. How should a Muslim respect others?

STORYTIME

One day, a rich man entered Al-Masjid An-Nabawi in Madinah to listen to Prophet Muhammad ﷺ speak. The rich man wore very expensive clothing. He sat right in front of Prophet Muhammad ﷺ . Other people also started to enter the Masjid because prayer time was drawing near. Now another man also came and sat by the side of the rich man. This man was poor and his clothing looked old and very cheap. The rich man disliked that he was sitting by the side of the poor man. The rich man pulled his clothing away from the poor man.

"Why did he do that?" thought the poor man. His feelings were hurt.

The Prophet ﷺ noticed what the rich man had done and said to him, "I have noticed that you have pulled away your clothes from this man. What is the reason for this? Is it because you were afraid that some of your wealth might go to him, or that his poverty might come to you?"

The rich man did not mean to hurt the poor man's feelings. He at once realized his mistake and told the Prophet ﷺ :

"Oh Prophet of Allah! I admit that I have made a big mistake. To make up for it, I am ready to give half of my wealth to this brother of mine."

The Prophet ﷺ asked the poor man, "What do you say about this?"

"Oh Prophet of Allah! I do accept the apology of my brother and forgive him, but I do not accept his wealth. I am happy with the living earned by my hard work. I do not want to become rich without earning it."

Respecting Others

The story tells you how respecting other people's feelings is important. As you learned earlier, respect is a special kind of caring. As a good Muslim you should always show the people around you that you care about them. When you respect them, they know that you love them and care about them. If you always do that, Allah سبحانه وتعالى will love you and make people love and respect you too. So by respecting others, you really respect yourself.

I respect you!

We should always remember that although others are different from us (e.g., they may have a different race or skin color or religion or clothing), it is still important to show respect to them all.

Here are few ideas about how you should respect others:

* Care about others' feelings.

* Treat all your friends kindly regardless of their looks, religion or color.

* Listen to your friends carefully, especially when they are sad or upset, and avoid interrupting them.

* Speak in a language that everyone around understands.

* Always knock before entering someone's home.

* Greet every Muslim with Assaalmu Alaykum, and greet non-Muslims the way they like.

* Greet others with a smile and kind words. Always look at them in the eye when you speak to them.

* Do for others whatever good things they like you to do as much as you can. Be a doer more than a talker.

Good Reasons to Respect Others

1. Showing respect to others pleases Allah سُبحان الله .

2. When you show respect to others, you follow the Sunnah (tradition) of the Prophet ﷺ .

3. When you show respect to others, they know that you have good manners, and that weighs a lot on the Day of Judgment.

4. Showing respect to others makes them respect you, too.

5. Your family and friends love to be with you when you respect them and their feelings.

Chapter Review

Did You Know?

The best way to respect others is to treat them as you like them to treat you!

1. How can a disrespectful person be dangerous to society?
2. List five differences between a respectful person and a disrespectful person.

1. What thing did Rasulullah ﷺ notice in his masjid that he disliked?
2. How did the action of the rich person affect the poor person?
3. What is respect?
4. List four ways that you can show respect for others.
5. Why should a person show sincere respect to others?

UNIT E CHAPTER 2 LESSON SIX

Respecting Yourself

Pre-reading Questions

1. What priceless gifts did Allah give you in this life?
2. How can you respect what Allah gave you?

Word Watch

amanah (Trust) أمانة
ghuroor (Arrogance) غرور

How should you respect yourself?

Respecting yourself means that you care about yourself the way Allah and the Prophet ﷺ taught you. When you respect yourself, people will also respect you. Respecting yourself does not mean that you show off and think that you are better than others. These are signs of **ghuroor** or arrogance. Actually, that will displease Allah and make people dislike you too.

You should never say bad things about yourself like, "I can never be a good person." To be nice to yourself, you should say instead, "I'll work harder on improving myself." Or, instead of saying, "I am weak, I can't do it," say, "I'll try again and again until I do it, inshaAllah." On the other hand, you should avoid saying, "I am good," "I am the best," and "I am never wrong." Instead, you should say:

"Alhamdulillah, Allah ﷾ gave me gifts and talents, but I am not perfect."

Respecting yourself means that you should take care of yourself the Islamic way.

In Islam we are taught that Allah ﷾ is the One Who created us and gave us everything we have. We do not own these gifts; rather, we are entrusted to use them the right way. They are an **amanah**, or a trust, that we are responsible for. Allah ﷾ will ask us on the Day of Judgment about how we used our bodies, our time, our brains, and everything He gave us.

This means taking care of your heart and spirituality, your body and health, your brain and education, your emotions, and your relationships with others.

Allah ﷾ gave you all of these priceless gifts, and you should thank Allah by developing them further, and taking care of them as Allah and the Prophet ﷺ taught you.

Let's learn some of what Allah ﷾ and Rasulullah ﷺ recommended as ways of respecting and taking care of yourself:

* Make sure to go to sleep early every night and wake up early in the morning for Salat Al-Fajr.

* Perform all prayers properly and on time.

* Say du'aa for yourself at the appropriate times.

* Learn your lessons well and develop the habit of continuous reading and gaining good knowledge.

* Develop good manners and treat people politely and respectfully.

* Avoid insulting others and hurting their feelings, so they will also avoid insulting you or hurting your feelings.

* Make sure that you are clean at all times, from the outside and the inside.

* Eat healthy foods and avoid junk food.

* Be careful not to put yourself in danger. For instance, do not cross the street without paying attention to the cars.

Chapter Review

Create, with a classmate, a table that shows ways to respect your:

1. Heart
2. Mind
3. Body

Try to list as many ways as possible.

What is the difference between respecting oneself and showing off?

1. Where do your heart, mind, and body come from?
2. Who is responsible for taking care of your heart, mind, and body the right way?
3. List seven ways of respecting yourself.

UNIT E CHAPTER 2

LESSON SEVEN

Respecting Nature

And He created gardens...palms and produce with fruits of various sorts like olives and pomegranates. Some are alike and some are different. Eat of its fruits when it bears fruit, and pay the due charity when you harvest it. And do not waste for Allah doesn't like those who waste.

Holy Qur'an 6:141

In all things of nature there is something of the marvelous.

Aristotle

Respecting The Environment

The environment is our big home that we all live in. Islam teaches us to respect the environment. The environment includes the wildlife and the buildings we live in or use. Taking care of our environment and keeping it safe, healthy, and clean are the best ways to respect the environment around us.

Taking Care of Nature

Do you see the blue sky up above? Can you smell the scent of the roses? What about the refreshing waterfalls and streams?

Nature around us is beautiful, but many people do not appreciate it. Respecting nature is very important because it is the creation and gift of Allah.

What would happen if the flowers stopped growing and birds stopped singing?

We would not have beautiful and colorful scenery. And the mornings would be quiet without the birds.

What if cows stopped producing milk, trees quit producing fruits, and plants ceased to give us vegetables?

Life would stop for many species, and we would not be able to live on Planet Earth.

Prophet Muhammad ﷺ ordered people to protect nature and keep the environment healthy and clean. He forbade Muslims from cutting trees without a good reason. He also prevented people from destroying parks, shade trees and sources of water. The Prophet also ordered Muslims to care for animals, feeding them and keeping them healthy.

Rasulullah ﷺ told us that taking care of animals will take us to Jannah. He also warned us that hurting animals may take us to Jahannam.

Hadeeth Shareef

عن أبي هريرة رضي الله عنه أن رسولَ اللهِ ﷺ قال:
اتَّقوا اللَّعَّانين. قالوا: وما اللَّعَّانان يا رَسولَ الله؟
قال: الَّذي يَتَخَلَّى في طَريقِ النَّاسِ وظِلِّهم " رواه مسلم

Abu Hurayarah narrated that the Prophet ﷺ said:
"Avoid two actions that hurt people and cause them to curse you."
The Sahabah asked: "What are they, Oh Rasulullah?"
"Don't urinate in the way of people, or under shade trees, or on objects where people sit."

(Reported by Muslim)

Conserving Natural Resources

Another important way to respect nature is to conserve natural resources. Many people waste water and throw food in the garbage. Wasting water, plants, animals and food is prohibited in Islam. Allah ﷻ said in the Qur'an:

﴿ وكُلُواْ وَاشْرَبُواْ وَلاَ تُسْرِفُواْ إِنَّهُ لاَ يُحِبُّ الْمُسْرِفِينَ ﴾

"...and eat and drink and be not wasteful; surely He [Allah] does not love wasteful people." [Surat Al-A'raf 7:31]

Once Rasulullah passed by Sa'd Ibn Abi Waqqas رضي الله عنه while he was making wudoo'. Sa'd was using more water than he actually needed for his wudoo'. So the Prophet asked Sa'd: "Why are you wasting water, Sa'd?" Sa'd then asked the Prophet ﷺ : "Is it bad to waste water?" The Prophet ﷺ quickly replied: "Yes, even if you are beside a river."

Following Safety Rules

Some careless people waste our natural resources and destroy the environment when they go outdoors for a picnic. They trash the parks, pick flowers, and even burn up forests. Every year thousands of trees and animals get burned up by careless campers. They cause fire to burn forests, killing animals and destroying thousands of trees and precious plants. Some children play with fire, and before they know it, they cause big fires to start. Following safety rules is an important way to care for nature and respect the environment.

Recycling

Recycling paper, cans, and plastic containers is one good way to take care of the environment. Recycling saves trees and many other natural resources. For example, paper factories cut millions of trees to produce paper and other products. When you dump newspapers, magazines, and discarded books in the recycling dumpster, you can help to save many trees from being chopped down. Recycling is a very good way to pay respect to our precious environment.

Healthy Habit

We show respect to animals, trees, and other living things when we....
* Keep them safe
* Feed and water them regularly
* Avoid harming them

Taking Care of Your Home and Other Facilities

Respecting the environment means also that you should keep your house safe, healthy and clean. We should keep our schools, streets, and other public places safe and clean too. Doing that is part of our Iman. The Prophet Muhammad ﷺ said: "Cleanliness is part of Iman (Faith)." This should be reflected in our daily actions. The Prophet ordered Muslims to keep streets, masajid, and front and backyards clean.

Respecting the environment also includes caring for and respecting the places of worship like the masjid. A masjid is the house of Allah سبحانه وتعالى . The Prophet ﷺ has said that the best places on Earth are those where the mosques are found. When we come to perform our prayer in the masjid, we must show respect inside and outside the masjid.

STORYTIME

Yousuf was ten years old when his dad took him and his friends to a nearby park to play. Beautiful trees grew everywhere in the park. Ducks and geese swam in a lake right in the center while the sun shone down on their colored feathers.

Yousuf, his dad and friends watched the ducks closely as they swam one behind the other. One duck walked out of the lake with ten baby ducklings following her every step of the way.

To make his friends laugh, Yousuf threw a rock at the duck and started to laugh. The duck rushed screaming away, and a tear settled in her eye. Yousuf's dad became very upset with him.

"Why did you do that?" asked his dad. "A person who does not appreciate the creation of Allah ﷻ does not need to be around it." Yousuf's friends were listening too. "We would never do that," they thought.

Yousuf felt that his dad and his friends disrespected him for what he had done. He apologized to everybody, and he vowed to respect nature and all living things after that.

Later, Yousuf learned to respect the environment and all creatures.

Healthy Habit

Things you can do to protect your environment:
* Do not litter: Throw trash in the proper places.
* Keep Earth clean: If you see trash, pick it up.
* Plant a tree: Trees give us oxygen to breathe
* Recycle: Do not waste resources.
* Conserve: The less you use now, the more you will have tomorrow. Turn off the lights and TV when you're not in the room. Don't waste water or food.

Chapter Review

Think about your usual day from the time you wake up until you go to bed. Think about some changes you can make in your daily routine to help the environment. Write a paragraph about some of these changes and how doing them can improve the environment.

Look at the changes you listed in your paragraph. Now choose one and put it into action!

Why do you think some people care about the cleanliness and safety of their homes, but they do not care about nature and the environment?

1. Why should we care about the environment we live in?
2. In what ways can we help take care of the environment?
3. What did the Prophet Muhammad ﷺ say about cleanliness?
4. Why should we take care of the places where we live, learn, and worship?

UNIT
E
CHAPTER
3
LESSON
ONE

Surat Al-'Insan 1 (The Human Being)

Allah, Creator of Man

This surah was revealed in Makkah. It has 31 ayaat, which describe what Allah has prepared for the believers in Jannah. When Jibreel taught Rasulullah ﷺ this surah, he also taught it to the person who was visiting with him. When the man heard the ayaat about Jannah, he passed away. The Prophet ﷺ said: "This man's heart was so hooked to Jannah." Rasulullah ﷺ used to love this surah and read it in Fajr prayer every Friday.

WORDS OF WISDOM

Holy Qur'an

سورة الإنسان

Surat Al-'Insan 1-3

﴿ هَلْ أَتَىٰ عَلَى ٱلْإِنسَٰنِ حِينٌ مِّنَ ٱلدَّهْرِ لَمْ يَكُن شَيْـًٔا مَّذْكُورًا ﴿١﴾ إِنَّا خَلَقْنَا ٱلْإِنسَٰنَ مِن نُّطْفَةٍ أَمْشَاجٍ نَّبْتَلِيهِ فَجَعَلْنَٰهُ سَمِيعًۢا بَصِيرًا ﴿٢﴾ إِنَّا هَدَيْنَٰهُ ٱلسَّبِيلَ إِمَّا شَاكِرًا وَإِمَّا كَفُورًا ﴿٣﴾ ﴾

TRANSLITERATION

Hal ata ala al-insani heenum-min-ad-dahri lam yakun shay-an mathkoora (76:1) Inna khalaqnal-insana min nut-fatin amshajin-nabtaleehi faja'alnahu samee'an baseera (76:2) Inna hadaynah-us-sabeela imma shakiraw-wa-imma kafoora (76:3)

UNDERSTOOD MEANING

(76:1) Has there a period of time when not passed upon the human being he was quite unknown?
(76:2) We created man (Adam and his children) from a little mixture to test him, then We gave him the gifts of hearing and sight.
[76:3] Then We taught him the path to go to Paradise; he chooses to be either thankful or ungrateful.

WORDS OF WISDOM

Holy Qur'an

سورة الإنسان

Surat Al-'Insan 4-6

﴿ إِنَّآ أَعْتَدْنَا لِلْكَٰفِرِينَ سَلَٰسِلَا۟ وَأَغْلَٰلًا وَسَعِيرًا ﴿٤﴾ إِنَّ ٱلْأَبْرَارَ يَشْرَبُونَ مِن كَأْسٍ كَانَ مِزَاجُهَا كَافُورًا ﴿٥﴾ عَيْنًا يَشْرَبُ بِهَا عِبَادُ ٱللَّهِ يُفَجِّرُونَهَا تَفْجِيرًا ﴿٦﴾ ﴾

TRANSLITERATION

Inna a'tadna lilkafireena salasila waaghlalaw wasaeera (76:4) Inna al-abrara yashraboona min ka'sin kana mizajuha kafoora (76:5) Aynay-yashrabu biha 'ibadullahi yufajjiroonaha tafjeera (76:6)

UNDERSTOOD MEANING

[76:4] For the ungrateful we have prepared chains and shackles and a burning fire [in the next life].

(76:5) The good people will enjoy a drink with a kafoor flavor, which

(76:6) comes from a fountain that the servants of Allah can drink from and it flows for them wherever they go.

Hadeeth Shareef

"Hell complained to its Lord, saying, 'O my Lord (I am so hot) that I am consuming myself.' So Allah allowed it to breathe out twice, a breath in the summer and a breath in the winter. That is where you get the severe heat and the zamhareer (which means severe cold)."

(Reported in Muslim)

WORDS OF WISDOM

Holy Qur'an

سورة الإنسان

Surat Al-'Insan 7-11

بِسْمِ اللَّهِ الرَّحْمَٰنِ الرَّحِيمِ

يُوفُونَ بِالنَّذْرِ وَيَخَافُونَ يَوْمًا كَانَ شَرُّهُ مُسْتَطِيرًا ﴿٧﴾ وَيُطْعِمُونَ الطَّعَامَ عَلَىٰ حُبِّهِ مِسْكِينًا
وَيَتِيمًا وَأَسِيرًا ﴿٨﴾ إِنَّمَا نُطْعِمُكُمْ لِوَجْهِ اللَّهِ لَا نُرِيدُ مِنكُمْ جَزَاءً وَلَا شُكُورًا ﴿٩﴾ إِنَّا نَخَافُ مِن رَّبِّنَا
يَوْمًا عَبُوسًا قَمْطَرِيرًا ﴿١٠﴾ فَوَقَاهُمُ اللَّهُ شَرَّ ذَٰلِكَ الْيَوْمِ وَلَقَّاهُمْ نَضْرَةً وَسُرُورًا ﴿١١﴾

TRANSLITERATION

Yoofoona binnathri wayakhafoona yawman kana sharruhu mustateera (76:7) Wayut'imon-at-ta'ama 'ala hubbihi miskeenaw-wayateemaw-wa'aseera (76:8) Innama nut'imukum liwajhillahi la nureedu minkum jaza'aw wala shukoora (76:9) Inna nakhafu mir-rabbina yawman 'aboosan qamtareera (76:10) Fawaqahumullahu sharra thalik-alyawmi walaqqahum nadrataw-wasuroora (76:11)

UNDERSTOOD MEANING

(76:7) They fulfill vows and fear a day of a great danger.
(76:8) And they love to feed people (even though they don't have much) out of love for Allah. They feed the poor, the orphan and the captive.
(76:9) They say [to the needy people], "We only do this so Allah will be happy with us. We don't want from you a reward or thanks."
(76:10) We fear from our Lord an upsetting and difficult day.
(76:11) So because of this (their fear and their giving) Allah protected them from the harm of that day and instead He gave them bright faces and happiness in their hearts.

UNIT E CHAPTER 3

LESSON TWO

Surat Al-'Insan 2 (The Human Being)

The Pious Will Win Paradise

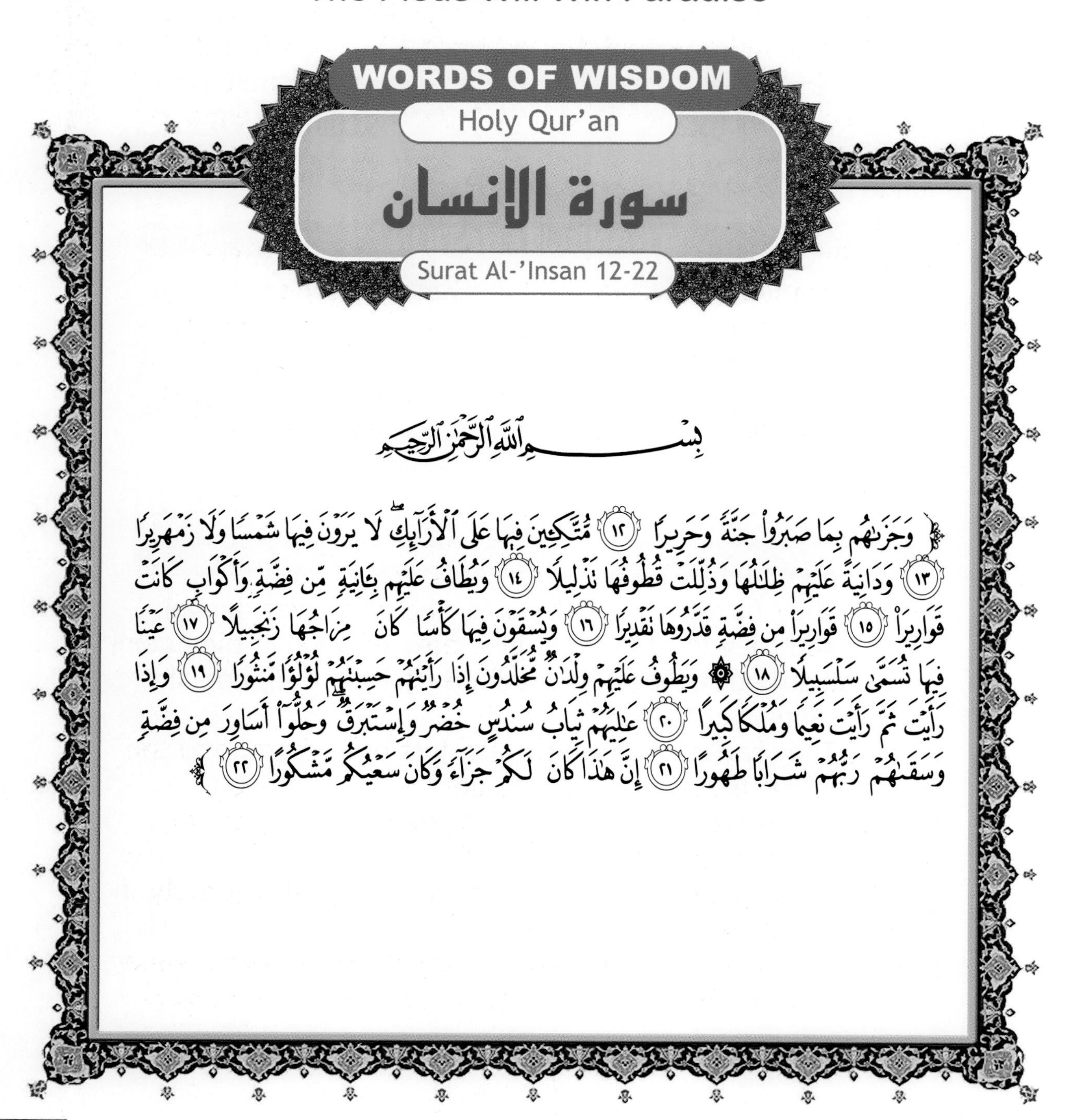

WORDS OF WISDOM

Holy Qur'an

سورة الإنسان

Surat Al-'Insan 12-22

بِسْمِ اللَّهِ الرَّحْمَٰنِ الرَّحِيمِ

﴿ وَجَزَاهُم بِمَا صَبَرُوا جَنَّةً وَحَرِيرًا ﴿١٢﴾ مُّتَّكِئِينَ فِيهَا عَلَى الْأَرَائِكِ ۖ لَا يَرَوْنَ فِيهَا شَمْسًا وَلَا زَمْهَرِيرًا ﴿١٣﴾ وَدَانِيَةً عَلَيْهِمْ ظِلَالُهَا وَذُلِّلَتْ قُطُوفُهَا تَذْلِيلًا ﴿١٤﴾ وَيُطَافُ عَلَيْهِم بِآنِيَةٍ مِّن فِضَّةٍ وَأَكْوَابٍ كَانَتْ قَوَارِيرَا ﴿١٥﴾ قَوَارِيرَ مِن فِضَّةٍ قَدَّرُوهَا تَقْدِيرًا ﴿١٦﴾ وَيُسْقَوْنَ فِيهَا كَأْسًا كَانَ مِزَاجُهَا زَنجَبِيلًا ﴿١٧﴾ عَيْنًا فِيهَا تُسَمَّىٰ سَلْسَبِيلًا ﴿١٨﴾ ۞ وَيَطُوفُ عَلَيْهِمْ وِلْدَانٌ مُّخَلَّدُونَ إِذَا رَأَيْتَهُمْ حَسِبْتَهُمْ لُؤْلُؤًا مَّنثُورًا ﴿١٩﴾ وَإِذَا رَأَيْتَ ثَمَّ رَأَيْتَ نَعِيمًا وَمُلْكًا كَبِيرًا ﴿٢٠﴾ عَالِيَهُمْ ثِيَابُ سُندُسٍ خُضْرٌ وَإِسْتَبْرَقٌ ۖ وَحُلُّوا أَسَاوِرَ مِن فِضَّةٍ وَسَقَاهُمْ رَبُّهُمْ شَرَابًا طَهُورًا ﴿٢١﴾ إِنَّ هَٰذَا كَانَ لَكُمْ جَزَاءً وَكَانَ سَعْيُكُم مَّشْكُورًا ﴿٢٢﴾ ﴾

TRANSLITERATION

Wajazahum bima sabaroo jannataw wahareera (76:12) Muttaki-eena feeha 'alaal-ara'iki la yarawna feeha shamsan wala zamhareera (76:13) Wadaniyatan alayhim thilaluha wathullilat qutoofuha tathleela (76:14) Wayutafu alayhim bi-aniyatim-min fiddatiw-wa-'akwabin kanat qawareera (76:15) Qawareera min fiddatin qaddarooha taqdeera (76:16) Wayusqawna feeha ka'san kana mizajuha zanjabeela (76:17) Aynan feeha tusamma salsabeela (76:18) Wayatoofu 'alayhim wildanum-mukhalladoona itha ra'aytahum hasibtahum lu'lu'am manthoora (76:19) Wa'itha raayta thamma ra'ayta na'eemaw-wamulkan kabeera (76:20) 'Aaliyahum thiyabu sundusin khudruw-wa-istabraq, wahulloo asawira min fiddatiw-wasaqahum rabbuhum sharaban tahoora (76:21) Inna hatha kana lakum jaza'aw wakana sa'yukum mashkoora (76:22)

UNDERSTOOD MEANING

(76:12) And Allah rewarded them, for their patience, Paradise and gave them (soft) silk [clothes to wear].
(76:13) [In the gardens of Paradise they will be] reclining on their canopy beds. They will not see [the heat of] the sun nor the bitter cold.
(76:14) The shades of the trees are just over them, and the fruits are made easy for them to get
(76:15) And servants will be around them with plates (of food) and big glass goblets.
(76:16) Glass goblets made from silver filled with exactly the amount of drink they want.
(76:17) And they will drink from a cup of (non alcoholic) wine mixed with zanjabeel (something that is like warm ginger)

UNDERSTOOD MEANING

(76:18) from a spring in Heaven called salsabeel (which means tasty smooth drink)
(76:19) And around them, the servants will be children who will stay young forever. When you see them they will look as beautiful as scattered pearls as they run to serve you.
(76:20) When you see Paradise, anywhere you look you will see delights and blessings for you and a magnificent huge kingdom (that will be yours).
(76:21) They, the people of Paradise, will have on them fine green silk and thick shiny silk. They will have bracelets of silver and their Lord will give them a purifying drink.
(76:22) It will be said to them, "This is your reward for what you did. Thank you for all your hard work and it is accepted."

When Allah thanks us for our deeds, it means He accepts them.

The Drinks of Jannah

This surah describes some of the drinks of Jannah. The people of Jannah will enjoy many drinks, including special kinds of wine with kafoor and ginger flavor. But the wine of Jannah does not cause people to get drunk or suffer headaches, like the wine of this life.

The higher you are in Paradise, the more you can drink from special springs. These springs or fountains follow where you go, so you get to drink your favorite drinks anytime, anywhere. Other drinks include special honey, milk, pure water and many other tasty drinks. Listen to how Allah describes the rivers of Jannah in Surat Muhammad, Ayah 15:

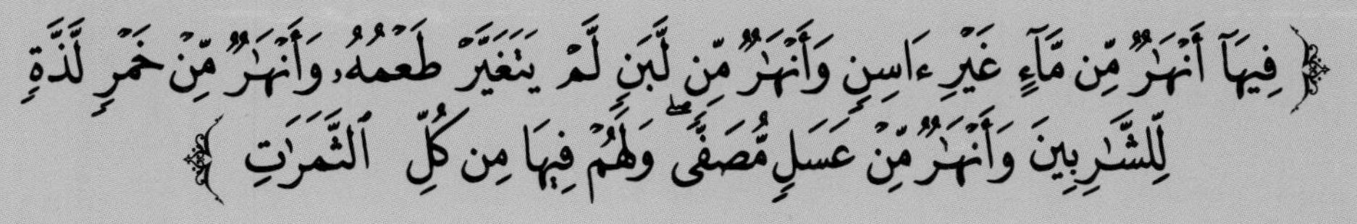

"Therein are rivers of fresh water, and rivers of milk the taste of which does not change, and rivers of wine delicious to those who drink, and rivers of clear honey and for them therein are all fruits." [Surat Muhammad 47:15]

In this world, glass is made from sand. In Paradise, the glass is made from silver. So it looks like silver, but you can see though it to see the drink inside.

UNIT E
CHAPTER 3
LESSON THREE

Surat Al-'Insan 3 (The Human Being)

Be Patient and Worship Your Lord

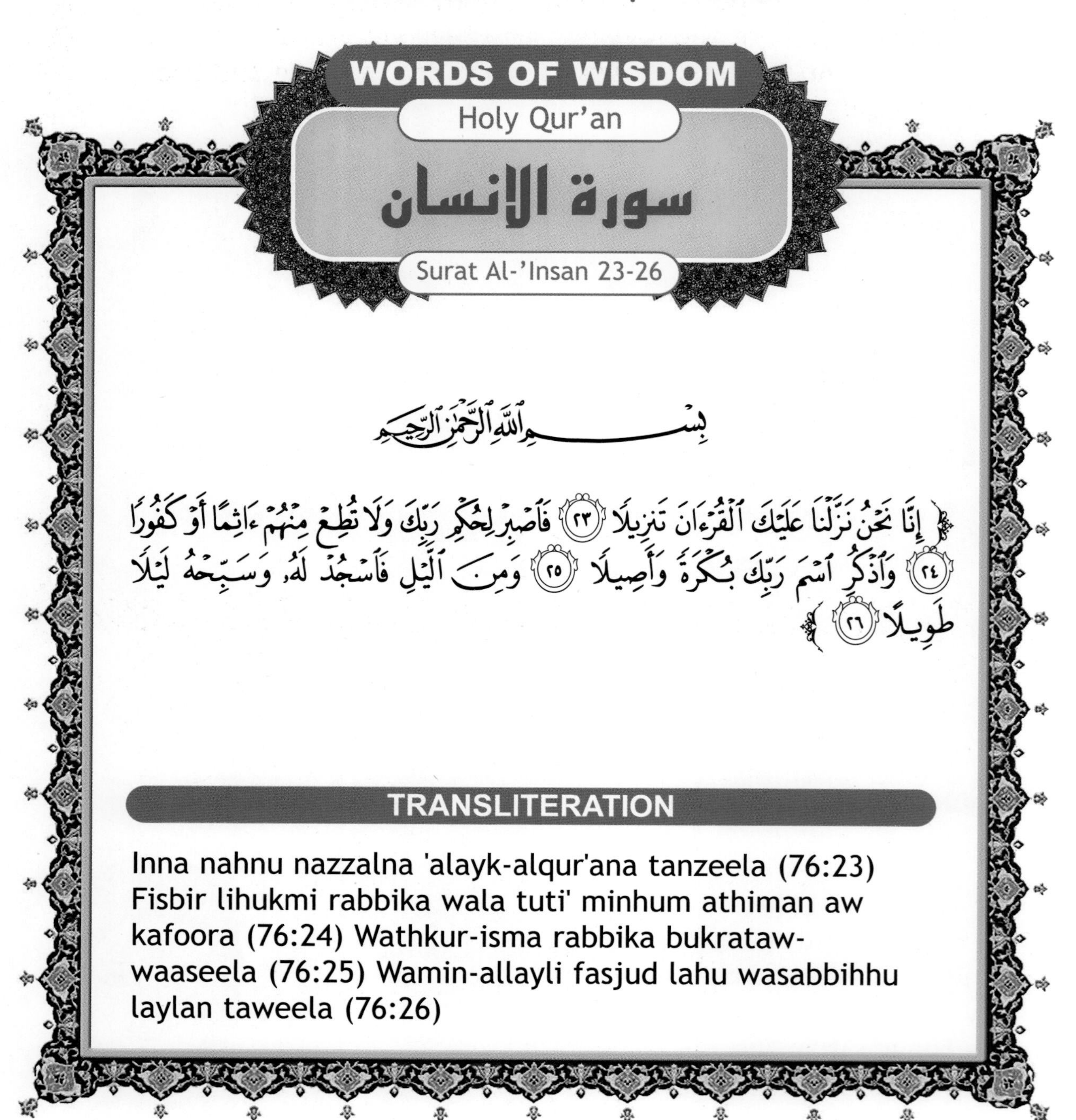

WORDS OF WISDOM

Holy Qur'an

سورة الإنسان

Surat Al-'Insan 23-26

بِسْمِ اللَّهِ الرَّحْمَٰنِ الرَّحِيمِ

﴿ إِنَّا نَحْنُ نَزَّلْنَا عَلَيْكَ الْقُرْآنَ تَنزِيلًا ﴿٢٣﴾ فَاصْبِرْ لِحُكْمِ رَبِّكَ وَلَا تُطِعْ مِنْهُمْ آثِمًا أَوْ كَفُورًا ﴿٢٤﴾ وَاذْكُرِ اسْمَ رَبِّكَ بُكْرَةً وَأَصِيلًا ﴿٢٥﴾ وَمِنَ اللَّيْلِ فَاسْجُدْ لَهُ وَسَبِّحْهُ لَيْلًا طَوِيلًا ﴿٢٦﴾ ﴾

TRANSLITERATION

Inna nahnu nazzalna 'alayk-alqur'ana tanzeela (76:23) Fisbir lihukmi rabbika wala tuti' minhum athiman aw kafoora (76:24) Wathkur-isma rabbika bukrataw-waaseela (76:25) Wamin-allayli fasjud lahu wasabbihhu laylan taweela (76:26)

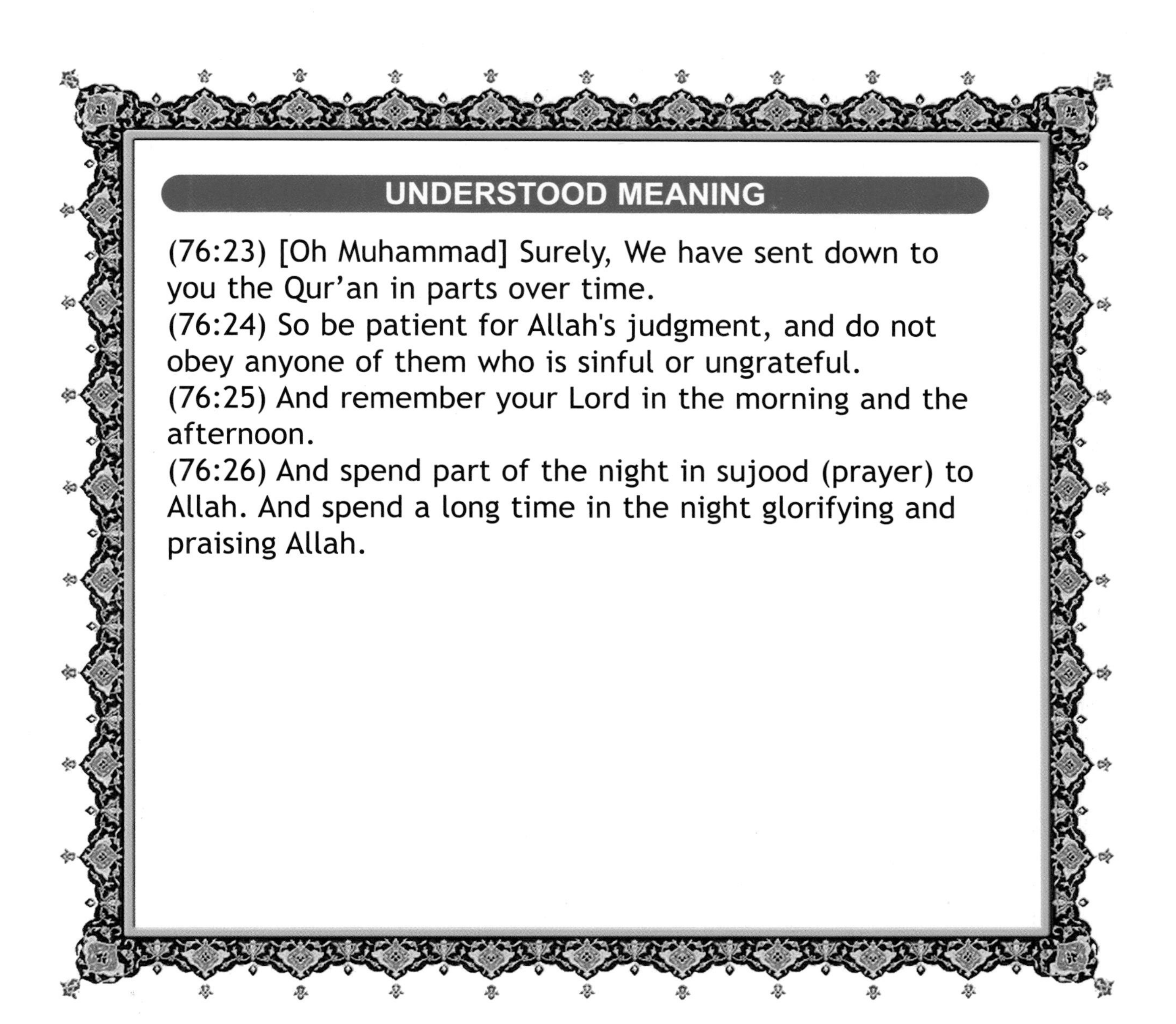

UNDERSTOOD MEANING

(76:23) [Oh Muhammad] Surely, We have sent down to you the Qur'an in parts over time.
(76:24) So be patient for Allah's judgment, and do not obey anyone of them who is sinful or ungrateful.
(76:25) And remember your Lord in the morning and the afternoon.
(76:26) And spend part of the night in sujood (prayer) to Allah. And spend a long time in the night glorifying and praising Allah.

Allah Can Replace the Disbelievers

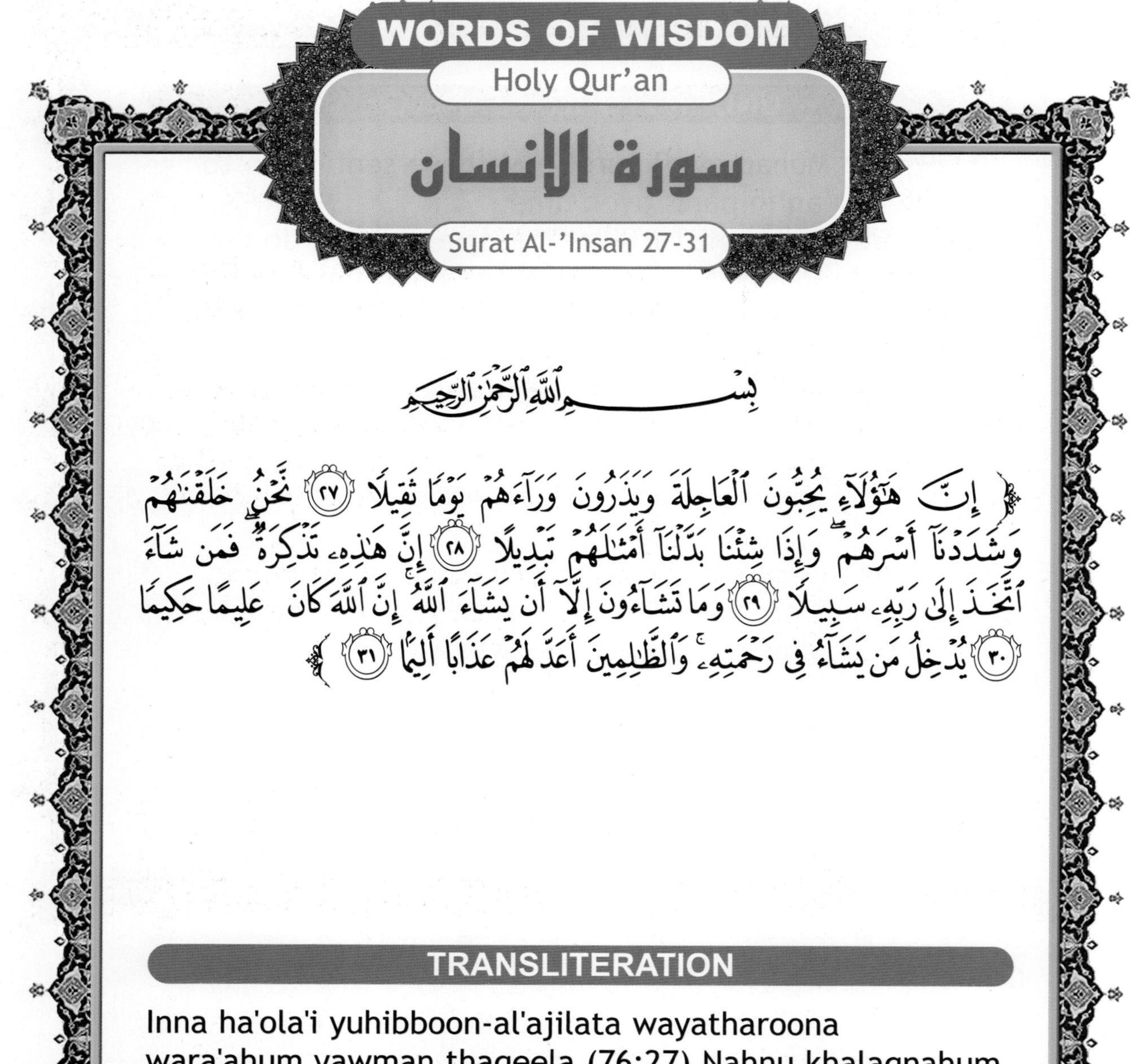

TRANSLITERATION

Inna ha'ola'i yuhibboon-al'ajilata wayatharoona wara'ahum yawman thaqeela (76:27) Nahnu khalaqnahum washadadna asrahum wa-itha shi'na baddalna amtha-lahum tabdeela (76:28) Inna hathihi tathkiratun faman shaa ittakhatha ila rabbihi sabeela (76:29) Wama tasha'oona illa ay- yasha'-Allahu inn-Allaha kana 'aleeman hakeema (76:30) Yudkhilu may-yashao fee rahmatih, waththalimeena a'adda lahum athaban aleema (76:31)

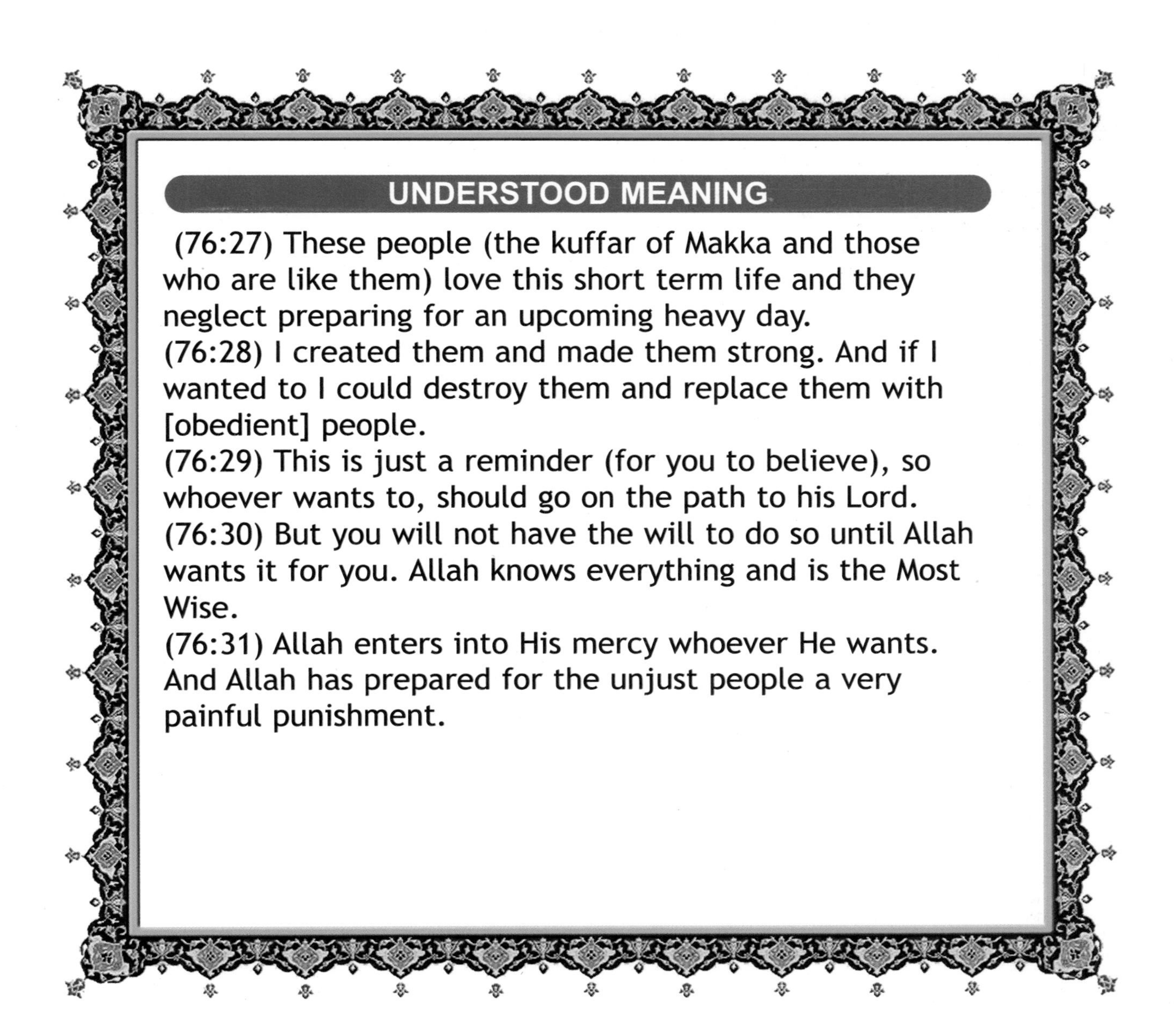

UNDERSTOOD MEANING

(76:27) These people (the kuffar of Makka and those who are like them) love this short term life and they neglect preparing for an upcoming heavy day.
(76:28) I created them and made them strong. And if I wanted to I could destroy them and replace them with [obedient] people.
(76:29) This is just a reminder (for you to believe), so whoever wants to, should go on the path to his Lord.
(76:30) But you will not have the will to do so until Allah wants it for you. Allah knows everything and is the Most Wise.
(76:31) Allah enters into His mercy whoever He wants. And Allah has prepared for the unjust people a very painful punishment.

Muslim Fashion

CHAPTER FOUR

Pre-reading Questions

1. What are the important rules for dressing in Islam?
2. Are there different rules for boys and girls?
3. Why is there a "dress code" for Muslims?

Word Watch

Hijab	حِجاب
Hayaa	حَياء
'Awrah	عَوْرَة

Leena Is Dressed For School

Leena looked at herself in the mirror. It was almost time for school, but she wanted to make sure she was dressed appropriately and that her clothes looked neat and presentable.

She had made sure that the clothes she was wearing were clean. As she looked in the mirror, she noticed that hair had fallen out of her hijab. She carefully tucked it back in. Leena knew how important it was for Muslim girls to wear hijaab.

Leena knew that Allah ﷻ and the Prophet ﷺ had made it mandatory for Muslim women to cover their bodies and their hair.

She understood that hijab was not a must on her yet, because she was still young. However, she wanted to start hijab early. This way she would win more hasanat and get used to it. Leena covered herself in the proper Islamic way because she wanted Allah ﷻ to be happy with her, and she wanted to listen to the Prophet ﷺ out of love.

Leena knew that her hijab was a protection for her, and that it made her personality more important than her looks. She loved wearing the hijab.

Zaid Is Dressed for School

Zaid looked in the mirror. He learned from Leena that it was important to check himself before he went out to make sure his clothes were in order. Zaid looked down to make sure his shorts were past his knees. He knew that the Prophet ﷺ had always worn a garment below the knees. He also knew that his 'awrah was from the bellybutton to his knees. Dad had taught Zaid about the 'awrah.

How Can You Dress the Islamic Way?

The Islamic dress should meet the following criteria:

1. Covers the 'Awrah

The **'awrah** عورة is the part of your body that needs to be covered in front of all people. It is different for boys and girls. For boys, the 'awrah is from the naval, or bellybutton, to the knees. For girls, it is the entire body, except the hands and the face when she is in mixed company. However, when she is with her family or other girls she doesn't need to cover as much.

Even though the 'awrah for boys is from the bellybutton to the knees, this does not mean that boys should walk around without their shirts on. If they need to do something without their shirts, they are allowed to.

Following the rules of 'awrah is mandatory once a child becomes an adult. Still, it is great to practice the rules before we grow up, so that we are used to dressing the right way when the time comes.

Understanding the 'awrah concept is important for us to follow the Islamic dress code. It tells us what parts of our bodies we are allowed to show, and what parts of our bodies we must cover. Covering properly is important because it shows that we have hayaa'. **Hayaa'**, or modesty, is very important in Islam. Modesty means we act in a humble way and that we dress in a humble way.

For girls, another part of covering the 'awrah and maintaining modesty is to not dress in an attractive way. This means that beside covering their 'awrah, the clothes should not be tight-fitting or see-through. Also, Girls should not wear make-up and perfume outside their homes, because this is attractive, too.

Boys should not wear tight-fitting or see-through clothes.

One part of modesty is that we act in a humble way. This means that we should not show off when we wear nice clothes. We should not go out of our way to wear name brands, and if we do, we should not brag about it.

2. Cleanliness

As you learned earlier, cleanliness is half of faith. Muslims must always be clean. The Muslim's body, clothes,

home and belongings are always clean. You should avoid getting your clothes dirty. Try your best to keep your clothes clean. If you want to play outside, wear your sports clothes. Also remember, your clothes must be clean inside and out. Some people care about how their clothes look from the outside but neglect their underwear. We sometimes sweat, and as a result we get our underwear and outfits dirty and smelly. We should be aware of that and change. Some people use the bathroom and do not clean themselves properly. Muslims should follow the etiquette of the bathroom properly and clean themselves very well. Being clean keeps you healthy and likeable.

3. Neatness

One day, Rasulullah ﷺ spoke about kibr, or arrogance. He advised the sahabah not to be arrogant. One Sahabi asked the Prophet, “Oh Rasulullah ﷺ we like to have neat clothes and look neat. Is that a kind of arrogance?” The Prophet ﷺ said, "No, Allah is beautiful and loves beauty." Therefore, a Muslim should be neat. Your shirt should be buttoned, your pants ironed, and your shoelaces tied. You can be neat in different ways, and your parents and teachers are the best ones to know when you look neat and when you don't.

4. Modesty

Being neat and wearing beautiful clothes doesn't mean you have to buy expensive items. Some people brag about their brand name and expensive outfits. That is unacceptable behavior.

If Allah gave you money to buy expensive clothes, you should thank Allah ﷻ and avoid talking about it, especially to people who don't have it. You will hurt their feelings if you do that because they cannot afford to buy similar clothes. It is even better not to spend too much money on clothes, shoes, or other things. It is better to buy good but inexpensive clothes and give the needy some money to buy clothes for themselves. This will please Allah and make you even happier.

Some people think that if they wear expensive clothes, they will be better than others; that is never the case. What makes you good is not your outfit; it is your manners. Great people are usually modest and hate to brag about their belongings.

Omar Ibn Al-Khattab used to wear a garment that had many patches. One day his son brought him an expensive garment as a gift. Omar wore the new garment but became restless. He didn't like to wear an expensive outfit while poor Muslims around him didn't have the same. He ordered his sons to bring him back his patched garment to wear. He felt happier wearing the old outfit.

5. Reflecting Islamic Personality

Another thing that we should keep in mind is that when we dress, we should not look to see what styles the non-Muslims are wearing. Many non-Muslims do not cover their 'awrahs, and many do not dress modestly.

Instead, we should be creative and think of our own Islamic styles that follow the principles of modesty. We should remember that being neat and presentable is always important.

Chapter Review

Hadeeth Shareef

عن عبدالله بن مسعود رضي الله عنه قال: قال رسول الله ﷺ :

"إنَّ اللّه جَميلٌ يُحِبُّ الجَمال." رواه مسلم

Abdullah Ibn Mas'oud narrated that the Prophet ﷺ said,
"Allah is beautiful and loves beauty."

(Narrated by Muslim)

1. Why isn't it a good idea for Muslims girls and boys to show their 'awrah?

2. Why is it important not to show off about our clothes? What might happen if we do?

1. What is the meaning of 'awrah? Why is it important?
2. What different things did Zaid and Leena check for in the morning? How did this show they were following the 'awrah rules?
3. Why should we not follow the way non-Muslims dress?
4. What are some rules both boys and girls must follow?

Muslims Online

CHAPTER FIVE

Pre-reading Questions

1. How many times a day do you go online? How many times a week?
2. How much time do you spend each day on the Internet?
3. What different things do you use the Internet for?

Word Watch

Hacker	
World Wide Web	الشبكة العنكبوتية
Parental Controls	مراقبة أبوية

In today's world, the Internet is a very big part of our lives. It is important to remember that the etiquette that Allah ﷻ taught us through Rasulullah ﷺ applies to all our actions, even when we're online. If we do this, then even surfing the Internet can be a way to worship Allah and get hasanat.

Healthy Habit

Start every session online by saying “Bismillah.”

The Biggest Thing to Remember

Even though you may feel like you're all alone when you're online, you and Allah سبحانه وتعالى are always close together. Allah knows everything you spend your time on. Once, Prophet Yaqoob عليه السلام gave a dessert to all of his children and told them to go eat it in a place that no one would see them. All of them went and hid themselves away somewhere to eat their treat happily. It was only Yousuf عليه السلام who came back to him slightly confused. He told his father that there was no place for him to go to eat where Allah wasn't watching him.

We should remember that Allah is always watching us. He knows what we see, think, hear, and say at all times. Remembering that Allah is always watching will help us do good things, and while avoid bad deeds at the same time.

Here are some internet rules to start off with:

1) Make your niyyah: All your work whether online or not should be for the sake of Allah.
2) Look at only what's clean, decent, and good.
3) Do not waste your time.
4) Avoid using foul language.

Different things are important to remember whenever we check our e-mail, surf the web, or sign into a chat room.

E-Mail

E-mail, or electronic mail, is a great and fast way for us to communicate. We can stay in touch with our friends and relatives, and we can also communicate to get our work done. Allah likes for us to be close to our families and to do good work, so e-mail can bring us good deeds if we use it properly.

What should we not do with e-mail?

We should not use it to communicate with members of the opposite gender if we do not have a legitimate reason. Girls should not e-mail boys, and boys should not e-mail girls, unless they have a good, Islamic reason to communicate. If you do need to communicate with someone of the other gender, make sure your parents know about it.

A good reason for e-mailing someone of the opposite gender is to get a homework assignment or do some committee work for your Muslim youth group.

We should not communicate with strangers, or anyone we do not know.

Even if we are communicating with someone we know, we should not give out personal information, such as our phone number or address. This is because it is easy for bad people to pretend to be our friends. There are also bad people, called hackers, who break into your computer and take your information.

We should not pay attention to junk mail. This mail either comes from bad people who want to show us bad things, from people who want to sell us items we do not need, or from bad people who want to send us viruses that will

damage our computers. Have a parent, teacher, or other trusted adult teach you how to figure out what is junk mail and what is not.

Chatting

Chatting online is similar to e-mail, but it is faster and has more instant answers. Chatting is like talking to someone, except you see what they are saying instead of hearing it. It is good to talk to family and friends, as long as we follow the rules.

What should we not do while chatting?

The rules for chatting are the same as with e-mail. We usually should not talk to members of the opposite gender, and never to strangers.

We should not give out our personal information, talk about bad things, or waste our time. It is really easy to lose track of time when we are chatting, so it is a good idea to put a clock near the computer so we can check. We can also set aside a small amount of time to chat. Not wasting time is important, because the time we waste chatting can be better spent doing things that will earn us more hasanat.

The World Wide Web

The World Wide Web, or WWW, is a gigantic place where nearly infinite amounts of information are stored. As with other things, the World Wide Web can be used for both good and bad things.

The best thing we can use the Web for is seeking and gaining knowledge. Allah ﷻ loves for us to learn good things, and using the internet for this reason can give us many good deeds. For example, we may use the internet for projects, papers, or just to learn something new. Going on the web is sometimes called "surfing."

We should follow the main rules in the beginning of this lesson about making our niyyah for the sake of Allah ﷻ , not to waste time, and to only look at good things.

What should we not do on the Web?

Just like with e-mail and chatting, there are bad people on the web that want to hurt our minds and our souls. We should be aware of this, because it is our responsibility to guard our sight.

Therefore, we should not look at anything bad that comes up while we are online, whether it is words, movies, or pictures. A good way to prevent this is to have your parent or teacher put in 'Parental Controls,' which keep most bad things from accidentally popping up. We should understand that 'Parental Controls' are for the protection of our souls. If we need to do something that 'Parental Controls' restrict, then it is a good idea to ask our parents to help us go online.

Overall, the internet can be a great tool for Muslims to communicate, learn, and even have fun. It is just as important to remember the rules, because if we don't, the internet can become a very bad thing.

Chapter Review

Make a list of five good Islamic websites forchil-dren and share it with your classmates.

1) Why is it most important to remember that Allah ﷻ is watching us when we are online?

2) What are some bad things that might happen if we do not follow the rules?

1. What are the rules that apply to everything we do online?
2. What is another common rule for e-mail, chatting, and web surfing?
3. Why are the rules important, and how do they protect us?